Suicide Attacks and International Humanitarian Law

Suicide Attacks and International Humanitarian Law

Culture, Agency, and Combatant Deaths

VISHAKHA V. WIJENAYAKE

Senior Research Equity Advisor, McGill University, Montreal, Canada

OXFORD
UNIVERSITY PRESS

OXFORD
UNIVERSITY PRESS

Oxford University Press is a department of the University of Oxford. It furthers the University's objective of excellence in research, scholarship, and education by publishing worldwide. Oxford is a registered trade mark of Oxford University Press in the UK and in certain other countries.

Published in the United States of America by Oxford University Press
198 Madison Avenue, New York, NY 10016, United States of America.

Library of Congress Cataloging-in-Publication Data
Names: Wijenayake, Vishakha V. author
Title: Suicide attacks and international humanitarian law : culture, agency, and combatant deaths / Vishakha V. Wijenayake.
Description: New York : Oxford university press, 2026. |
Includes bibliographical references and index.
Identifiers: LCCN 2025042808 (print) | LCCN 2025042809 (ebook) |
ISBN 9780197812143 hardback | ISBN 9780197812167 updf | ISBN 9780197812150 epub |
ISBN 9780197812174 online
Subjects: LCSH: Humanitarian law | Combatants and noncombatants (International law) | Suicide bombers—Legal status, laws, etc. |
Warfare, Conventional
Classification: LCC KZ6471 .W55 2026 (print) | LCC KZ6471 (ebook)
LC record available at https://lccn.loc.gov/2025042808
LC ebook record available at https://lccn.loc.gov/2025042809

DOI: 10.1093/9780197812174.001.0001

Printed by Integrated Books International, United States of America

The manufacturer's authorized representative in the EU for product safety is Oxford University Press España S.A. of Parque Empresarial San Fernando de Henares, Avenida de Castilla, 2 – 28830 Madrid (www.oup.es/en or product.safety@oup.com). OUP España S.A. also acts as importer into Spain of products made by the manufacturer.

Note to Readers

This publication is designed to provide accurate and authoritative information in regard to the subject matter covered. It is based upon sources believed to be accurate and reliable and is intended to be current as of the time it was written. It is sold with the understanding that the publisher is not engaged in rendering legal, accounting, or other professional services. If legal advice or other expert assistance is required, the services of a competent professional person should be sought. Also, to confirm that the information has not been affected or changed by recent developments, traditional legal research techniques should be used, including checking primary sources where appropriate.

(Based on the Declaration of Principles jointly adopted by a Committee of the American Bar Association and a Committee of Publishers and Associations.)

This book is dedicated to family.
Amma, Sandya Kumuduni De Silva, a beloved and selfless teacher.
Thaththa, Pemasiri Wijenayake, who encouraged debates at the dinner table.
My partner, Alex Boulanger, who keeps me grounded.
Dusty (2016–2024), Rengar, Fern, and Bodhi, who remind me that a little silliness goes a long way.

Contents

Preface

This book will appeal to diverse audiences. First, and most evidently, the target audience for this book is those with an interest in International Humanitarian Law (IHL), including practitioners, government officials, academic researchers, and students studying this field of law. For those within militaries, this book offers critical insights into how they treat their combatants as well as helpful cultural understandings of diverse actors on the battlefield at a time when militaries' adversaries and partners are ever evolving. In a similar vein, for humanitarian professionals and international legal practitioners, this work offers tools to deconstruct complex phenomena and understand actors with whom they engage, encouraging them to reflect on who is considered a victim worthy of protection during the conduct of hostilities.

It is my hope that the book will resonate with researchers in international law from diverse geographies and cultures, given that it studies conflicts in multiple contexts. Its critical and plural lens toward IHL invites legal scholars, especially those who are critically leaning, to envision a normative framework for warfare that challenges key assumptions of international law, offering new critical and culturally informed frames for unpacking notions such as agency. For IHL scholars belonging to a more positivist tradition of law, what it offers is an opportunity to reflect on the silences of their discipline and their positionality in relation to its practices.

Given the interdisciplinary nature of this work, it is accessible to scholars in social sciences, including anthropology, gender studies, moral philosophy, and religious studies. The work borrows insights from these disciplines and connects them to legal norms applicable during armed conflicts. It studies why IHL has not interacted with insights into suicide attackers' deaths found in other scholarly disciplines. However, similarly, there is a lack of interaction on the part of these disciplines with legal norms governing warfare. This book bridges this gap. Therefore, it offers an opening for scholars from diverse disciplines to bring their disciplinary concepts into conversation with legal scholarship on warfare.

The book views law as being influenced by plural normative frameworks, including those norms that are embedded in local cultural practices. Therefore, it has a theoretical commitment to making the law more accessible to communities outside the traditional domains in which legal discourse resides. I have made efforts to adopt a style of writing that makes scholarly content more accessible to nonlawyers and those outside academia. Narratives on suicide attackers that have remained invisible in legal scholarship can resonate not only among lawyers and scholars but with a larger public interested in exploring and learning from stories of war, death, and agency. I hope that this book will not only carry intellectual but also emotional resonance, appealing to a wider audience.

Writing a book about suicide was a daunting endeavor. This work grapples with the intricate ways in which individuals exercise agency in violent and hierarchical environments. I cannot presume how the reader might feel engaging with this book, including to what extent these feelings would be disquieting. What I can share, however, is that for me, while this project was an intellectual exercise undertaken voluntarily, it was not without its emotional and moral challenges.

To me, the value of reading and writing lies in their capacity to facilitate unique encounters with ideas and, at times, with emotions. In writing this book, I hope to challenge the reader to think critically about how agency is constructed and understood, as well as the silences and assumptions that shape these constructions. In doing so, I seek to open a conversation which, while not necessarily pleasant, is important.

Vishakha Wijenayake, Montreal, January 31, 2025

Acknowledgments

This book marks the culmination of a seven-year journey, shaped by the support of countless individuals and communities. Their insights and kindness have enriched the ideas within these pages. Even though academic conventions limit who can be acknowledged in formal citations, these boundaries placed for what is valorized as legitimate knowledge are limiting. I wish to recognize contributions that, although not cited, have been integral to this work.

The foundation for this book lies in my Doctor of Civil Law thesis, completed at McGill University's Faculty of Law from 2018 to 2022. This period of intensive research and reflection provided the theoretical framework and critical approach that underpin the book's core arguments. The vibrant academic environment at McGill University, combined with the guidance of mentors and peers and the financial support provided, played a pivotal role in ensuring this work was completed.

I am especially grateful to my supervisor, Professor René Provost, who provided unwavering support throughout my doctoral journey. He gave me the necessary guidance and the space to develop my scholarly thinking and consistently held me to high standards. He also helped me see the law through a plural lens, broadening my understanding of its cultural and contextual dimensions. Most importantly, he preserved and nurtured my individuality in legal thinking and writing, empowering me to express my unique academic voice.

My thesis committee members, Professors Angela Campbell, Alana Klein, and Ronald Niezen offered timely, detailed, and insightful feedback. Their guidance was not only intellectually rigorous but also considerate of my well-being. Prof. Mark Drumbl, the external examiner of my doctoral thesis, provided generous constructive feedback, which was pivotal in advancing my doctoral thesis to a publishable book. Professors Niezen and David Howes kindly allowed me to audit and engage in their anthropology courses at McGill University, which enriched my interdisciplinary approach and significantly influenced the direction of this book.

I was fortunate to have strong mentors throughout this journey. At McGill University, I had the luxury of observing and learning from female scholars who are leaders in their field: Professor Nandini Ramanujam offered opportunities for collaboration, checking on my well-being, and instilling confidence in me as an academic; Professor Shauna Van Praagh was a transformative educator; and Professor Angela Campbell was an understanding guide in both my academic and professional journey. Many former supervisors and advisors have instilled in me a love for research, including Dr. Jean-Marie Henkaerts, Legal Adviser in the Legal Division of the International Committee of the Red Cross and Head of the project to update the Commentaries on the 1949 Geneva Conventions and the Additional Protocols of 1977, Professor Steven Ratner, University of Michigan, Ann Arbor, and Professor Sharya Scharniguivel, University of Colombo. These mentors offered lessons on leadership through their empathy and guidance.

During the process of writing this book, I benefited from the support of several institutions and services, both within and beyond McGill University. The Centre for Human Rights and Legal Pluralism was instrumental, offering me the O'Brien Fellowship, a vibrant intellectual community, and a collaborative workspace. I am grateful to its leadership, including Professors Nandini Ramanujam, Frédéric Mégret, and François Crépeau, and to Ms. Sharon Webb for fostering opportunities for meaningful research. I also thank the Fonds de Recherche du Québec—Société et Culture (FRQSC) for funding my work during this pivotal phase, which enabled me to dedicate crucial time to refining the ideas that underpin this research.

The graduate office of the Faculty of Law, under the leadership of former Deans Richard Gold, Andrea Bjorklund, and Darren Rosenblum, has been a tremendous source of support throughout this journey. I thank Pascalina Chiarelli, Bianca Bourgeois, Silvana Soltiero, and Dalia Charafeddine for their assistance with my grant applications and thesis defense, and for consistently going above and beyond to help. Mariève Isabel at Graphos (McGill writing services) made academic writing a social activity. McGill's therapists and Local Wellness Advisors helped me stay balanced and mentally healthy.

I had the luxury of having Michael Mendis, who is both an award-winning fiction writer and a brilliant legal scholar, edit the final drafts of this book. This work also benefited from the meticulous proofreading and indexing work by Charlie Sauvourel and Emma Beilouny. I am also indebted to all those who read and provided thoughtful feedback on my drafts throughout the development of this book. This includes my doctoral cohort, participants in the workshops organized by the McGill Writing Centre, attendees of the intensive doctoral week seminar at Sciences Po in 2021, and everyone who was part of Ronald Niezen's ethnographic writing seminar.

Certain segments of this work have been included in the following previously published articles and chapters: Vishakha Wijenayake, "Limiting the Risk to combatant Lives: Confluences between International Humanitarian Law and Buddhism" in Andrew Bartles-Smith et al. (eds.) *Buddhism and International Humanitarian Law* (Taylor & Francis 2023) 213, and Vishakha Wijenayake "To Live or Not to Live: International Human Rights Law's Biases on Agency in Suicide" (2023) 3 intergentes at https://intergentes.com/

to-live-or-not-to-live-international-human-rights-laws-biases-on-agency-in-suicide/. I am grateful to the editors and reviewers who provided insightful feedback.

I am profoundly indebted to the friendships forged during my doctoral journey, most importantly, Professor Maya Ceballos, Nivedita Raju, Atagun Kejanlioglu, Dr. Ling Chen, Dr. Amy Preston-Samson, and Professor Upasana Dasgupta. I also wish to express my heartfelt thanks to Dr. Madhawee Fernando, Anushka Gunewardena, Audrey Mackay, and Luwie Ganeshathasan, who have been my reliable support system for many years and continue to offer their encouragement from afar.

I am finally grateful to the city of Montreal, with its serene parks, musicians at the metro stops, and cozy coffee shops (particularly Café Pistache in St Lambert and Clarke Café where some of the chapters were written). It is a communal place that supports without imposing. Thank you for allowing me to be myself and for keeping me emotionally, culturally, and intellectually fulfilled.

Table of Cases and Instruments

INTERNATIONAL DOCUMENTS

INTERNATIONAL CASES

NATIONAL CASES

NATIONAL STATUTES AND CODES

Abbreviations

ECHR	European Convention on Human Rights
ECtHR	European Court of Human Rights
ICJ	International Court of Justice
ICL	International Criminal Law
ICRC	International Committee of the Red Cross
IHL	International Humanitarian Law
IHRL	International Human Rights Law
IS	Islamic State
ISIS	Islamic State of Iraq and Syria
LTTE	Liberation Tigers of the Tamil Eelam
PIJ	Palestinian Islamic Jihad
TNT	Trinitrotoluene
TWAIL	Third World Approaches to International Law
UDHR	Universal Declaration of Human Rights
UN	United Nations
US	United States of America

1
The Narrative Nuances of IHL

1.1. Introduction

To me, as a child, it was a certainty that my father would always be home after work in time for dinner. On the last day of January 1996, however, this sense of normalcy constructed by my nine-year-old self was put to the test, as the evening stretched on in his absence. That morning, the Central Bank of Sri Lanka, located in Colombo, had been struck by a bomb explosion carried out by a suicide attacker belonging to the Liberation Tigers of the Tamil Eelam (LTTE). The blast was so powerful that it damaged the buildings around it, including the Bank of Ceylon's iconic Head Office building. My father was, at the time, an Assistant Bank Manager of that bank's Matara branch, a city more than 150 kilometers south of Colombo. But, on that day, he had taken an early morning train to visit the Head Office on official duty.

By evening, after news of the attack had broken, my mother, sister, and I sat next to a radio, listening to announcements of the deceased and injured. We oscillated between a sense of expectation, waiting to see the familiar sight of my father arriving home, and a sense of dread that, instead, we might hear his name on a list of victims. Mobile phones were not yet a common possession, so we had no information about his whereabouts. The relief we felt when he finally returned home, in time for a relatively late dinner, was enormous.

All things considered, I was fortunate that my childhood experiences of war were peripheral, even trivial. It is true that, for years, fear of clandestine attacks kept us away from crowded places. Schoolchildren, me included, were required to buy schoolbags made of transparent plastics, to prevent anyone from using an unsuspecting child's schoolbag to transport a bomb. To me, all of this seemed normal. Everyone growing up with me shared similar or worse experiences of war. I was grateful that my father came back home, that I had all my limbs, was never recruited to fight, or made to strap a bomb around my body.

Too eager to move on with our lives, which we had the privilege of doing, my family and friends, with whom I had shared war-adjacent experiences, shied away from discussing them. Amidst this reluctance to unpack wartime emotional upheavals, I recall being inhabited by a mixture of victimhood and vigilance, on

Suicide Attacks and International Humanitarian Law. Vishakha V. Wijenayake, Oxford University Press.
 DOI: 10.1093/9780197812174.003.0001

account of constantly living in fear of clandestine attacks, which mingled with a deep-seated sense of guilt for having been spared worse terrors of war.

The Central Bank bombing of 1996 was the first time I had to confront wartime violence personally, and more specifically, suicide attacks. Over time, other memories of war have also become sedimented in the recesses of my memory, accumulations of reported information of various suicide attacks depicting the suicide attacker from a vantage point of fear, casting them in a unidimensional and macabre otherness.

That I chose to focus on the death of suicide attackers in this book may reflect how, either despite or because of the negative emotions I have about the phenomenon, the image of the suicide attacker in my mind's eye has stayed with me since childhood, and continues to subvert my attempts to construct an organized reality. Just as much as my indirect experience of the Central Bank bombing destabilized my childhood sense of security, my intellectual engagements with suicide attacks also continue to challenge the limits of what is within my realm of knowing. A deeper investigation into the phenomenon of suicide attacks has urged me to raise questions, specifically, about the intentionality of suicide attackers' deaths, and to deepen my understanding of how persons exercise agency in relation to their own deaths.

1.1.1. The intrigue of silences

The plethora of legal norms with which I engaged during my legal education and professional life, including those of International Humanitarian Law (IHL), has directly or indirectly shaped the way I see the world, including how I assess my past engagements with war. Yet, neither in IHL provisions nor in related scholarship did I encounter any express mention of suicide attackers. While navigating this silence in IHL, I was compelled to hypothesize that, perhaps like my memories of war, IHL's image of warfare too was not comprehensive. How else would wartime experiences that featured predominantly in my lived reality remain obscure in this branch of the law, the objective of which was to mitigate suffering during warfare? Therefore, my attempts to unpack this phenomenon through the lens of IHL led me to critique the way in which IHL fulfills its function of regulating wartime violence. I was, thus, drawn to examining whether IHL builds its own story of warfare, whether there is some deliberateness behind which practices are deemed worthy of its attention, and which ones are left invisible in the eyes of the law.

At the center of this book is a silence that made me uncomfortable: IHL's silence regarding suicide attacks evoked in me a sense that it did not speak to my memories of war. Silences at times indicate avoidance or denial. I considered that perhaps IHL's silence on suicide attackers, too, was such a denial. However, I recognize that silence is an essential aspect of the law's relation with human agency. If laws regulated all aspects of human behavior, they would deny persons any degree of choice and agency. For example, Jorge Luis Borges provides an extract from "Travels of Praiseworthy Men" by J. A. Suárez Miranda in his short story "On Exactitude in Science":

> In that Empire, the craft of Cartography attained such Perfection that the Map of a Single province covered the space of an entire City, and the map of the Empire itself an entire Province. In the course of Time, these Extensive maps were found somehow wanting, and so the College of Cartographers evolved a Map of the Empire that was of the same Scale as the Empire and that coincided with it point for point. Less attentive to the Study of Cartography, succeeding Generations, came to judge a map of such Magnitude cumbersome, and not without Irreverence, they abandoned it to the Rigours of sun and Rain.[1]

Like this map, which replicated reality point for point, became too cumbersome to handle, a law that is so meticulous and detailed in providing for all eventualities would become cumbersome for the lack of space it affords to human agency. Silences in the law can keep the law's regulatory power minimal, not extending any more than is exactly required, allowing people to enjoy their freedom without any superfluous imposition of norms from external sources. Nevertheless, despite the general utility of silences and indeterminacy in the law, their occurrences in otherwise detailed bodies of law like IHL may also indicate bias in terms of what is worthy of regulation and what is considered beyond its scope. They may also shed light on the kinds of situations in which the law assumes people to be capable of making decisions autonomously, free of prescriptions by the law.

Boaventura de Sousa Santos evokes Borges to examine what silent spaces reveal about the biases that undergird legal rules. The brilliance and intrigue of both maps and laws lie in their omissions.[2] The fact that the geographical space cannot be plotted on a map in all its detail means the cartographer must make value judgments in deciding which details to include. A map omits some aspects of physical space to prioritize others as being more relevant to a potential navigator. Those who create laws, too, are selective about what they see as central to the law, and aspects they consider peripheral, or beyond the remit of legal regulation, are omitted. For example, as feminist legal scholars have shown, the law

[1] Jorge Luis Borges, *A Universal History of Infamy* (Norman Thomas di Giovanni trans., Penguin Books 1975) 131.

[2] Boaventura de Sousa Santos, "Law: A Map of Misreading. Toward a Post-Modern Conception of Law" (1987) 14:3 Journal of Law and Society 279, 283.

has been historically reluctant in regulating what it deemed to be the private affairs of individuals, resulting in its silence on abuses within the domestic sphere. Thus, by highlighting certain issues while shunning others to the periphery, the law projects a constructed reality shaped by, and fitting the worldview of, those with the power to make and interpret laws.[3]

In international law, particularly in the formation of treaty or customary law, disagreements among States based on differences in deeply held cultural beliefs or ways of seeing the world can lead to gaps in the law.[4] Agreements are crucial when creating legal rules because of the bivalent nature of the law; that is, legal rules can only either allow or prohibit behavior, and are not adept in capturing plural views that may fall in between or outside the scope of a binary logic.[5] Where cultural diversity engenders a plurality of positions or practices, rather than adopting a nonbinary or multivalent logic, international law prefers to stay silent. As will be shown in this book, the bivalent logic of IHL struggles to engage with the culturally plural narratives on the death of suicide attackers.

Silences in the law also reveal aspects of human behavior that cultures view as predictable, so much so that legal rules are unnecessary to regulate it. Marianne Constable, in her book *Just Silences,* uses the example of the sign commonly seen in libraries calling for "silence."[6] The absence of such a sign in a particular library may allow one of two interpretations: that everyone knows a library is a quiet place, or that the lack of an express requirement of silence creates an ambiguity with respect to this particular library, that it perhaps never required, or no longer requires, those who use it to always maintain silence.

Like Constable's example, IHL's lack of engagement with suicide attackers' deaths demonstrates a silence on an integral part of warfare: combatant deaths. This silence may stem from IHL taking for granted that States deal with combatant deaths in a uniform manner. The Commentary to Common Article 3 of the Geneva Conventions assumes that how a State treats its troops may not have to be regulated by IHL because militaries would naturally be inclined to treat them humanely, claiming that nevertheless, Common Article 3 would also apply to one's own forces.[7] The assumption that States are inclined to treat their

[3] Ibid. 292.

[4] Dustin A. Lewis, Naz K. Modirzadeh, & Gabriella Blum, "Quantum of Silence: Inaction and *Jus ad Bellum*" (2019) Harvard Law School Program on International Law and Armed Conflict iv.

[5] Patrick Glenn, *The Cosmopolitan State* (Oxford University Press 2013) 262.

[6] Marianne Constable, *Just Silences: The Limits and Possibilities of Modern Law* (Princeton University Press 2005) 12.

[7] International Committee of the Red Cross, *Commentary on the First Geneva Convention: Convention (I) for the Amelioration of the Condition of the Wounded and Sick in Armed Forces in the Field (Commentaries on the 1949 Geneva Conventions)* (Cambridge University Press 2016) paras. 548–549: "In many cases, of course, recourse to common Article 3 may not be necessary to make a Party to a conflict treat its own armed forces humanely, be it because a Party to a conflict will feel under a natural obligation to do so, because it will do so out of self-interest, or because, at least in the case of a State Party, domestic law and international human rights law require treatment at least

combatants humanely dilutes the diversity of combatant experiences, including the fact that not all parties governed by Common Article 3 belong to State armed forces. Therefore, at the root of IHL's understanding of combatants' experiences of death, is the assumption that combatants' experiences of war as part of an armed force tend to be homogeneous.

1.1.2. The silence on suicide attackers in IHL

Although its dynamism has failed to account for suicide attacks as a wartime tactic, IHL has not been a static body of law. Treaties and declarations regulating warfare in the late nineteenth century and at the dawn of the twentieth century depicted war as occurring mainly between State armed forces.[8] With time, the international community, in this context primarily consisting of States, the International Committee of the Red Cross (ICRC), the Red Cross Movement, and other international, nongovernmental, and civil society organizations, has tried to ensure that IHL evolves with changing realities. The 1949 Geneva Conventions were partly an attempt by this international community to update IHL rules to reflect the experiences of World War II.[9] Since then, IHL has adopted a multitude of treaties and soft-law documents to respond to emerging developments in warfare—for example, the Convention on Cluster Munitions

equivalent to that of humane treatment in the sense of common Article 3. Nevertheless, insofar as a specific situation has a nexus to a non-international armed conflict, as in the examples given above, all Parties to the conflict should, as a minimum, grant humane treatment to their own armed forces based on common Article 3."

[8] Declaration Renouncing the Use, in Time of War, of Explosive Projectiles Under 400 Grammes Weight, 11 December 1868, International Military Commission, Saint Petersburg; Project of an International Declaration concerning the Laws and Customs of War, August 27, 1874, Brussels Conference of 1874, Brussels; Convention (III) for the Adaptation to Maritime Warfare of the Principles of the Geneva Convention of August 22, 1864, July 29, 1899, International Peace Conference 1899, The Hague; Declaration (IV,1), to Prohibit, for the Term of Five Years, the Launching of Projectiles and Explosives from Balloons, and Other Methods of Similar Nature, July 29, 1899, International Peace Conference 1899, The Hague; Convention for the Amelioration of the Condition of the Wounded and Sick in Armies in the Field, July 6, 1906, Conference for the revision of the Geneva Convention of 1864, Geneva; Convention (X) for the Adaptation to Maritime Warfare of the Principles of the Geneva Convention, October 18, 1907, International Peace Conference 1907, The Hague; Manual of the Laws of Naval War, August 9, 1913, Institute of International Law, Oxford; Convention for the Amelioration of the Condition of the Wounded and Sick in Armies, in the Field, July 27, 1929, Diplomatic Conference convened by The Swiss Federal Council with a view to the revision of the Geneva Convention for the Amelioration of the Condition of the Wounded and Sick in Armies in the Field of July 6, 1906, and the elaboration of a Code relating to the Prisoners of War, Geneva; Convention relative to the Treatment of Prisoners of War, Geneva, July 27, 1929, Diplomatic Conference convened by The Swiss Federal Council with a view to the revision of the Geneva Convention for the Amelioration of the Condition of the Wounded and Sick in Armies in the Field of July 6, 1906, and the elaboration of a Code relating to the Prisoners of War, Geneva.

[9] Nils Melzer, *International Humanitarian Law: A Comprehensive Introduction* (International Committee of the Red Cross 2019) 36.

(2008), the Montreux Document on Private Military and Security Companies (2008), and the Tallinn Manual on the International Law Applicable to Cyber Warfare (2013).[10] However, it has not made any attempt to create rules expressly governing suicide attacks. Given IHL's meticulous regulation of most aspects of warfare, this silence on suicide attacks becomes an outlier.

Rather than being a peculiar practice of a handful of actors operating in a specific space and time, suicide attacks constitute a practice with a long history which is now spread out across the globe. Some scholars trace suicide attacks to as far back as Jewish Zealots and Sicarii, with the leader of the Zealots persuading the mass suicides in Masada, and from 1090 to 1256, assassins belonging to the Nizari Isma'ilis, a group said to have carried out suicidal missions using daggers.[11] In 1881, Ignaty Grinevitsky, a member of the Russian revolutionary group called the People's Will, threw a fatal bomb at Tsar Alexander II, killing himself in the process.[12] During World War II, the Japanese military conducted Kamikaze attacks, a program of aerial suicide operations that instilled terror in the allied forces. However, the drafting history of the Geneva Conventions of 1949 suggests that representatives of States did not, during the diplomatic negotiations, discuss Kamikaze operations as being distinctive from other attacks.

Suicide attacks have increased in frequency since the 1980s as many non-State armed groups have adopted them as a useful tactic in asymmetrical warfare.[13] For example, Boko Haram has used this tactic while operating primarily in Nigeria, Cameroon, Chad, and Niger; the Chechnyan rebels have employed them in their insurgency against Russia; Hezbollah has been accused of carrying out suicide bombings in Lebanon, Israel, Palestine, and Syria; the LTTE has conducted suicide attacks in Sri Lanka and South India; Hamas has used suicide operations as a tactic in its conflict with Israel; Taliban has frequently used suicide bombings, as have Al-Qaeda in numerous countries across the globe, and more recently ISIS (the Islamic State of Iraq and Syria) has inspired attacks by

[10] Convention on Cluster Munitions, Dublin, May 30, 2008, 2688 U.N.T.S. 39; Montreux Document on Pertinent International Legal Obligations and Good Practices for States Related to Operations of Private Military and Security Companies during Armed Conflict, Montreux, UN doc. A/63/467-S/2008/636, September 17, 2008; Michael N. Schmitt (ed.), *Tallinn Manual on the International Law Applicable to Cyber Warfare* (Cambridge University Press 2013).

[11] Riaz Hassan, *Suicide Bombings* (Routledge 2011) 8–10; Diego Gambetta, "Can We Make Sense of Suicide Missions?" in Diego Gambetta (ed.) *Making Sense of Suicide Missions* (Oxford University Press 2006) 279.

[12] Candice D. Ortbals & Lori M. Poloni-Staudinger, *Gender and Political Violence: Women Changing the Politics of Terrorism* (Springer 2018) 55.

[13] For more on the spread of suicide attacks as a wartime tactic, Michael C. Horowitz, "The Rise and Spread of Suicide Bombing" (2015) 18 Annual Review of Political Science (Palo Alto) 69; Efraim Benmelech, Claude Berrebi, & Esteban F. Klor, "Economic Conditions and the Quality of Suicide Terrorism" (2012) 74:1 Journal of Politics 113; Mia Bloom, *Dying to Kill: The Allure of Suicide Terror* (Columbia University Press 2007).

individuals and small cells in various countries. Given the widespread occurrence of suicide attacks, critically engaging with IHL's silence on the subject may be useful to any practitioner.

One may argue, indeed, that while suicide attacks warrant IHL's attention, there is no need for provisions expressly tackling suicide attacks. According to this view, IHL's general provisions sufficiently regulate suicide attacks, for instance, when the limited scholarship within IHL and the *opinio juris* of States on suicide attacks apply general rules pertaining to the legality of attacks in war to suicide attacks.[14] One of these rules is that parties to a conflict must distinguish between civilian populations and combatants, and between civilian and military objects.[15] Accordingly, a suicide attack that directly targets civilians is prohibited under general rules of IHL. If an attack is directed against a military objective but causes incidental harm to civilians, it would be legal if such harm done from an attack was not expected to be excessive in relation to its anticipated military advantage.[16] Under the current treaty and customary IHL, a suicide attack conducted in a manner that directly targets civilians, or is perfidious,[17] indiscriminate,[18] or disproportionate,[19] would violate IHL. According to these general rules, suicide attacks directly targeting combatants and military objectives would be allowed.[20] The position taken by most, if not all, international law scholars is that suicide attacks, if they respect the general rules of distinction in IHL, would not in and of themselves be illegal.[21] Within this view, suicide attacks are sufficiently regulated inasmuch as their effects on civilians and the adversary are regulated, while apparently deeming irrelevant the unavoidable

[14] Demian Casey, "Breaking the Chain of Violence in Israel and Palestine: Suicide Bombings and Targeted Killings Under International Humanitarian Law" (2005) 32:2 Syracuse Journal of International Law and Commerce 311; Dieter Fleck, "International Humanitarian Law a Decade after September 11: Developments and Perspectives" (2011) 14 Yearbook of International Humanitarian Law 349; Michael Schmitt, "Precision attack and international humanitarian law" (2005) 87:859 International Review of the Red Cross 445; Muhammad Munir "Suicide Attacks: Martyrdom Operations or Acts of Perfidy?" in Marie-Luisa Frick & Andreas T. Müller (eds.) *Islam and International Law* (Brill Nijhoff 2013) 99.

[15] Protocol Additional to the Geneva Conventions of August 12, 1949, and relating to the Protection of Victims of International Armed Conflicts (Additional Protocol I), June 8, 1977, 1125 U.N.T.S. 3, Arts. 48, 51(2) and 52(2). No reservations have been made to these articles. *Legality of the Threat or Use of Nuclear Weapons*, Advisory Opinion, I.C.J. Reports 1996, 226, International Court of Justice (ICJ), July 8, 1996, para. 434: The ICJ stated that the principle of distinction was one of the "cardinal principles" of international humanitarian law and one of the "intransgressible principles of international customary law."

[16] Additional Protocol I (n. 15) Art. 51(5) (b).

[17] Ibid. Art 37(1).

[18] Ibid. Art 51 (4).

[19] Ibid. Art 51 (5) (b).

[20] Switzerland, Federal Council, "Report on IHL and Armed Conflict," September 17, 2010, section 3.4, 12.

[21] Donna E. Arzt, "Can Law Halt the Violence—Palestinian Suicide Bombings and Israeli Targeted Assassinations under International Humanitarian Law" (2005) 11 ILSA Journal of International & Comparative Law 357, 360; Casey (n. 14) 333.

and characteristic effect of a suicide attack, which is its impact on the combatant carrying it out (i.e., that of causing their death).

The premeditated nature and relative certainty accompanying the death of the person carrying out a suicide attack set it apart from all other military attacks governed under IHL.[22] In the latter, minimizing the harm caused to one's own combatants in the course of an attack is a natural part of planning the attack. The high risk or probability of fatality is not unknown by either those planning the attack or those carrying it out, but the intention to cause the death of the combatants carrying out the attack is not part of its plan. As such, the intentionality underlying the death of the suicide attacker warrants specific examination in terms of how it is treated in IHL, and categorizing suicide attacks under the more general banner of "attacks" may preclude such examination.

As will be discussed in more detail in chapter 2, although death is a common effect of warfare, IHL offers little consideration to how dying may be perceived differently in various cultural contexts, remaining relatively blind to the distinctive narratives built within cultures around how a suicide attacker faces intentional and certain death, at times depicting the attacker as an agentic actor, naming them a hero or martyr for sacrificing their lives for a significant cause, or in contrast, painting them as victims, cogs in the wheel of armies or armed groups, or as perpetrators who carry out violence that is deviant and extreme. In failing to engage with the position that suicide attackers' deaths occupy in these narratives, IHL tacitly dismisses their relations to the culture and context within which they occur. In this way, IHL avoids the questions their deaths raise regarding the exercise of agency by combatants who navigate profoundly hierarchical structures and the heterogeneous ways in which agency is depicted in diverse contexts.

Another approach to using existing IHL rules to evaluate suicide attacks is through the application of the provisions regulating the means and methods of warfare. In the conduct of hostilities, IHL regulates targeting enemy combatants to the extent that IHL allows such targeting within specific limits.[23] However, IHL prohibits the use of means or methods of warfare that are of a nature to cause superfluous injury or unnecessary suffering.[24] In the following chapters, I will expose the ambiguities in IHL on whether rules regulating superfluous suffering apply to the treatment of one's own armed forces. Briefly, under the means-of-war approach, suicide attacks are regulated to the extent of their

[22] Bloom, *Dying to Kill* (n. 13) 76: "violent, politically motivated attack, carried out in a deliberate state of awareness by a person."

[23] "Customary IHL—Rule 1. The Principle of Distinction between Civilians and Combatants" *ICRC—IHL Database* (January 1, 2022) online: ICRC https://ihl-databases.icrc.org/customary-ihl/eng/docs/v1_rul_rule1 accessed January 5, 2025.

[24] Additional Protocol I (n. 15) Art 35. Not, however, that Art. .35(2) also applies to civilians: Nuclear Weapons Case (n. 15) para. 78.

impact on adverse parties or civilians, but not in terms of their impact, including death, on one's own combatants. In those chapters, I will also delve into specific provisions of IHL governing methods of warfare, such as those pertaining to the prohibitions of denial of quarter and perfidy, to understand how IHL's treatment of suicide attackers' deaths can be gleaned from these provisions.

In relation to provisions governing weapons of war, it is notable that many current scholarly accounts of suicide attacks have primarily focused on suicide "bombings."[25] Accounts of suicide bombings often begin with the car filled with around 100 kilograms of explosives that crashed into the Iraqi embassy in Beirut in 1981, killing 61 persons including the attacker.[26] Yet, the term "suicide bombings" limits the discussion to a time when explosive technology, especially trinitrotoluene (or TNT), made it possible to blow oneself up along with an intended target.[27] Suicide attacks predate such bombs. Kuyuli was a female army commander under Rani Velu Nachiar, a queen who ruled the Indian city of Sivaganga during colonial times. In 1780, Kuyuli covered herself in oil, set herself on fire, and walked into a British ammunition storehouse—causing it to explode, and allowing her queen to defeat the British and regain her territory.[28] In this instance, she used her body to make a bomb out of an ammunition storehouse, intertwining her body and the weapon, blurring the line between the two. Governing suicide attacks through rules applicable to weapons, thus, excludes the unique role of the attacker who intentionally gives up their life, which presents a type of embodied violence. Likewise, limiting the narrative of suicide attacks to the use of a weapon (e.g., by using the term "suicide bombings") shifts the attention away from the attacker who dies in the process of carrying out the

[25] Debra D. Zedalis, *Female Suicide Bombers* (University Press of the Pacific 2004); Meytal Grimland, Alan Apter, & Ad Kerkhof, "The phenomenon of suicide bombing: a review of psychological and nonpsychological factors" (2006) 27:3 Crisis 107; Horowitz (n. 13); Benmelech, Berrebi, & Klor, (n 14) 113–128; Bloom, *Dying to Kill* (n. 13): while Bloom recognizes historical cases where bombs were not used in suicide attacks, her substantive case studies primarily deal with instances where suicide attacks have been carried out with the use of explosives; Mia Bloom, *Bombshell: Women and Terrorism* (University of Pennsylvania Press 2011).

[26] Gambetta, "Can We Make Sense of Suicide Missions?" (n. 11) 287; Horowitz (n. 13) 72; Daniel Pipes, "The Scourge of Suicide Terrorism" (1986) 4 The National Interest 95, 96; Nora Boustany, "20 Killed, 100 Injured in Explosion at Iraqi Embassy in Lebanese Capital" *The Washington Post* (December 16, 1981) online: https://www.washingtonpost.com/archive/politics/1981/12/16/20-killed-100-injured-in-explosion-at-iraqi-embassy-in-lebanese-capital/271c59ca-126f-4a4f-bee0-9f47d2192f46/ accessed January 5, 2025. For more data on suicide bombings, see Paul Gill, "A Multi-Dimensional Approach to Suicide Bombing" (2007) 1:2 International Journal of Conflict and Violence 142, 144.

[27] Gambetta, "Can We Make Sense of Suicide Missions?" (n. 11) 282.

[28] "Tamil Nadu to Build Memorial for Freedom Fighter Kuyili" *The Times of India* (May 6, 2013) online: http://timesofindia.indiatimes.com/articleshow/20075937.cms?utm_source=contentofinterest&utm_medium=text&utm_campaign=cppst accessed January 5, 2025; Priya S. Lekshmi, "Velu Nachiyar & Kuyili: The Women Who Took Down the British 85 Yrs before 1857!" *The Better India* (28 August 2018) online: https://www.thebetterindia.com/157316/news-india-independence-women-fighters-british-raj/ accessed January 5, 2025.

operation, toward an object, namely, the bomb. This shift can depersonalize and dilute the cultural meanings given to these attacks which are often constructed around the death, the motivations, and the agency exercised by the attacker, rather than the type of weapon they used to commit the attack.

My approach to understanding the silence on suicide attackers' deaths in IHL is to acknowledge that while legal rules influence wartime practices, the law does not have a monopoly over dictating how an individual or society engages with wartime death. Therefore, the intention of this book is not to fill a silence with a new universal norm. Rather, it critically examines why no express provisions exist in IHL regarding suicide attackers' deaths and what it says about the assumptions that determine the scope of the body of law that regulates wartime violence. Accordingly, in the following chapters of this book, I venture to show that IHL's silence on suicide attackers' deaths is a result of its inability to engage with the nuanced ways in which diverse cultures understand combatants' agency over their own deaths. I posit that this failure on the part of IHL renders invisible in its eyes those who do not fit neatly into its boxes.

In examining IHL's silence about the deaths of suicide attackers and what it reveals about IHL's assumptions on how combatants exercise agency when dying in combat, I raise the following questions: What narratives of combatants' agency over their deaths emerge from IHL? What are the cultural frameworks that undergird IHL's narratives of combatant deaths? Do suicide attackers' deaths occurring in diverse contexts challenge the narratives on combatant agency embedded in IHL, and if so, how?

To answer these questions, I examine narratives on suicide attacks in three geographical and cultural contexts: Kamikaze pilots in World War II, female suicide attackers in the Sri Lankan Civil War, and martyrdom operations carried out by jihadist non-State armed groups. These case studies of suicide attacks are selected with a view to examining historical, gender, and religious biases in IHL about how combatants die in battle. The narratives of deaths by suicide attacks in these three contexts offer varied understandings of suicide attackers' agency while subverting IHL's victim-perpetrator binaries and complicating its image of combatants and the types of agencies that they exercise. In this manner, I seek to enrich IHL with pluralistic depictions of combatant agencies in war.

The next sections of this chapter unpack the concept of narratives and their location within cultural contexts as well as larger discursive structures of IHL. First, I will elaborate on why I adopt a narrative approach to law in this book and explain how this approach opens avenues to studying agency and resistance to dominant normative structures. Second, I examine IHL through a narrative approach to law. Through this exercise, I challenge IHL's claim to universality and investigate the *locus* of suicide attackers in IHL's normative framework.

1.2. The importance of narrative constructions

Growing up, I observed how members of my community filled gaps in their knowledge with assumptions about suicide attackers' motivations, weaving together, among others, political propaganda, religious narratives, and historical myths and legends to create a story that made sense to them. For example, in the late 1990s, with limited access to the internet or satellite television, my childhood was dominated by local media reports and informal oral accounts of how the LTTE had been the first and only non-State armed group to employ clandestine suicide attacks against civilians. While this portrayal was not nuanced or even accurate, it generated an image of unparalleled brutality of the LTTE, which was perhaps intended to draw more attention to and sympathy for the victims of their attacks. These narratives played a role in how I and those around me made sense of wartime experiences, in a manner that cannot be divorced from how they interact and negotiate with the diverse normative frameworks that governed warfare. In this section, I explore the concept of narratives and their location within specific cultural contexts. In doing so, I also elaborate how a narrative approach to law opens avenues to studying agency and resistance to dominant normative structures, thereby allowing me to critically analyze IHL's relationship with combatant agency.

1.2.1. Unpacking the idea of narratives

Narratives, simply put, are the stories that are intrinsically tied to how we construct our reality.[29] They provide an avenue for a community to negotiate and find a sense of meaning and ownership over how it structures its ways of seeing the world.[30] In doing so, narratives can play a normative role, meaning they can influence individuals' behavior and guide communities in understanding what is ordinarily allowed, what actions deviate from the norm, and in what cases exceptional behavior may be accepted.[31] For example, as a child, I experienced shock at realizing that my life or the lives of my loved ones could be taken away by a combatant willing to give up theirs. This sense of shock cannot be decoupled

[29] Robert M. Cover, "Foreword: Nomos and Narrative" (1983) 97:1 Harvard Law Review 4, 10; Michel Foucault, "The Order of Discourse" in Robert Young (ed.) *Untying the Text* (Routledge & Kegan Paul 1981) 48, 57. In this book, I have avoided formal constructions of narrative that subscribe to binary thinking. For example, see Seymour Chatman, "Towards a Theory of Narrative" (1975) 6:2 New Literary History 295.

[30] Philipp Kastner, *Legal Normativity in the Resolution of Internal Armed Conflict* (Cambridge University Press 2015) 37: According to Kastner, narratives are viewpoints and experiences told in the form of a story, over which an individual or a collective can claim ownership.

[31] Jerome Bruner, *Acts of Meaning* (Harvard University Press 1990) 47.

from how I have been taught to value life, and my beliefs about death, which placed suicide in the margins of how people are expected to die. These beliefs were complemented by stories I had heard about the LTTE, which depicted them as deviant, violent actors, as opposed to the State military, who were fulfilling a seemingly legitimate role in exercising their acts of violence. Likewise, these communal narratives demarcating whose lives were worth protecting, who was permitted to engage in violence, and which type of deaths were considered abhorrent, shaped my childhood understandings of suicide attackers' deaths.

Narratives, including my childhood narrative of suicide as a type of deviant death, rarely project comprehensive realities. Instead, they can often obfuscate nuances in human behavior and simplify complex social structures by depicting "representations" of reality.[32] For example, Ronald Niezen and Sarah Federman write that the narratives that attempt to make sense of violence and conflict can label people as victims, heroes, or perpetrators, portraying "groups as uniform, bounded entities, with a coherent structure of decision-making and shared political aspirations."[33] Phenomena that are complex in a way that challenge assumptions and tropes embedded in such narratives can "create a cognitive dissonance," particularly when they require a nuanced "understanding of political victimization and vulnerability."[34] To avoid this cognitive dissonance, narratives tend to pursue coherence and simplicity while excluding or distorting certain aspects of life.[35]

Excluding certain realities from a narrative can result in controlling the lived experiences of those whose realities do not fit the norm.[36] Mary Douglas, in her ethnographic study *Purity and Danger* examines how categorizing and classifying things can lead to condemnation of and anxiety around those realities that do not "fit" or are "likely to confuse or contradict cherished classifications."[37] When categories are challenged, those that do not fit with the established framework can be labeled dangerous,[38] or condemned as irrational.[39] In my personal experience, this meant that the death of suicide attackers, by challenging my understanding of how individuals were "normally" meant to die, led me to perceive

[32] Edward Said, *Orientalism* (Vintage Books 1979) 21.
[33] Ronald Niezen & Sarah Federman, "Introduction: Narrative in the Aftermath of Mass Atrocity" in Ronald Niezen & Sarah Federman (eds.) *Narratives of Mass Atrocity: Victims and Perpetrators in the Aftermath* (Cambridge University Press 2022) 6.
[34] Charli Carpenter, *Forgetting Children Born of War: Setting the Human Rights Agenda in Bosnia and beyond* (Columbia University Press 2010) 43.
[35] James Boyd White, "Economics and Law: Two Worlds in Tension" (1987) 54Tennessee Law Review 161, 166; Said (n. 32).
[36] White, "Economics and Law" (n. 35) 174.
[37] Mary Douglas, *Purity and Danger: An Analysis of Concepts of Pollution and Taboo* (Routledge & Kegan Paul 1966) 36–37.
[38] Ibid. 40; Lawrence Rosen, *Law as Culture: An Invitation* (Princeton University Press 2008) 70.
[39] Foucault, "The Order of Discourse" (n. 29) 53.

their actions as "extreme" and provoked a sense of fear in a way that other wartime deaths did not.

Likewise, narratives inform how we respond to complex phenomena. Charli Carpenter notes that one of the reasons certain issues gain more attention over others has to do with how easily they can be framed "so as to resonate with policymakers and publics."[40] She explains how representations of children born of war "functioned not to promote their human rights as war-affected people but instead to frame sexual atrocities in Bosnia as crimes against women."[41] Therefore, even in cases where legal provisions are available within the human rights regime, it can garner less attention due to its inability to fit within the existing narratives surrounding the issue that impact the decision-making of human rights actors. This shows how communally constructed narratives on complex phenomena have a direct bearing on how institutions, policymakers, or funding agencies respond to them, and guide their decisions regarding whether such phenomena are deemed to require regulation or are deserving of sympathy.

Rather than being merely stories told by individuals, narratives are constructed around communal beliefs and value structures, including historical, social, and political dynamics, and they are deeply embedded within broader contexts, reflecting, borrowing from, and reinforcing their norms and ideologies. As such, the notion of culture is vital to a discussion of narratives. Legal anthropologist Lawrence Rosen notes how "culture" encompasses a society's "capacity for creating the categories of our experience" across multiple domains of life, "successfully stitching together these seemingly unconnected realms" to the end of adding a sense of orderliness and logic to collective experiences.[42] Similarly, James Boyd White pays attention to how culture can be defined as the practice of collective "habits of mind and expectations."[43] According to Douglas, culture provides order and meaning to human existence by structuring social relationships, defining roles and statuses, and regulating behavior, creating and perpetuating in this process hierarchies of power through symbolic means and through mechanisms of social control.[44]

The notion of culture cannot be understood in isolation of "configurations of power" given that culture is not simply a reflection of social reality but is actively produced and maintained through systems of power and knowledge.[45] Accordingly, Edward Said, in his seminal work *Orientalism,* unpacks the role

[40] Carpenter (n. 34) 43.
[41] Ibid. 52.
[42] Rosen (n. 38) 4.
[43] James Boyd White, *The Legal Imagination* (abridged version) (University of Chicago Press 1985) xiii.
[44] Mary Douglas, *Risk and Blame: Essays in Cultural Theory* (1st ed., Routledge 1992) 126.
[45] Said (n. 32) 5.

of political and systemic power in how narratives are created, spread, and help structure epistemological frameworks.[46] His discussion pertains specifically to Orientalism as a discourse that gained its relevance because it was created from the point of view of the Western imperialist project to serve its interests. Thus, hegemonic societies, meaning societies where oppressive power is used to suppress the diversity of ideas, such as "the Industrial West," that imbued Orientalism with "strength" and "durability" produce and prioritize narratives in service of those who hold power.[47] Discourses, in this context, can be seen as the organizing power structures that signal toward a narrative's acceptability and influence within a culture. There are multiple competing narratives within any given culture, reflecting diverse perspectives, interests, and power dynamics. Discourses signify the relationships and structures that mediate the prominence given to these narratives, determining which voices are heard, which experiences are validated, and which forms of knowledge are considered legitimate.[48] Analyzing narratives as mediated through discourses permits us to understand how existing power hierarchies shape the assumptions, categories, and biases that drive the stories we tell ourselves, as individuals or as communities, in diverse cultural contexts.

In the critical analysis of cultural narratives in this book, I have no intention to use the notion of culture as a tool to view complex societies through a singular lens, or to portray suicide attacks as defining or being defined by these contexts.[49] I operate with the understanding that a culture is not a monolith and that while cultural contexts remain diverse when compared with one another, there is also significant diversity within each culture. The notion of culture is furthermore characterized by its dynamism.[50] These recognitions are key in finding room for individual agency and communal resistance within hegemonic cultural spaces, providing for the possibility of challenging and subverting existing cultural narratives. They also allow me to acknowledge the types of agencies that can operate within cultures while not being bound by them.

1.2.2. A narrative approach to law

Despite having a dominant influence on legal scholars and practitioners, positivist and natural law traditions fall short of addressing the nuanced relationship between law and the cultural contexts that law occupies. Scholars belonging to

[46] Ibid.
[47] Ibid. 6.
[48] Foucault, "The Order of Discourse" (n. 29) 53.
[49] Arjun Appadurai, "Theory in Anthropology: Center and Periphery" (1986) 28:2 Comparative Studies in Society and History 356, 358.
[50] See Michel Foucault, *The Order of Things: An Archaeology of the Human Sciences* (Vintage Books 1970) 50; Clifford Geertz, *The Interpretation of Cultures* (Basic Books 1973).

both positive and natural law traditions recognize the normative functions of law in that the effect of law on society is to shape human behavior. However, these two legal theories differ in their understanding of the relationship law has with other normative frameworks. Positivist legal scholars tend to emphasize the autonomy of law from culture, arguing that legal norms are distinct from cultural ones and should be analyzed and evaluated based on their own internal criteria of validity.[51] While natural law theorists often view law as deeply intertwined with morality, they often posit the existence of universal moral principles that transcend specific and varied cultural contexts.[52] Likewise, as Boyd White notes, "[b]oth positivist and natural law theories conceive of law as a distinct social and cultural entity with a structure, life, and importance of its own."[53]

Scholarship by legal anthropologists have challenged this approach to law. Rosen thus posits that

> while it is no mystery that law is part of culture, it is not uncommon for those who, by profession or context, are deeply involved in a given legal system to act as if "The Law" is quite separable from other elements of cultural life.[54]

Anthropology of law propounds the unity existing between legal and cultural systems, attempting to understand the law in the context of the cultural frameworks that feed them with meaning.[55] Thus, it challenges preconceived notions about the autonomous nature of the law, including the idea that it is "unaffected by social and economic relations, political forces, and cultural phenomena."[56]

Both natural law and positivist traditions have contributed to forming the foundation for principles of international law. On the one hand, pioneering international law theorists such as Francisco de Vitoria, Hugo Grotius, and Emmerich de Vattel have argued for the universality of fundamental principles of international legal principles pertaining to relations between States, often founded in Christian morality.[57] On the other hand, reflecting a positivist approach to law,

[51] See Hans Kelsen, *Pure Theory of Law* (University of California Press 1967); H. L. A. Hart, *The Concept of Law* (Oxford University Press 1994): especially chapters 7 and 8; Joseph Raz, *The Authority of Law: Essays on Law and Morality* (Oxford University Press 1979).

[52] See John Finnis, *Natural Law and Natural Rights* (Oxford University Press 1980); Hugo Grotius, *De Jure Belli ac Pacis* (Francis W. Kelsey trans., The Carnegie Institution 1925).

[53] White, *The Legal Imagination* (n. 43) xiii.

[54] Rosen (n. 38) 6.

[55] Annelise Riles, "Anthropology, Human Rights, and Legal Knowledge: Culture in the Iron Cage" (2006) 108:1 American Anthropologist 52, 54: "One example would be the consequences of anthropology's disciplinary commitment to context when anthropological discourse enters the human rights field. Anthropologists sometimes invoke context in debates about human rights when they assert that different geographical and social contexts produce entities of different orders."

[56] Laura Nader, *The Life of the Law* (University of California Press 2005) 28: "In the eighteenth century, European intellectuals had treated law as universal and easily identified in all societies."

[57] See Francisco de Vitoria, *Relectiones Theologicae* (Joseph B. Bogen trans., Bobbs-Merrill 1964); Emmerich de Vattel, *Le droit des gens ou Principes de la loi naturelle, appliqués à la conduite et aux affaires des nations et des souverains* (1758); Grotius, (n. 52).

international law limits the primary sources that can be used to identify legal rules to those mentioned in Article 38 of the Statute of the International Court of Justice, which are treaties, international custom, and the general principles of law, recognized by civilized nations.[58]

As René Provost notes, these sources reflect a notion of law that, first, is grounded in "monism (the claim that law is a unified, coherent regime)".[59] This is so as it is geared toward determining general agreements, as is the case in customary law and general principles which look for agreements among States that would unite different regions and cultures.[60] Second, international law is focused on "centralism (associating the power to create valid legal standards with state sovereignty)": the agreements one looks for in international law are those as consented to or practiced by States.[61] In this manner, positivism in international law determines the scope of its regulation by looking for narrow and preexisting legal standards, which makes it challenging to bring the ignored silences in law within its ambit.[62] Finally, embedded in international law is prescriptivism, which treats legal norms as dictating and modifying the behavior of States and, through States, the behavior of those persons coming under their jurisdiction(s). Individuals, therefore, become objects in international law, with limited agency in shaping and creating laws based on their culturally specific realities. The creation of customary law is also centered on State practice, and non-State actors are merely the objects of its prescriptions. Thus, international law does not consider non-State actors including individuals as agentic actors with the power to shape law through their actions and choices. As Sandesh Sivakumaran argues, not only is the capacity of non-State armed groups to obey the law not always considered in creating IHL rules, their views on the law are also not given much significance, as they are seen "solely as a problem rather than also as part of the solution."[63]

[58] Statute of the International Court of Justice, United Nations, April 18, 1946, 33 U.N.T.S. 993, Art. 38: "1. The Court, whose function is to decide in accordance with international law such disputes as are submitted to it, shall apply: a. international conventions, whether general or particular, establishing rules expressly recognized by the contesting states; b. international custom, as evidence of a general practice accepted as law; c. the general principles of law recognized by civilized nations[.]"

[59] René Provost, *Rebel Courts: The Administration of Justice by Armed Insurgents* (Oxford University Press 2021) 11.

[60] Annyssa Bellal & Ezequiel Heffes, "Yes I Do: Binding Armed Non-State Actors to IHL and Human Rights Norms through Their Consent" (2018) 12 Human Rights and International Legal Discourse 120, 121.

[61] Provost, *Rebel Courts* (n. 59) 11; René Provost, "Interpretation in International Law as a Transcultural Project" in Andrea Bianchi, Daniel Peat, & Matthew Windsor (eds.) *Interpretation in International Law* (Oxford University Press 2015) 290, 291: "While all governments are different, all states share in a culture rooted in the idea of sovereignty, such that the transcultural dimensions of international law is in many ways limited."

[62] Provost, *Rebel Courts* (n. 61) 11–12.

[63] Sandesh Sivakumaran, *The Law of Non-International Armed Conflict* (Oxford University Press 2012) 4.

Despite the general State-centricity of international law, it has still evolved to recognize the role of some non-State actors in the practice and interpretation of international law, such as international nongovernmental organizations. In the case of IHL, the role of non-State actors in interpreting the law can be clearly seen in ICRC's role in determining customary rules, writing commentaries, and providing interpretive guidance.[64] However, the key actor in international law, responsible for its formation and implementation, remains the State.

The narrative approach further steps outside this State-centric, positivist, monist, and prescriptivist view of international law, recognizing that law cannot be decoupled from narratives, given how intrinsically tied they are with how we construct reality.[65] Robert Cover notes that rather than being a set of rules sanctioned by State power or setting out an objective truth, laws are a collection of multiple narratives: laws are a part of "a complex normative world," and therefore, our actions cannot be interpreted purely as influenced by laws but by a web of plural norms.[66]

Legal pluralism provides a framework to see the law as a construct specific to each society, which, therefore, interacts with cultural understandings prevalent in different contexts. As Brian Z. Tamanaha notes, scholarship on legal pluralism emerged within legal anthropology and was then adopted by international law scholars, who used legal pluralism to extend international law beyond State action to other actors as well as plural and coexisting normative structures.[67] As such, it provides an alternative to strictly positivist approaches that view the law as a coherent and self-contained system of rules, arguing instead that the law cannot be separated from societies, social practices, and the beliefs of people.[68]

Positivist or natural law approaches tend to create legal categories in which persons are then placed. For example, within IHL, this categorical approach to identity[69] is seen where an individual's role and capacity are determined based on where they fall within the singular distinction between combatant and civilian. Legal victimhood is a process where a narrow category of persons is recognized

[64] Marko Milanovic & Sandesh Sivakumaran, "Assessing the Authority of the ICRC Customary IHL Study" (2022) 104 (920–921) International Review of the Red Cross 1856, 1863: the authors argue that ICRC's customary study has created a "positive feedback loop" of authority that gives it legitimacy, rather than States and international tribunals verifying its accuracy.

[65] Cover (n. 29) 10; Kastner (n. 30) 37: According to Kastner, narratives are viewpoints and experiences told in the form of a story, over which an individual or a collective can claim ownership.

[66] Cover (n. 29) 9; Geertz (n. 50) 5.

[67] Brian Z. Tamanaha, *Legal Pluralism Explained: History, Theory, Consequences* (Oxford University Press 2021) 2.

[68] Martha-Marie Kleinhans & Roderick A. Macdonald, "What Is Critical Legal Pluralism?" (1997) 12 Canadian Journal of Law & Society 25, 27.

[69] Margaret R. Somers, "The narrative constitution of identity: A relational and network approach" (1994) 23:5 Theory and Society 605, 605.

as visible in the eyes of the law based on the harms they have experienced.[70] Such classifications fail to appreciate the plural identities that rest within a person and the relational nature in which cultural identities operate. As Provost and Myriam Denov point out, the sympathy and positive attention one is offered for being labeled a victim come with associations of "powerlessness, vulnerability, and lack of agency."[71] For example, children are considered quintessential victims of war based on the perception that they embody all the attributes of victimhood just mentioned.[72] A cognitive dissonance emerges when child soldiers who engage in combat functions become legitimate targets or liable for the commission of war crimes.[73] The narratives separating victims and perpetrators converge and the agentic nature of the child rests in the balance. Suicide attackers' deaths are another occasion where representations of victimhood of a person conflict with their acts of violence, thereby raising dilemmas about the agency of the relevant actor.

Critical legal pluralism delves into the character of the legal subject, treating them as complex selves with multiple, heterogeneous identities consisting in agency.[74] As such, critical legal pluralism challenges the law's insistence on fitting persons into boxes to make its own operation possible. Provost and Colleen Sheppard's critical approach to legal pluralism acknowledges the agency of individuals, as non-State actors, to create and give meaning to law.[75] The legal subject can "produce legal knowledge and . . . fashion the very structures of the law that contribute to constituting their legal subjectivity."[76] If law controls its subjects, then critical legal pluralism posits that they also control the law.[77] Through their actions and choices, as well as through their relationships with others, they negotiate their place within the law.[78] This is consistent with the idea

[70] Sara Kendall & Sarah Nouwen, "Representational Practices at the International Criminal Court: The Gap Between Juridified and Abstract Victimhood" (2014) 76:3 Law and Contemporary Problems 235, 241.

[71] René Provost & Myriam Denov, "From Violence to Life: Children Born of War and Constructions of Victimhood" (2019) 53:1 New York University Journal of International Law and Politics 1, 35.

[72] See René Provost and Vishakha Wijenayake, "Collateral Kids: Weighing the Lives of Children in Targeting" (2024) 37:4 Leiden Journal of International Law 1018, https://doi.org/10.1017/S0922156524000219.

[73] See René Provost, "L'attaque directe d'enfants-soldats en droit international humanitaire" (2018) 55 Annuaire canadien de droit international 33; René Provost, "Enfants-soldats, civils ou combattants? Expériences et réflexions canadiennes" in Oonagh Fitzgerald, Valerie Hughes, & Mark Jewett (eds.) *Réflexion sur le passé, le présent et l'avenir du Canada en droit international* (CIGI Press 2018) 309.

[74] Kleinhans & Macdonald (n. 68) 36.

[75] René Provost & Colleen Sheppard (eds.) *Dialogues on Human Rights and Legal Pluralism* (Springer Netherlands 2013) 4.

[76] Kleinhans & Macdonald (n. 68) 37–38.

[77] Ibid. 40.

[78] Ibid. 42.

that communal negotiations of meaning generate narratives, which allow for a dynamic understanding of identities rather than them being fixed. As Margaret R. Somers points out, "[n]arrative identities are constituted by a person's temporally and spatially variable place in culturally constructed stories composed of (breakable) rules, (variable) practices, binding (and unbinding) institutions, and the multiple plots of family, nation, or economic life."[79] Narratives help us understand how the attribution of agency to an act, including the act of death by a suicide attacker, is facilitated by negotiating that act's meaning at a social and communal level.

By acknowledging that obedience to law is a personal reflection, critical legal pluralism recharacterizes the legal subject as an actor with agency or a person with the power to negotiate, through their choices and actions, the way they give meaning to law.[80] However, this does not mean that power structures do not have an impact on how normative regimes operate, mainly where coercive measures are involved.[81] Such coercive measures can diminish the capacity of a person to act freely. Provost and Sheppard subject their argument on the agentic nature of non-State actors to this concession:

> the suggestion of agency cannot be taken as a claim of absolute liberty in which legal actors are free to make unconstrained choices about the norms to which they will adhere. That normative universe encases the range of options which we feel are legitimate and open to rational interpretive option.[82]

In this book, I explore the subtle contours that divide these two ideas: recognizing the agency of the suicide attacker to negotiate their actions and acknowledging the possibility that their agency may be influenced by the strict military structures into which they are integrated.

While acknowledging that coercive structures can impose limitations on how individuals and communities exercise their agency, understanding law through the lens of narratives has provided tools for marginalized communities to subvert existing power structures.[83] Federman notes that "narrative approaches operate

[79] Somers (n. 69) 625.

[80] Roderick A. Macdonald & David Sandomierski, "Against Nomopolies" (2006) 57:4 Northern Ireland Legal Quarterly 610, 627.

[81] Ibid.

[82] Provost and Sheppard (n. 75) 4.

[83] Andrew D. Case & Carla D. Hunter, "Counterspaces: A Unit of Analysis for Understanding the Role of Settings in Marginalized Individuals' Adaptive Responses to Oppression" (2012) 50 American Journal of Community Psychology 257; Donald Brenneis, "Telling Troubles: Narrative, Conflict and Experience" (1988) 30:3 Anthropological Linguistics 279, 286: "When others gain legitimate access to such stories, however, personal experience becomes public record, serving as explanatory information, moral example or informal precedent. As such these tales redefine one's relationship to others and one's moral and political stature."

at a story level", with the capacity to be adapted to diverse cultures and provide an opportunity for marginalized peoples to voice their experiences.[84] In the legal discipline, stories have become a way for outgroups or "groups whose marginality defines the boundaries of the mainstream, whose voice and perspective—whose consciousness—has been suppressed, devalued, and abnormalized" to subvert an ingroup reality, projected through existing legal frameworks.[85] Recognizing this capacity of individuals and communities to rely on culturally generated narratives, I take a step further in the next section, to examine how narratives not only shape communal realities external to the law but also have been intertwined into how legal frameworks are framed, including becoming an integral part of IHL.

1.3. The narratives of IHL

As a branch of law that regulates militaries, IHL's narratives are sustained by interacting with stories, myths, and practices such as religious beliefs, military and honor codes, and other cultural rituals that feed it with meaning.[86] The underlying narratives of IHL tend to be specific to a particular State-centric, gendered, and secular cultural understanding of war. For example, European codes of chivalry through historical practice and incorporation into texts have influenced the way in which IHL has developed, thereby prescribing the behavior of soldiers to date.[87] Acknowledging these cultural narratives, I challenge the claim that IHL is neutral, objective, and universal, and then inquire into the *locus* of the suicide attacker within IHL's narratives.

1.3.1. The conventional and critical narratives of IHL

IHL, also called the Law of Armed Conflict (*jus in bello*) by some scholars,[88] seeks to limit the effects of armed conflict by providing protections to those

[84] Sarah Federman, "Narrative Approaches to Understanding and Responding to Conflict" (2016) International Journal of Conflict Engagement and Resolution 154, 166.

[85] Richard Delgado, "Storytelling for Oppositionists and Others: A Plea for Narrative" (1989) 87 Michigan Law Review 2411, 2412.

[86] Amanda Alexander, "Narrative Contingency and International Humanitarian Law" in Ingo Venzke and Kevin Jon Heller (eds.) *Contingency in International Law* (Oxford University Press 2021) 351.

[87] Frédéric Mégret, "The Laws of War and the Structure of Masculine Power" (2018) 19:1 Melbourne Journal of International Law 200, 207–208: "the laws of war can be seen as a sort of apotheosis of then prevalent ideas about what it meant to be manly in war."

[88] Gary D. Solis, *Law of Armed Conflict: International Humanitarian Law in War* (3rd ed., Cambridge University Press 2022); Leslie C. Green, *The Contemporary Law of Armed Conflict*

affected by it. At the oft-told origins of IHL is a vivid account of one man's memories of war. "What tragic, dramatic scenes of every kind, what moving catastrophes were enacted!" wrote Henry Dunant, having witnessed the Battle of Solferino during a journey through Northern Italy in 1859.[89] Fought between Austrian and French troops, the battle left more than forty thousand wounded soldiers. Dunant describes the battle with ample reference to the shattered skulls, dismembered limbs, and walls of wounded and dead bodies.[90] Michael Ignatieff notes how for Dunant, Solferino was a "moral puzzle" about the "myths of a nation's gratitude to its soldiers."[91] Dunant's account of the battle of Solferino inspired the creation of the International Committee for Relief to the Wounded, which preceded the ICRC.[92] His memoir, *A Memory of Solferino*, also persuaded nations to adopt an international treaty to alleviate the suffering of war, namely, the Geneva Convention for the Amelioration of the Condition of the Wounded in Armies in the Field of 1864.[93] Since then, numerous treaties have expanded IHL's contents, at the heart of which rest the four Geneva Conventions of 1949.[94] All United Nations (UN) member and observer States have ratified them, contributing to a narrative of universal acceptance of IHL principles.[95]

To describe IHL with this singular narrative, however, is to simplify a nuanced and contentious account of how laws came to regulate wars. Amanda

(Manchester University Press 2018); William H. Taft IV, "The Law of Armed Conflict after 9/11: Some Salient Features" (2003) 28:2 Yale Journal of International Law 319.

[89] Henry Dunant, *A Memory of Solferino* (American Red Cross trans., American Red Cross 1959) 24.
[90] Ibid.
[91] Michael Ignatieff, *The Warrior's Honor: Ethnic War and the Modern Conscience* (Metropolitan Books 1997) 110.
[92] Henry Dunant (1828-1910) *International Committee of the Red Cross* (April 6, 1998) online: ICRC, https://www.icrc.org/en/doc/resources/documents/misc/57jnvq.htm accessed July 31, 2024.
[93] Convention for the Amelioration of the Condition of the Wounded in Armies in the Field, August 22, 1864, Diplomatic Conference, 08.08.1864–22.08.1864, Geneva.
[94] International Committee of the Red Cross (ICRC), *Geneva Convention for the Amelioration of the Condition of the Wounded and Sick in Armed Forces in the Field (First Geneva Convention)*, August 12, 1949, 75 U.N.T.S. 31; International Committee of the Red Cross (ICRC), *Geneva Convention for the Amelioration of the Condition of Wounded, Sick and Shipwrecked Members of Armed Forces at Sea (Second Geneva Convention)*, August 12, 1949, 75 U.N.T.S. 85; International Committee of the Red Cross (ICRC), *Geneva Convention Relative to the Treatment of Prisoners of War (Third Geneva Convention)*, August 12, 1949, 75 U.N.T.S. 135; International Committee of the Red Cross (ICRC), *Geneva Convention Relative to the Protection of Civilian Persons in Time of War (Fourth Geneva Convention)*, August 12, 1949, 75 U.N.T.S. 287.
[95] Final Declaration of the International Conference for the Protection of War Victims, September 1, 1993, 31st International Conference of the Red Cross and Red Crescent, Geneva, part II, para. 4: "Consider or reconsider, in order to enhance the universal character of international humanitarian law, becoming party or confirming their succession, where appropriate, to the relevant treaties concluded since the adoption of the 1949 Geneva Conventions"; Hans-Peter Gasser, "Universal Acceptance of International Humanitarian Law: Promotional Activities of the ICRC" (1994) 302 International Review of the Red Cross 450.

Alexander notes that the chosen nomenclature "International Humanitarian Law" emphasizes the humanitarian aspect of regulating warfare. However, "this orthodox narrative tends to conflate a long history of varied approaches to the laws of war with modern international humanitarian law,"[96] the former having objectives that were more geared towards satisfying military interests. The result of simplifying a contentious history of how the laws of war developed, according to her, is that "the values of international humanitarian law appear universal and ahistorical."[97]

This narrative also projects an aura of neutrality not only onto IHL rules but also onto its advocates, such as the ICRC, thereby downplaying the role of imperialism and colonialism that featured heavily in how and when IHL rules took shape and were implemented on the ground.[98] Anthony Anghie traces the development and spread of international law as tied to Western colonialism. In his influential article titled *Evolution of International Law: Colonial and Postcolonial Realities*, he notes that this endeavor consisted of establishing "a universal system of order among entities characterised as belonging to different cultural systems."[99] This creation of a universal system rooted in coloniality is what Anghie refers to as "dynamic of difference":

> [I]nternational law posits a gap, a difference between European and non-European cultures and peoples, the former being characterised, broadly, as civilised and the latter as uncivilized.... This gap having been established, what follows is the formulation of doctrines that are designed to efface this gap: to bring the uncivilized/aberrant/violent/backward/oppressed into the realm of civilisation, the universal order governed by (European) international law.... Colonialism, then, far from being peripheral to the discipline of international law, is central to its formation. It was only because of colonialism that international law became universal; and the dynamic of difference, the civilising mission, that produced this result, continues into the present.[100]

This critique of the foundation of international law is one to which many scholars, particularly scholars adopting Third World Approaches to International Law

[96] Amanda Alexander, "A Short History of International Humanitarian Law" (2015) 26:1 European Journal of International Law 109, 112.

[97] Ibid. 113.

[98] Boyd van Dijk, "Internationalizing Colonial War: on the Unintended Consequences of the Interventions of the International Committee of the Red Cross in South-East Asia, 1945–1949" (2020) 250:1 Past and Present 243, 248; also see Frédéric Mégret, "From 'Savages' to 'Unlawful Combatants': A Postcolonial Look at International Humanitarian Law's 'Other'" in Ann Orford (ed.) *International Law and Its Others* (Cambridge University Press 2006).

[99] Antony Anghie, "The Evolution of International Law: Colonial and Postcolonial Realities" (2006) 27:5 Third World Quarterly 739, 742.

[100] Ibid.

(TWAIL) subscribe.[101] As Luis Eslava and Sundya Pahuja posit, international law's preoccupation with achieving normative coherence is intertwined with the type of universalist ideology it projects: a regulatory framework grounded in specificity which seeks "to bring about a certain way of being."[102]

IHL's universalism rests, on the one hand on moral foundations, and on the other hand, on a positivist legal justification based on the consent of States (treaties) and of the general practice of States. As Jean Pictet, the drafter of the original commentaries of the 1949 Geneva Conventions states, IHL has a "universal vocation" "since it applies to all men and countries."[103] This element speaks to the positivist universality based on the Geneva Conventions' universal ratification by States. He further states that IHL's rules are "acceptable to all because they are fully consistent with human nature."[104] Here, he appeals to understandings of humanity and argues that from a moral standpoint, IHL evokes principles that are shared by all.[105] As Patrick Glenn's analysis of legal traditions posits, universality "teaches truths, or a truth, which must be respected, and by everyone."[106] This is also a succinct explanation of a foundational premise of IHL, which requires that all parties to the conventions respect and "ensure respect" for the Conventions "in all circumstances."[107]

Accordingly, IHL's claim to universality indicates that it is comprehensive in its geographical, as well as moral and sociopolitical reach in regulating conflicts around the world. This understanding that all societies accept IHL's rules fails to respond to the ways in which war is practiced in various geographical and cultural contexts. It conceals both diverse cultural practices in wartime contexts and cultural assumptions within its own framework that take certain aspects of warfare for granted. IHL, like the larger international law project, emerged as a European construct, despite its attempts to project seemingly objective rules.[108]

[101] Makau Mutua, "What Is TWAIL?" (2000) 94 Proceedings of the ASIL Annual Meeting 31; Luis Eslava & Sundhya Pahuja, "Beyond the (Post)Colonial: TWAIL and the Everyday Life of International Law" (2012) 45:2 Verfassung Und Recht in Übersee [Law and Politics in Africa, Asia and Latin America] 195; Kwadwo Appiagyei-Atua, "Ethical Dimensions of Third-World Approaches to International Law (TWAIL): A Critical Review" (2015) 8:3–4 African Journal of Legal Studies 209.

[102] Luis Eslava & Sundhya Pahuja, "Between Resistance and Reform: TWAIL and the Universality of International Law" (2011) 3:1 Trade Law & Development 103, 108.

[103] Jean Pictet, "Humanitarian Ideas Shared by Different Schools of Thought and Cultural Traditions" in Henry Dunant Institute, *International Dimensions of Humanitarian Law* (Martinus Nijhoff, 1988) 3.

[104] Ibid.

[105] Also see Theodor Meron, "The Humanization of Humanitarian Law" (2000) 94:2 The American Journal of International Law 239.

[106] Patrick Glenn, *Legal Traditions of the World: Sustainable Diversity in Law* (5th ed., Oxford University Press 2014) 365.

[107] First Geneva Convention (n. 94) Art. 1; Second Geneva Convention (n. 94) Art. 1; Third Geneva Convention (n. 94) Art. 1; Fourth Geneva Convention (n. 94) Art. 1.

[108] Martti Koskenniemi, *The Gentle Civilizer of Nations* (Cambridge University Press 2001) 51; Christine Chinkin & Mary Kaldor, *International Law and New Wars* (Cambridge University Press 2017) 90.

However, IHL is no longer a European project but one that is applicable across culturally diverse battlefields. With the universal ratification of the Geneva Conventions these Eurocentric principles of IHL have been adopted by States around the world and given them the aura of neutrality and objectivity. By not expressly acknowledging diversity in wartime practices, IHL's universal narrative implicitly others cultural practices in war that may be inconsistent with its own rules and the cultural biases that undergird them. In this light, IHL's adoption of a universalist normative framework impacts how it responds to diversity on the battlefield.

IHL regulates wars when violence threatens to destroy established worldviews. Therefore, it tends to lean on its constructed reality with set categories and roles that hold it together. To further this pursuit of maintaining stability during warfare, IHL uses classifications in which objects and people have recognizable roles.[109] Rosen states that culture plays a key role in creating organizing categories that help communities conduct their affairs in an orderly manner.[110] As a product of culture, IHL too is deeply enmeshed in this process, its categories being universally applied across global conflicts without critically investigating the cultural contexts that engendered them. The argument has been made that on the battlefield, where a moment of indecision or miscommunication may be the difference between life and death, acknowledging culturally diverse wartime practices could entail chaos and loss of life.[111] This logic makes it possible for IHL to suppress diverse practices of war by disseminating its universalist normative framework.

Although IHL creates universally applied categories, these categories are bound to the cultural context that inspired their creation. For example, the Third Geneva Convention classifies combatants into officers and soldiers, "reminiscent of the different treatment accorded in Medieval warfare to knights and foot soldiers".[112] Accordingly, in IHL rules, officers are provided treatment based on their rank as compared to prisoners of lower ranks.[113] These categories have gained credibility with time and through State practice. They continue to

[109] Douglas, *Purity and Danger* (n. 37) 37.
[110] Rosen (n. 38) 170.
[111] *The Laws of War on Land* (Oxford Manual) (Institute of International Law September 9, 1880) at Preface: "In fact so long as the demands of opinion remain indeterminate, belligerents are exposed to painful uncertainty and to endless accusations. A positive set of rules, on the contrary, if they are judicious, serves the interests of belligerents and is far from hindering them, since by preventing the unchaining of passion and savage instincts—which battle always awakens, as much as it awakens courage and manly virtues—it strengthens the discipline which is the strength of armies; it also ennobles their patriotic mission in the eyes of the soldiers by keeping them within the limits of respect due to the rights of humanity."
[112] Rain Liivoja, "Chivalry without a Horse: Military Honour and the Modern law of Armed Conflict" in Rain Liivoja & Andres Saumets (eds.) *The Law of Armed Conflict: Historical and Contemporary Perspectives* (Tartu University Press 2012) 75, 82–83.
[113] Third Geneva Convention (n. 94) Arts 44-45.

entrench the cultural biases that created them within the system of IHL. When IHL's rules conflict with other wartime cultural practices, IHL's categories are also challenged. The universalization of IHL requires that its tightly woven narrative constructed around neat categories does not come undone through practices that challenge its bivalent logic.

IHL's simplified narratives place people in mutually exclusive categories diluting the complexity of wartime identities.[114] Civilians do not carry weapons and have not become part of an armed group with the intent of fighting in battle. Therefore, they are prone to be victimized in war. One of the cornerstones of IHL is that civilians are protected from being targeted. Combatants move in and out of victimhood depending on their circumstances. For example, a sick or wounded combatant who can no longer fight is a victim of war and, therefore, deserving of protection. They cannot be legitimately targeted. The victim is vulnerable to being harmed while not having the capacity to harm others. This raises challenges in understanding and legally presenting intricate wartime identities including suicide attackers who, as the book will note in following chapters, eschew such binary categorizations of victim or perpetrator.

1.3.2. The place of suicide attackers in the narratives of combatancy in IHL

Looking at IHL as performing narrative functions necessitates an inquiry into what narrative devices it uses to maintain its silence on suicide attackers. This section precedes and facilitates a more elaborate and contextualized analysis in later chapters of tropes embedded in IHL that provide us with cues about the role that suicide attackers play within the wartime landscape and the limits of their agency.

Prior to embarking on uncovering the *locus* of IHL's image of the suicide attacker or specific causes for its absence, it is apt to consider the generalized image of a combatant that this body of law projects. The image of a combatant is bound within the scope of armed conflicts and the confines of the battlefield as designed by IHL rules. IHL's projection of combatants has been created based on European values of an ideal soldier/warrior. Likewise, Michael Walzer refers to the professional soldier, as the descendant of the feudal knight.[115] As will be further elaborated in the upcoming chapters, IHL's image of a combatant is rooted in cultural narratives that are gendered, influenced by chivalric traditions

[114] Saira Mohamed, "Of Monsters and Men: Perpetrator Trauma and Mass Atrocity" (2015) 115:5 Columbia Law Review 1157, 1161.

[115] Michael Walzer, *Just and Unjust Wars: A Moral Argument with Historical Illustrations* (3rd ed., Basic Books 2000) 34.

of Medieval Europe, and State-centric. It would be wrong to say, however, that in the various interpretations of IHL provisions, one can identify a singular image of combatants. While States under international law have the primary capacity to develop IHL and, therefore, its narrative, this does not translate to them creating a coherent narrative of war in interpreting IHL. Given that States themselves are diverse, they tend to interpret and create images of IHL that would align with their interests.

In pursuit of its "war on terror," the United States (US) began constructing its own narrative of war that justified inhumane detention practices of "unlawful combatants."[116] In doing so, the US interpreted IHL to create its narrative of combatants and the conditions of their treatment. While the reality on the battlefield rarely remains tidy, ICRC has developed ways to manage these diverging interpretations of the existing framework. The interpretive guidance the ICRC published in 2009 was a guideline on how to treat civilians who directly take part in hostilities. It created new concepts, such as the continuous combat function and metaphors like the revolving door, which exist between civilian and combatant categories. This generated a new plot and characters to help make sense of the original narrative of IHL and sustain it in the face of evolving realities on the battlefield.[117]

IHL's structure is facilitated by the military context which carries a persuasive institutional narrative. Émile Durkheim suggests that out of the many institutions that form a society, the military's narratives can be indoctrinating and coercive, at least in relation to those internal to it.[118] The military ethos is one of hierarchy, subordination, and obedience.[119] This opens a debate about the extent to which there is space in the military for an agentic subject. Jeff McMahan highlights how exigencies of war demand that the individuality of combatants be surrendered to larger objectives. According to him, in the case of a soldier, the notion of duty overrides their moral autonomy, converting themselves into the instruments of others.[120] IHL mirrors this highly collectivized structure. Within IHL, a combatant is required to belong to an organized armed group of a party

[116] Office of the Deputy Assistant Attorney General, "Re: Military Interrogation of Alien Unlawful Combatants Held Outside the United States" U.S. Department of Justice, March 14, 2003.

[117] International Committee of the Red Cross (ICRC), "Interpretive Guidance on the Notion of Direct Participation in Hostilities under International Humanitarian Law" May 2009.

[118] Émile Durkheim, *On Suicide* (Robin Buss trans., Penguin Books 2006) 253.

[119] Samuel P. Huntington, *The Soldier and the State: The Theory and Politics of Civil-Military Relations* (Harvard University Press 1956) 90.

[120] Jeff McMahan, *Killing in War* (Clarendon Press 2009) 72: "The exigencies of war may afford no time for those lower down to engage in careful reflection, and the necessity of classifying information may in any case deprive them of resources necessary for informed deliberation. Military institutions may thus be better able to achieve their morally vital aims if those who occupy the various positions in the chain of command surrender their autonomy and defer entirely to the authority of those above them."

to the conflict or spontaneously take up arms against an approaching enemy (*levée en masse*).[121] This signifies the importance of combatants being part of a collective. In turn, IHL provisions fail to give direct expression to how individual combatants exercise agency on the battlefield.

However, in the eyes of the law, the actions of individual combatants do have consequences. As will be elaborated in later chapters, combatants are called to exercise agency on the battlefield, for example, to disobey manifestly unlawful orders. They can also be held accountable under international and domestic criminal law for violating the rules of IHL and committing war crimes. Therefore, there is tension between the idea that combatants operating within the military environment have limited agency and the legal consequences attributed to their actions. The suicide attacker's death, given that suicide is often considered a voluntary act, stands at the crossroads of the debate on whether a combatant who is strictly part of the collective dynamic of a military can exercise individual agentic acts, in this case, the act of dying.

The agency that combatants exercise regarding their own deaths cannot be decoupled from their primary function in warfare. Combatants must carry weapons openly as a sign that their function is to attack, shoot, or even kill. For instance, a person who is part of an organized armed group in the capacity of a medical officer would not be considered a combatant because they are not in the business of killing, which in IHL is a defining feature of combatants.[122] But the weapon and the capacity to kill others also distinguishes combatants as legitimate targets, who can be legally killed.[123] Despite this relationship that combatants have with killing and dying, IHL does not directly regulate how combatants negotiate agency while engaging in hostilities. This silence in IHL conceals a thick narrative of soldiers' sacrifice that can be found implicitly embedded in its principles and shape IHL's approach to agency in combatant deaths.

While not expressly mentioned in IHL provisions this notion of warriors' sacrifice underlies IHL's ethos. Ignatieff notes that "codes of a warrior's honor" served as a "deeper moral source" for IHL Conventions.[124] While admitting that "codes vary of culture to culture," he claims that they are "a common feature" of human morality.[125] One example of an underlying assumption of a combatant's sacrifice in IHL principles is its ban on mercenaries. Additional Protocol I to the Geneva Conventions defines a mercenary as a person who takes

[121] Third Geneva Convention (n. 94) Art. 4 (A).

[122] Customary IHL Study, "Customary IHL Rule No. 3: Definition of Combatants," online: ICRC—IHL Database https://ihl-databases.icrc.org/customary-ihl/eng/docs/v1_rul_rule3#Fn_91C058A1_00015 accessed January 5, 2025.

[123] Melzer (n. 9) 85.

[124] Ignatieff (n. 91) 116.

[125] Ibid. 117.

part in hostilities motivated primarily by the desire for private gain.[126] The commentary to Additional Protocol I notes that selfless foreign volunteers are not considered to be mercenaries and monetary gain is integral to how a mercenary is defined.[127] Implicit in these requirements is the idea that IHL's image of a soldier is of a person fighting due to a reason that goes beyond pure monetary gain which equates to self-interest. Accordingly, a soldier putting his or her life at risk is meant to be carrying out, at least to some extent, a selfless act of sacrifice.

Contrary to narratives that frame combatant deaths as a sacrifice, not much documentation is available on suicides that occur in Western military contexts, specifically during the conduct of hostilities. While examples of suicides in military contexts exist, Western militaries have reserved the term "suicide" for agentic deaths lacking the purpose of serving their nation and therefore are mutually exclusive with sacrificial deaths. For example, Patricia E. Prestwich notes the relative silence in official records on the suicides within the French ranks during World War I. She specifies that in the French military at the time, a soldier who committed suicide was considered to have deserted the forces, and failed attempts at suicide resulted in harsh sanctions.[128] Militaries often considered suicide as an abandonment of the larger purpose of serving one's nation or community: "[s]uicidal soldiers were cowards" on account of failing to exercise their efforts to support their peers.[129] It speaks to how the French military approached the issue of individual agency of its soldiers: agentic acts, when it contradicted the aspirations of the military's normative framework, were not entertained. These narratives of suicides by combatants can be distinguished from the cultural narratives constructed around suicide attackers' deaths. This is so, as unlike the deaths considered cowardly in militaries, suicide attackers die while engaging in hostilities rather than to escape from them.

To understand how suicide attacks become a sacrifice for the collective rather than an individual's escape route, it is crucial to examine cultural understandings of suicide as a collective act. Niezen argues that in some cultural contexts, suicide can become the source of "interpersonal connection and identity":[130] an act of individual agency that is directed toward social belonging. Likewise, suicide can be seen as building social solidarity.[131] The act could also

[126] Additional Protocol I to the Geneva Conventions (n. 15) Art. 47(1).

[127] Bruno Zimmermann et al., *Commentary on the Additional Protocols of 8 June 1977 to the Geneva Conventions of 12 August 1949* (Brill 1987) paras. 1809–1810.

[128] Patricia E. Prestwich "Suicide and French Soldiers of the First World War: Differing Perspectives 1914-1939"' in John C. Weaver & David Wright (eds.) *Histories of Suicide: International Perspectives on Self-Destruction in the Modern World* (University of Toronto Press 2009) 135.

[129] Ibid.

[130] Ronald Niezen, "The Durkheim-Tarde Debate and the Social Study of Aboriginal Youth Suicide" (2015) 52:1 Transcultural Psychiatry 96, 108.

[131] Ibid. 111.

be social because it is an individual agentic act exercised to protest a social injustice. Lisa Stevenson's work on "the psychic life of biopolitics" critiques the State's desire to make live at the population level, in the context of the Inuit youth suicide epidemic. Her article evokes the possibility that those who kill themselves may be acting as agentive subjects by refusing to cooperate with a regime that purports a truth that life is always worth living.[132] Michael J. Kral who explores how the idea of suicide is internalized through culture, argues that suicide is a type of social logic and that the method by which people kill themselves can be highly local and deeply embedded in the cultural system of ideas.[133] However, this embeddedness to culture does not take away from the agency of this act. Kral insists that it is important to hold on to the idea of suicide as a conscious choice.[134]

Natalia Linos presents theoretical entryways for anthropology to engage with the topic of suicide attacks. Linos indicates how the body can be the site of political control and oppression.[135] She employs Michel Foucault's elaboration of governmentality and biopolitics, which details how in modernity, laws began to be used to control what human populations did with their lives and bodies. Linos hypothesizes that "severe political and structural violence that threatens the body and identity of an individual and his group can be rejected through the 'reclaiming of the body' which, in its most extreme form, happens by self-directed violence—in this case, suicide."[136] Likewise, suicide attacks can indicate a person's resistance against the control of one's body and the bodies of one's community by an alien sovereign power. This act expresses the agency of the individual attacker and speaks for their community, oppressed by a sovereign power whose identity they do not recognize as conforming to their own. Therefore, by using their body for violence, the suicide attacker keeps the agency of their community alive. The act of suicide becomes not merely a death but a performative exercise of agency.

[132] Lisa Stevenson, "The Psychic Life of Biopolitics: Survival, Cooperation, and Inuit Community" (2012) 39:3 American Ethnologist 592, 601: "One of the persistent questions of this article is, what does it mean to cooperate in survival? To see life as a value in itself? To get up out of the snow and go back to the residential school where a 'rehabilitation' program was in full swing? To eat, as the doctor urged Michael K to do—so that he could resume the jumping jacks and flag salutes of his reeducation center? . . . And what does it mean to resist such cooperation? The irony, of course, is that by the 1970s, after Inuit health had undergone increasing surveillance, when fewer Inuit were dying in childbirth, of starvation, and of tuberculosis, a suicide epidemic among Inuit youth erupted. On some level, Inuit youth were not willing to cooperate."

[133] Michael J. Kral, "Suicide as Social Logic'" (1994) 24:3 Suicide and Life-Threatening Behavior 245, 248.

[134] Ibid.

[135] Natalia Linos, "Reclaiming the Social Body through Self-Directed Violence: Seeking Anthropological Understanding of Suicide Attacks" (2010) 26:5 Anthropology Today 8, 8.

[136] Ibid. 9.

1.4. Conclusion

Through this chapter, I have demonstrated that the shock or anxiety that suicide attacks generate cannot be analyzed as an isolated phenomenon, but only through the place it occupies in a more extensive system.[137] Chapter 2 sets the thematic and conceptual setting for the case studies by exploring how culturally nuanced articulations of agency related to death are more adept at depicting how IHL can relate to the narratives of agency constructed around suicide attackers. I trace the notions of killing and death that vary across history and geographical or cultural contexts and juxtapose them with the understanding of death that emerges within IHL provisions. Then, I examine how suicide generates narratives that can be distinguished from other types of deaths, especially regarding the agency attributed to this act. I present the narratives built around the deaths of suicide attackers that depict them as engaging in agentic acts.

Chapters 3 to 5 contain my case studies. Namely, I study the Kamikaze pilots during World War II, the LTTE's female suicide attackers, and martyrdom operations that have been carried out in the name of *jihad*. These are not the only contexts in which suicide attacks have taken place. My choice of the case studies was based on how they challenged three assumptions about combatant deaths in IHL. First was the reciprocal risk taken in combatant deaths and how this assumption is tied to a Eurocentric image of warfare. The case of the Kamikaze pilots with a policy of fighting till death presented a State armed force that challenged the extent to which IHL considers a combatant can assume risk to oneself while also being an agentic actor. Second, IHL adopts a gendered view on combatants' exercise of agency. The female suicide attackers of the LTTE, an armed group that facilitated a narrative of female liberation, reveals points of friction with this gendered image of agency that tends to place women in the category of victims. Finally, I delve into IHL's concept of combatants as rational actors operating in a secular construct of war. I challenge this image by counterposing it with martyrdoms carried out in the name of *jihad* and how subjective intentionality becomes a key feature in narratives surrounding these attacks. I conclude by uncovering IHL's understanding of combatant agency and by providing a more constructive and culturally plural understanding of IHL that could prevent it from remaining silent on diverse approaches to agency as seen in suicide attackers' deaths.

[137] Douglas, *Purity and Danger* (n. 37) 36: "Dirt is the by-product of a systematic ordering and classification of matter, insofar as ordering involves rejecting inappropriate elements."

2
The Contested Agency in Suicide Attackers' Deaths

2.1. Introduction

Despite death being a universal experience, the diverse ways in which people die and the contexts surrounding death remain complex.[1] Suicide represents one such form of death. As Hector N. Qirko notes, "Why any given individual commits to suicidal action is influenced by many factors, including adherence to group and community norms and ideologies as well as personal disposition and circumstances, and so can never be fully known or predicted."[2] It would, therefore, be reductive to make categorical claims regarding the agency exercised by suicide attackers in relation to their own deaths. Rather than seeking to provide definitive statements about the psychological conditions that may contribute to their behavior, this chapter examines the narrative construction of agency in the context of suicide attacks, and the extent to which these narratives shape perceptions of suicide attackers as either deviant yet agentic actors or victims of circumstance.

Owing to their public and political nature, wartime suicide attacks differ from peacetime suicides, which are considered personal and stemming from psychological conditions. Both the attacker and the armed group or military to which they belong aim to create public narratives that extend beyond the act itself. When compared with how militaries and armed groups talk about the ordinary deaths of combatants, suicide attackers' deaths generate significant agentic narratives. In Palestine, each act of martyrdom by a suicide attacker tends to generate new posters that commemorate the life and death of the martyr.[3] The suicide attackers were invited to a ritual dinner with the leader of the Liberation Tigers of Tamil Eelam (LTTE) enhancing their individual recognition.[4] These narratives often glorify the death of the suicide attacker as an agentic act. This is not to say that other soldiers' deaths are any less agentic than the deaths of

[1] Glennys Howarth, *Death and Dying: A Sociological Introduction* (Wiley 2007) 2.
[2] Hector N. Qirko, "Altruism in Suicide Terror Organizations" (2009) 44:2 Zygon 289, 292.
[3] Mia Bloom, *Dying to Kill: The Allure of Suicide Terror* (Columbia University Press 2007) 30.
[4] Diego Gambetta, "Can We Make Sense of Suicide Missions?" in Diego Gambetta (ed.) *Making Sense of Suicide Missions* (Oxford University Press 2006) 277.

Suicide Attacks and International Humanitarian Law. Vishakha V. Wijenayake, Oxford University Press.
 DOI: 10.1093/9780197812174.003.0002

suicide attackers. However, the narratives generated around the individual deaths of the latter group elevate the individuality and the agency of the attacker in a way that is less often seen in the depiction of the general combatant deaths. Their agency is not ascertained by factually delving into the attacker's intention but is attributed *ex post facto* by the social symbolization of the act by the community that supported it. Not all narratives grant the attacker full agency in their deaths. Scholarly and political discourse have framed these attackers instead as victims of coercion, ideological indoctrination, or socioeconomic desperation. This chapter explores how the *locus* of power over death becomes a critical point of tension in understanding the agency of suicide attackers.

In interpretations of International Humanitarian Law (IHL) that follow the positivist tradition in international law, non-State armed groups and individual combatants are seen as having minimal agency to create or influence legal norms. The power to shape laws rests primarily with States, leaving out the lived experiences and normative choices of those who do not occupy State-centric positions of power. However, it is not possible to sequester agency from social and cultural norms that influence human behavior.[5] Legal pluralism recognizes that individuals engage with diverse normative frameworks, meaning agency encompasses the individual's capacity to navigate and shape these frameworks. This broader understanding of agency is critical in analyzing the actions of suicide attackers, whose deaths are shaped by complex and often competing narratives of choice and coercion.

IHL's engagement with agency exercised by individual combatants has been nuanced by the jurisprudence of International Criminal Law (ICL). ICL holds combatants accountable for their actions on the battlefield, imposes individual criminal responsibility on combatants, and, therefore, recognizes that they exercise agency over their acts.[6] This accountability is consistent with the customary IHL rule that obliges combatants to exercise free will to refuse to obey manifestly unlawful orders.[7] However, casebooks are not filled with accounts of combatants refusing to commit war crimes. Indeed, instances where combatants refused to commit war crimes may evade scholarly attention for that very reason. On the other hand, when combatants are tried for war crimes they committed, the prosecutorial process delves into their *mens rea* or the intention or knowledge, as a necessary condition of criminal responsibility.[8] This results

[5] Laura M. Ahearn, "Agency" (1999) 9:1/2 Journal of Linguistic Anthropology 12, 13.

[6] Gabriella Blum, "The Individualization of War: From War to Policing in the Regulation of Armed Conflicts" in Austin Sarat, Lawrence Douglas, & Martha Merrill Umphrey (eds.) *Law and War* (Stanford University Press 2013) 48, 67.

[7] Customary IHL Study, "Customary IHL Rule No. 154: Obedience to Superior Orders," online: ICRC—IHL Database https://ihl-databases.icrc.org/customary-ihl/eng/docindex/v1_rul_rule154 accessed January 5, 2025.

[8] Rome Statute of the International Criminal Court, U.N. General Assembly, July 17, 1998, Art. 30.

in a narrative where the agency of combatants only becomes a focus when they deviate from the norms of IHL. Thus, judicial and scholarly discourses engaging with combatant agency become dominated by criminal conduct, which taints the concept of combatant agency with negative connotations of illegality. Thus, in legal accounts, an agentic combatant becomes almost synonymous with a war criminal. More nuanced accounts of agency remain outside the blackletter of the law.

The overemphasis on agency exercised in violation of international rules does not mean that the law does not provide space for combatants to exercise agency when conforming to international law rules, albeit within a limited scope. For example, if an order is manifestly unlawful within international law, a combatant is required to exercise agency to disobey such order, thereby showing allegiance to international legal rules. International law, however, does not go so far as to acknowledge that the individual combatant as capable of creating new legal norms, especially when they are subversive to existing legal rules, or when they draw on different cultural understandings of how to operate on the battlefield.

While recognizing that agency is a multifaceted concept discussed across various scholarly disciplines, this chapter approaches it through the lens of legal pluralism. This perspective is particularly relevant to the book's aim of navigating points of tension where we locate agency in death, but also to how these understandings of agency are translated into legal norms in IHL. As outlined in chapter 1, critical legal pluralism seeks to explain how individuals exercise agency by choosing to be bound by particular normative frameworks and depicts the legal subject as an individual endowed with relative degrees of agency, even in contexts where coercion is present.[9] As Roderick A. Macdonald and David Sandomierski argue, "all obedience to law is, . . . the fruit of personal reflection, greater or lesser, conscious or tacit, according to the case, and a judgment about what justice requires."[10] In this context, an agentic individual is "capable of purposive action," engaging with the law in ways that go beyond mere compliance.[11] Thus, critical legal pluralism contributes to the discussion on the agency of suicide attackers by acknowledging that even those who lack formal

[9] Martha-Marie Kleinhans & Roderick A. Macdonald, "What Is Critical Legal Pluralism?" (1997) 12 Canadian Journal of Law & Society 25, 40. This is not to deny structures of domination and their effect, nor is it to deny the coercive operations that are masked by attention to law, but rather to emphasize the resistance to domination that is evidenced in subjects' creative capacity. René Provost & Colleen Sheppard, "Introduction: Human Rights through Legal Pluralism" in René Provost & Colleen Sheppard (eds.) *Dialogues on Human Rights and Legal Pluralism* (Springer Netherlands 2013).

[10] Roderick A. Macdonald & David Sandomierski, "Against Nomopolies" (2006) 57:4 Northern Ireland Legal Quarterly 610, 627

[11] Kristen Rundle, *Forms Liberate: Reclaiming the Jurisprudence of Lon L. Fuller* (Bloomsbury Publishing 2012) 9–10; Lon L. Fuller, "Freedom: A Suggested Analysis" (1955) 68 Harvard Law Review 1305, 1307.

lawmaking power can still exercise agency in choosing and influencing the normative frameworks that guide their actions.[12]

Legal pluralism recognizes that agency can be understood not only as an individual choice but also through the normative frameworks shaped by communities and shared interpretations. As Robert Cover posits, legal norms are held together through interpretive commitments: a community exercises agency in interpreting legal norms and then chooses to be bound by these commitments. In legal adjudication, an act is deemed agentic, to some extent, based on how others view this act. For example, criminal courts would ascertain the agentic quality of an act based on how the evidence is presented and the narratives constructed by legal counsel fit with the applicable legal norms, making the determination of agency a highly interpretive enterprise. Cultural narratives play a key role in how or whether deaths, including suicides, are depicted as agentic acts with legal meaning. Suicide is an act through which a person prioritizes commitment to a normative order even in death, providing an extreme instance of seizing control over one's own life.[13] Anthropologist Bronislaw Malinowski examined how suicide in the South Pacific Trobriand Islands was considered a socially accepted way to seek redress for problems. He narrates the story of a sixteen-year-old Trobriand who threw himself off a coconut tree as a response to a failed romantic relationship that garnered negative public attention. Through this example, Malinowski argues that in specific contexts, suicide can operate as a social institution that enables a person to escape obligations, to express protest or vengeance, or to seek rehabilitation. Therefore, although it is "by no means a purely juridical institution, suicide possesses incidentally a distinct legal aspect."[14] Using suicide as a protest does not occur only in the South Pacific Islands. The Bosnian Croat war criminal Slobodan Praljak took potassium cyanide in the International Criminal Tribunal of Yugoslavia Courtroom seconds after having lost his appeal. In reaction to his death, leading Croat politicians have called the suicide a sacrifice that Praljak took to demonstrate he was not a war criminal and that it is a statement against the profound moral injustice of the trials.[15]

These narratives depict the person committing suicide not as a mere subject of law but as someone taking self-destructive action to take control over the normative framework that governs them. This chapter further explores narrative

[12] Kleinhans & Macdonald (n. 10) 38: "Legal subjects are not wholly determined; they possess a transformative capacity that enables them to produce legal knowledge and to fashion the very structures of law that contribute to constituting their legal subjectivity."

[13] Robert M. Cover, *Narrative, Violence, and the Law: The Essays of Robert Cover*, Martha Minow, Michael Ryan, & Austin Sarat (eds.) (University of Michigan Press 1995) 208.

[14] Russell Smith & Bronislaw Malinowski, *Crime and Custom in Savage Society* (1st ed., Routledge 2013) 111, 97–99.

[15] "Slobodan Praljak Suicide: War Criminal 'Took Cyanide' in Hague Court," *BBC News* (December 1, 2017) online: https://www.bbc.com/news/world-europe-42204587 accessed January 5, 2025.

constructions of agency and how they can depict the suicide attacker as someone prioritizing commitment to a normative framework as set out by an armed group, a military, or a community at large against the adverse party to an armed conflict who wishes to impose their authority or sovereignty over a community. It explores how interacting with such narratives would require IHL to recognize combatants as legal agents making "conscious and deliberate action" in choosing which normative framework they adopt when conducting hostilities.[16]

2.2. Agency in understandings of suicide

Discourses on suicide have evolved across time and vary by cultural context. In some cultures, at specific points in history, suicide was morally and legally sanctioned, portraying the act of committing suicide as a deviant exercise of agency. Some other cultures have considered it an honorable agentic act, particularly in circumstances where the person ended one's life for the betterment of others. The current dominant approach medicalizes suicide and treats the person as the victim of a pathological condition. The pathologizing of suicide in the sciences has become intertwined with broader narratives which challenge the capacity of the person committing suicide to engage in agentic acts. While acknowledging the importance of medicalization of suicide in general, and its role in removing legal sanctions placed on this act, the chapter notes that essentializing suicides, even for the purpose of decriminalization, may lead to disregarding the agency attached to such acts in different cultural contexts.

2.2.1. Historical overview of suicide as an agentic act

Today, suicides are often seen as private acts which become public to the extent that medical intervention becomes necessary.[17] Medicalization has become a central feature of modernity's approach to suicide. Scientific disciplines such as psychology, psychiatry, and sociology have also presented their own relatively siloed narratives on this topic. For instance, scholarship in psychiatry argues that common biological or genetic factors and psychiatric disorders can cause suicidal tendencies in individuals.[18] Sociological scholarship deems

[16] Jeremy Webber, "Legal Pluralism and Human Agency" (2006) 44:1 Osgoode Hall Law Journal 167, 169.

[17] Katrina Jaworski, "Suicide, Agency, and Limits of Power" in Ludek Broz & Daniel Münster (eds.) *Suicide and Agency: Anthropological Perspectives on Self-Destruction, Personhood, and Power* (Routledge 2016) 183.

[18] Lil Traskman-Bendz & J. John Mann, "Biological Aspects of Suicidal Behaviour" in Keith Hawton & Kees van Heeringen (eds.) *The International Handbook of Suicide and Attempted Suicide*

explanations for suicide that are rooted in studies of individual biological or psychological factors to be insufficient. It focuses on sociocultural factors that can cause suicide.[19] It is at times hard to reconcile these different narratives, such as the medicalized account of suicide, which views it as an individual condition, and that of sociology, which highlights the social conditions in which suicides take place.[20]

Discourses surrounding suicide have evolved over the years. In Western cultures, prior to Medieval times, suicide was not always treated with connotations of social and moral deviance.[21] Stoic philosophers in ancient Greece accepted that suicide was a reasonable way of dying in some circumstances, especially where obligations to others or deterioration of one's quality of life were involved.[22] Early Roman society valorized committing suicide under certain conditions as being honorable, including when commanders or soldiers killed themselves when faced with being captured by enemies.[23] In early Judeo-Christian texts, suicides were not always subject to moral disapprobation.[24] One such well-known account from the Old Testament is that of Samson, the last judge of the ancient Israelites, who, with the strength granted to him by God, knocked down the pillar of a temple, killing himself and three thousand Philistines.[25] Here, not only was there self-harm but there was also killing of others in the process. Samson's story has inspired narratives for Israeli soldiers to sacrifice themselves.[26]

Often, the value attached to suicide was measured in relation to the social good it was intended to serve. Kay Redfield Jamison notes that "the Eskimo, Norse, Samoan, and Crow Indian [cultures] accepted, and even encouraged 'altruistic' self-sacrifice among the elderly and sick."[27] Ancient Chinese communities

(Wiley 2000) 65, 65–93; Jouko K. Lonnqvist, "Psychiatric Aspects of Suicidal Behaviour: Depression" in Hawton & van Heeringen (*supra*) 107, 107–120: "The risk of suicidal behaviour has always been connected with depressive disorders."

19 Unni Bille-Brahe, "Sociology and Suicidal Behaviour" in Hawton & van Heeringen (n. 18) 193, 193–207.

20 Daniel Münster and Ludek Broz, "The Anthropology of Suicide: Ethnography and the Tension of Agency" in Daniel Münster and Ludek Broz (eds.) *Suicide and Agency: Anthropological Perspectives on Self-Destruction, Personhood, and Power* (Routledge 2016) 5.

21 Jennifer Michael Hecht, *Stay: A History of Suicide and the Philosophies Against It* (Yale University Press 2013) 2.

22 Walter Englert, "Seneca and the Stoic View of Suicide" (1990) The Society for Ancient Greek Philosophy Newsletter 184, 186.

23 Hecht (n. 21) 3; Makiko Sato, "The Prohibition of Suicide for Affirmation of Human Beings by Augustine" (2015) 11 Journal of Patrology and Critical Hagiography 135, 136.

24 Kay Redfield Jamison, *Night Falls Fast: Understanding Suicide* (Vintage 1999) 13.

25 Judges 16:28–30, JPS (1917).

26 Rachel S. Harris, "Samson's Suicide: Death and the Hebrew Literary Canon" (2012) 17:3 Israel Studies 67, 68: "[H]is final suicide (martyred sacrifice) underpinned the drama of the Samson narrative. The symbolism of Samson soldiers willing to sacrifice themselves for the modern nation state altered as attitudes towards sacrifice for the collective changed."

27 Jamison (n. 24) 12–13.

morally and socially accepted some suicides primarily due to the influence of Confucianism.[28] The Confucian philosopher Mencius (372 BC–289 BC) propounded: "Life is what I want; dutifulness is also what I want. If I cannot have both, I would choose dutifulness rather than life."[29] Mencius seems to perceive suicide as a choice made by a dutiful person and therefore recognizes agency on the part of the person committing suicide. Sri Lankan historical narratives, too, valorize the story of King Sri Sangha Bodhi (252–254 AD), a devout Buddhist who is said in the *Mahawamsa* to have abdicated the throne. Knowing that the new occupant of the throne has offered a reward for his head, Sangha Bodhi, to repay a poor peasant who shared a meal with him, decapitates himself and offers the peasant his head. This act of self-sacrifice is honored in Sri Lankan culture granting him a saint-like quality.[30] These narratives across cultures demonstrate that suicide is not viewed purely as a morally or legally sanctionable act. Nor do these narratives indicate that suicide was inherently the result of a psychological condition. Rather they depict suicides as acts committed by exceptional persons, their intrinsic altruism not negating their agentic nature.

Even when not framed as a social good, suicide can represent an ethical choice for the individual who undertakes it, particularly when considered through a more individualistic lens.[31] Enlightenment-era philosophers, for instance, championed a view that values the autonomy expressed in the act of suicide. David Hume, in his essay "On Suicide," argues that suicide should not be criminal given that it does not constitute a "transgression of our duty either to God, our neighbour, or ourselves."[32] According to Hume, a person may use reason to decide that dying may cause more happiness to them rather than living, and that, given the survival instinct, such a decision to end one's life will be the result of serious deliberation.[33] Friedrich Nietzsche, in Zarathustra's speech "On Free Death," considered suicide as an assertion of freedom and will, including from conforming to societal norms and values.[34] In this light, suicide can be seen as an existential choice—a deeply personal act through which an individual negotiates the structural and cultural forces around them to define their understanding of

[28] Justin A. Chen, Andrew Courtwright, & Kevin Chien-Chang Wu, "The Role of Stigma and Denormalization in Suicide-Prevention Laws in East Asia: A Sociocultural, Historical, and Ethical Perspective" (2017) 25:5 Harvard Review of Psychiatry 229, 231.

[29] Mencius, *Mencius* (D.C. Lau trans., Penguin 2004) V. A. 10.

[30] Douglas Boulis, *Mahanamasthavira Thera's The Mahavamsa: The Great Chronicle of Sri Lanka* (Jain Publishing 1999) 352.

[31] Susan K. Morrissey, *Suicide and the Body Politic in Imperial Russia* (Cambridge University Press 2007) 1.

[32] David Hume, *On Suicide* (Penguin 2005) para. 5.

[33] Ibid.

[34] Friedrich Nietzche, *Thus Spake Zarathustra* (Thomas Common trans., Dover Publications, 1999) 46–48.

life and death.[35] However, even when considered a private act, suicide remains influenced by the societal norms it resists, highlighting the tension between individual autonomy and the surrounding normative frameworks.

By the Medieval and early modern eras, most Judeo-Christian religions had begun to prohibit or morally condemn suicide, labeling it an inappropriate exercise of agency. A clear indication of this shift in the context of Christianity is found in the writings of St. Augustine (354–430 AD), who interpreted Moses's prohibition against killing as encompassing self-killing.[36] Those who committed suicide were not granted Christian burial rites or sacred burial grounds.[37] Jewish custom, too, did not grant funeral orations to those who committed suicide.[38] These religious sanctions evolved over time into a legal sanction, reinforcing the idea that individuals were not free to choose their manner and time of death. The Roman civil law in the Late Roman Empire allowed the Emperor to confiscate the property of those who committed suicide, a practice that spread to other parts of Europe.[39] These sanctions reflect how power over life and death was perceived as granted to God alone, which later shifted to the King as sovereign, and eventually to the State as the exclusive authority over such decisions.[40]

John Austen, a central figure of legal positivism, posits in his command theory of law, that laws are essentially commands issued by a sovereign authority to those under its rule, backed by the threat of sanctions or penalties for noncompliance.[41] The State enforced this authority through criminal law, designating suicide as a crime against the State's control over life and death.[42] By labeling suicide a crime, the State reinforced its own normative framework, where unauthorized acts such as suicide were viewed as deviant and criminal. This legal and moral condemnation had far-reaching implications on how society was to treat those who committed suicide, even beyond their death. Early Norwegian laws demanded the bodies of those who committed suicide to be buried in the forest with criminals.[43] Many Western countries criminalized suicide, prior to it being decriminalized in the late nineteenth and twentieth centuries, remaining a crime

[35] Francesca Di Marco, "Act or Disease? The Making of Modern Suicide in Early Twentieth-century Japan" (2013) 39:2 The Journal of Japanese Studies 325, 327.

[36] St. Augustine, *The City of God* (Henry Bettenson trans., Penguin Classics 2003) para. 1.24.

[37] Thomas F. Tierney, "The Governmentality of Suicide: Peuchet, Marx, Durkheim, and Foucault" (2010) 10:4 Journal of Classical Sociology 357, 365; Jamison (n. 24) 15.

[38] Jamison (n. 24) 14.

[39] Tierney (n. 37).

[40] Chloë Taylor, "Birth of the Suicidal Subject: Nelly Arcan, Michel Foucault, and Voluntary Death" (2015) 56:2 Culture, Theory and Critique 187, 193.

[41] John Austin, *The Province of Jurisprudence Determined* (Wildrid E. Rumble ed., Cambridge University Press 2009).

[42] See Ian Marsh, *Suicide: Foucault, History and Truth* (Cambridge University Press 2010); Georges Minois & Lydia G. Cochrane, *History of Suicide: Voluntary Death in Western Culture* (Johns Hopkins University Press 1999).

[43] Jamison (n. 24) 16.

in England and Wales until 1961 and in Ireland until 1993.[44] Despite England's decriminalization of suicide, through its colonial promulgation of criminal statutes, its own cultural values criminalizing suicide were replicated and continue to be preserved in the penal codes of its former colonized communities.[45]

These narratives that morally and legally condemn suicide disallowed the exercise of agency over one's own death. This was an act not authorized by the State, the promulgator of the prevailing dominant normative framework over life-and-death decisions. Therefore, suicide became an inappropriate exercise of agency, depicting the person committing suicide as a deviant perpetrator of a crime. Though criminalization marked suicide as a deviant act, this very act of criminalization paradoxically recognized the agency of the individual undertaking it, given that criminal law generally assumes that for actions to be punishable, they must be carried out with intent, thereby implicitly acknowledging that suicide involves choice.

2.2.2. Dilution of agency in medicalized understandings of suicide

In contrast to the criminalization seen in the Medieval period until the nineteenth century, the dominant approach to suicide today is defined by its medicalization.[46] As early as 1821, the *Dictionnaire des sciences médicales* published Jean-Etienne Esquirol's article, "Suicide," which provided medical symptoms presented by the suicidal person.[47] According to professionals studying mental diseases at the time, suicide was considered "preventable given appropriate medical oversight", making suicidality "a pathological symptom of ill individuals, something to be identified, classified, institutionalized, and prevented."[48] Today, suicidology remains relatively monolithic in pathologizing suicide as a problematic condition suffered by individuals.[49] Medical professionals consider it a behavior caused by psychological issues affecting individuals, at times aggravated by social factors.[50] The capacity to make rational decisions on the part of the

[44] Ibid. 18.

[45] Mensah Adinkrah, "Anti-Suicide Laws in Nine African Countries: Criminalization, Prosecution and Penalization" (2016) 9:1 African Journal of Criminology and Justice Studies 729, 279.

[46] Di Marco (n. 35) 325.

[47] Jean-Étienne Dominique Esquirol, "Suicide" *Dictionnaire des Sciences Médicales* 53 (Panckoucke 1821) 213; Ian Marsh, "The Uses of History in the Unmaking of Modern Suicide" (2013) 46:3 Journal of Social History 744.

[48] John C. Weaver & David Wright, "Introduction" in John C. Weaver & David Wright (eds.) *Histories of Suicide: International Perspectives on Self-Destruction in the Modern World* (University of Toronto Press 2009) 4.

[49] Margaret Pabst Battin, *Ending Life: Ethics and the Way We Die* (Oxford University Press 2005) 242.

[50] Marsh (n. 42) 56–57.

person committing suicide is thereby questioned, creating a narrative that denies this person agency over their own death.[51] The advancements that medical sciences have made in diagnosing, decriminalizing, and preventing suicide cannot be dismissed. However, it is possible to simultaneously critique the essentializing effect medicalization has had in undermining the depiction of suicides as agentic acts in various cultural contexts.

By characterizing a person committing suicide as lacking the capacity sufficient to exercise agency due to some mental pathology, medical sciences gradually countered the rationale for legal sanctions attributed to this act. This is exemplified by the fact that "[i]n 1487, Henry VII required coroners in England to convene a jury in all cases of suspected suicide, to determine whether the person who died was not of sound mind and therefore not subject to punishment."[52] The World Health Organization notes that while

> [a]t the beginning of the nineteenth century, most countries around the world had laws that provided for punishment, including jail sentences, for persons who attempted suicide, . . . in the last 50 years the situation has changed significantly. Most, but not all, countries have decriminalized suicide.[53]

Implicit in these developments relating to the decriminalization of suicide is that the law attributes accountability to agentic acts alone. For example, the defense of insanity, which is enshrined in most criminal law codes and Article 31 of the Rome Statute, excludes criminal responsibility if "at the time of that person's conduct: (a) The person suffers from a mental disease or defect that destroys that person's capacity to appreciate the unlawfulness or nature of his or her conduct, or capacity to control his or her conduct to conform to the requirements of law[.]"[54] What sets attempted suicide apart from other crimes where the defense of insanity would come into question is that in the case of suicide, there is always a presumption that the act was caused by an unsound mental condition. Rather than applying a defense of insanity to each case of suicide, pathologizing suicide as a mental condition has removed the *prima facie* rationality and agency of the person committing suicide, leading to its decriminalization. In this process, the person committing suicide has moved from being an agentic yet deviant actor, a perpetrator of a crime, to a pathologized

[51] Dariusz Galasinski & Justyna Ziółkowska, *Discursive Constructions of the Suicidal Process* (Bloomsbury Academic 2020) 45: "[T]he dominant suicidological discourse can be seen as removing the agency of the person involved in suicide."

[52] Tierney (n. 37).

[53] World Health Organization, *Preventing Suicide: A Global Imperative* (Geneva World Health Organization Press 2014) 51.

[54] Rome Statute (n. 8).

victim incapable of exercising agency, creating a binary, mutually exclusive construction of agency and victimization.

The scientific narrative of suicide is constructed in an objective language and then treated as being universally applicable. This universalistic narrative pathologizing suicide also views it as an individual condition. It has thereby diluted the importance of the social factors that contribute to suicide and the way cultural discourses surrounding suicide frame it as an agentic act.[55] Ian Marsh critiques this empiricist discourse that is articulated as and accepted by scientific experts to be universal truths that are "acultural and ahistorical."[56] On the contrary, cultural assumptions are embedded in this seemingly objective view of understanding suicides. One such premise deemed universal that undergirds the scientific narrative of suicide is the idea that ending one's own life cannot be a rational decision. This stems from modernity's assumption that "healthy people would not choose to take their own lives unless they were not healthy. Life thereby becomes the ultimate value, the right to reject it denied."[57] This tendency to essentialize all types of suicides prevents critical investigation into how pathologizing suicide reveals cultural biases that may conflict with how various societies understand death and suicide.

Debates over the decriminalization of suicide and the need for its medicalization have been the site for multiple normative frameworks on agency and death to contend with one another. For example, the Indian Penal Code, which was introduced as Act No. 45 of 1860 during the British Colonial period, in Section 309, criminalizes attempted suicide. In 2008, in its proposal to decriminalize attempted suicide, the Law Commission of India described suicide as an act that is "a manifestation of a diseased condition of mind deserving of treatment and care rather than punishment."[58] The Law Commission of India, therefore, patently subscribes to the idea that a person who attempts to commit suicide is not within a mental state to exercise agency over their act. The issue of suicide also came before the Supreme Court of India in 2020 when it sought to resolve the conflict between Section 309 of the Indian Penal Code which criminalizes attempts to commit suicide, and the Mental Healthcare Act of 2017, which bars the prosecution of a person trying to take their own life under severe mental stress.[59] The arguments entailed whether there can be a blanket presumption on intentions and the mental stress experienced by a person who

55 Marsh (n. 42) 72–74.
56 Ibid. 32, 39.
57 Morrissey (n. 31) 1.
58 Law Commission of India, "Humanization and Decriminalization of Attempt to Suicide," Report No. 210 (October 7, 2008) 38.
59 India, Supreme Court, *Red Lynx Confereration v. Union of India & Others*, Record of Proceedings Petition(s) for Special Leave to Appeal (Crl.) No(s). 3185/2020, September 11, 2020.

is committing suicide. This was particularly relevant in the cultural context of India, where priests and monks have killed themselves as a form of protest. Moreover, as was noted by the Chief Justice of India, the practice of *Santhara* among Jains (a religious ritual of voluntary death by fasting), is intended to liberate oneself from the material world rather than to commit suicide due to a mental illness.[60] Accordingly, modern Western science presumes that a mentally healthy individual would choose to preserve life rather than end it, a view that conflicts with cultural practices where ending one's life is deemed an agentic act.

The shift toward medicalizing suicide redefined it as a condition of mental pathology, with the effect of removing agency from the act. Unlike earlier frameworks where suicide was criminalized as an intentional defiance of State or divine authority, medicalization, by portraying suicidality as a symptom of psychological distress, cast individuals who attempt suicide as patients lacking rational agency. This pathologizing view established a binary between agency and victimization: if suicide stems from mental illness, it cannot be seen as a rational, agentic act. Treating suicide as a pathology open to universal and objective assessment minimized cultural narratives on suicide that perceive it a meaningful act imbued with agency. Thus, while medicalization has promoted compassionate responses to suicide, it has also obscured culturally embedded notions of agency and autonomy attributed to the act.

2.3. Ways of dying in wartime and peacetime

Narratives surrounding death are invariably shaped by the sociocultural contexts in which people die. Due to advances in health and well-being, death has become a more sequestered and controlled phenomenon, often removed from the fabric of everyday life—particularly in peacetime. However, this was not always the case. During the world wars, the constant reminders of human mortality disrupted the attempt to treat death as an exceptional event. In wartime, and especially among combatants, death is situated in a vastly different context from that of peacetime civilians. The relationship to death in such settings is imbued with a different set of social and cultural meanings.

[60] Badra Sinha, "Is Attempt to Suicide Punishable? Two Laws Have Opposing Views, SC Seeks Govt's Response" *The Print* (September 11, 2020) online: https://theprint.in/judiciary/is-attempt-to-suicide-punishable-two-laws-have-opposing-views-sc-seeks-govt-response/500905/ accessed January 5, 2025; "SC Looks at Clash in Legal Clauses on Suicide," *The Hindu* (September 12, 2020) online: https://www.thehindu.com/news/national/sc-looks-at-clash-in-legal-clauses-on-suicide/article32586469.ece accessed January 5, 2025.

2.3.1. Cultural narratives on ways of dying

Tony Walter identifies three paradigms of death: traditional, modern, and postmodern.[61] Traditional death, he argues, was shaped by religious and spiritual frameworks, where communal rituals guided the process. At the same time, medical professionals hold power over norms and knowledge relating to death in modern times.[62] The dying person is often excluded from the decision-making process, with personal feelings becoming isolated from the bureaucratic, medical procedures that now dominate death.[63] According to Walter, while this medicalization of death has been widely accepted by modern society, it has come at the cost of marginalizing the agency of the dying individual.[64] In postmodern death, however, the individual regains control to some extent over their deaths, making more informed choices about medical and spiritual interventions relating to the dying process.[65]

Tony Walter's schema for understanding the sociocultural meanings of death, which categorized death into traditional, modern, and postmodern paradigms,offers a helpful framework to explore how the agency of the dying person is shaped by social contexts. However, it is overly simplistic to treat these paradigms as a linear progression. Cultural interpretations of death are diverse and intertwined with beliefs about the afterlife and concepts of the self, and influenced by notions of agency. Walter's model also overlooks wartime contexts where proximity to death and reminders of mortality are more present, challenging modern constructions of death as a private phenomenon to be managed individually. Therefore, while Walter's model aids in understanding death's evolving social context, it fails to capture the complexity and variation in how agency around death is constructed. For example, to classify suicide attacks as a postmodern experience of death would ignore that these deaths are not merely personal but also framed through the political and communal narratives that shape and valorize them.

This limitation reflects a broader critique raised by scholars regarding Western-centric approaches in death studies. Kit Ying Lye and Terence Heng note that there is a gap in the scholarship as to culturally diverse understandings of death and that "when there are publications on death in non-western contexts, they are often positioned as either an interesting but supplementary case study, an issue of anthropological curiosity, or bounded by region-centric sub-disciplines."[66]

[61] Tony Walter, "Facing Death without Tradition" in Glennys Howarth & Peter C. Jupp (eds.) *Contemporary Issues in the Sociology of Death, Dying and Disposal* (St. Martin's Press 1996) 193–194.
[62] Ibid. 193.
[63] Ibid. 194.
[64] Ibid. 197.
[65] Ibid. 194.
[66] Kit Ying Lye & Terence Heng, "Introduction" in Kit Ying Lye & Terence Heng (eds.) *Death and the Afterlife: Multidisciplinary Perspectives from a Global City* (Routledge 2024) 1.

Likewise, despite modernity's understanding of end-of-life decisions, including suicide, as being acultural and objective, the criteria adopted to determine when such decisions are acceptable are intrinsically intertwined with cultural biases on death.[67] As anthropologist Lisa Stevenson elaborates in her analysis of bureaucratic forms of care seen in Canada's efforts to tackle the issue of suicides in indigenous communities, "[t]he self-evident truth of the 'suicide apparatus,' its unquestioned certainty, is that life is worth living, that life itself is its own value.... To be a good citizen means to cooperate in this regime of life."[68]

While she appreciates the work that goes into confronting and preventing suicides among the Inuit in Nunavut, Stevenson challenges the universality of the narrative of a "suicide epidemic" and that a person who commits suicide was suffering from mental illness. She underscores the importance of acknowledging other cultural perspectives that view life and death with greater uncertainty.[69] In this manner, suicide becomes a point of underlying contention among various cultural narratives on uncertainties about the agency of the dying person.

These Western-centric assumptions regarding the agency of the person experiencing death can also be observed in international law jurisprudence on end-of-life decisions. For instance, International Human Rights Law (IHRL) has discussed when decisions to carry out assisted suicide or euthanasia do not violate protected rights. The capacity of the person wishing to die to exercise agency is central to both active and passive euthanasia. Passive euthanasia, which entails the removal of life-supporting devices, is often premised on the idea that loss of autonomy equates to an undignified existence.[70] In active euthanasia, the European Court of Human Rights (ECtHR) has agreed, at least in principle, that

> [t]he ability to conduct one's life in a manner of one's own choosing may also include the opportunity to pursue activities perceived to be of a physically or morally harmful or dangerous nature for the individual concerned and even where the conduct poses a danger to health or, arguably, life[.][71]

[67] Morrissey(n. 31) 4–8: "A cultural history of suicide in the twentieth century has not been written, which is a striking lacuna. The making of modern suicide has apparently presented a more straightforward historical problem than the ambiguous faces of modern suicide itself, which have been shaped by the paradigms advanced by Durkheim, Freud, Camus, and others.... In both Russia and the West, the condemnation of self-killing as a terrible sin has faded (though not disappeared), a process shaped in part by new cultural and scientific paradigms, which, in turn, created new contexts for suicide."

[68] Lisa Stevenson, *Life Beside Itself: Imagining Care in the Canadian Arctic* (University of California Press 2014) 8.

[69] Ibid. 10.

[70] Gianluca Montanari Vergallo & Matteo Gulino, "End-of-Life Care and Assisted Suicide: An Update on the Italian Situation from the Perspective of the European Court of Human Rights" (2022) 21 Ethics, Medicine and Public Health 2, https://doi.org/10.1016/j.jemep.2022.100752.

[71] *Pretty v. the United Kingdom*, Application No. 2346/02, Council of Europe: European Court of Human Rights, April 29, 2002, para. 62.

Despite this broad claim, conditions apply in deciding whether a patient can be allowed to end their lives, including a requirement that they should be suffering from a severe and irreversible illness, be in intolerable physical or psychological pain, or kept alive through life support. These conditions indicate that the patient has to present themselves as a victim of circumstances often beyond their control, to be allowed to die.[72] Furthermore, the ECtHR has acknowledged that "[m]any terminally ill individuals will be vulnerable," for instance, to external influences and that it is legitimate for a State to deny such person agency over their end-of-life decisions through laws that restrict their access to assisted suicide.[73] Here, vulnerability to external influence is viewed as antithetical to agentic choice.

Discussions on assisted suicide reveal some of modernity's measurements and biases of when life ceases to be worth living. Gianluca Montanari Vergallo and Matteo Gulino state that passive euthanasia can be justified because it is universally accepted that "advanced life-supporting procedures may preserve a biological and artificially sustained survival, . . . which is difficult to define from an ethical perspective."[74] This is consistent with judicial determinations on assisted suicide that consider the essence of the European Convention on Human Rights (ECHR) to be that of preserving "respect for human dignity and human freedom."[75] Implicit in these statements is that autonomy over one's own body is a crucial aspect of a dignified life. In active euthanasia, "the right of an individual to decide how and when to end his life," is granted if the "said individual was in a position to make up his own mind in that respect and to take the appropriate action[.]" This right is considered to form part of the right to respect for private life.[76] These statements reveal specific cultural biases. First, life is only worth living when certain physical conditions are met, such as being in control of one's bodily autonomy and not undergoing unbearable physical pain. Second, life-and-death decisions are individual ones, disregarding these decisions' communal or relational dimensions. Finally, death is considered an aspect of private life. All these cultural assumptions of modernity's understanding of end-of-life decisions contrast with suicide attackers' deaths, which are often carried out by a person in good physical health in a public manner for a political purpose and engender communal narratives.

A notion that challenges the Western-centric understanding of death is the understanding that agency in death can extend beyond the individual and the

72 Montanari Vergallo & Gulino (n. 70) 3.

73 *Pretty v. the United Kingdom* (n. 71) para. 79.

74 Montanari Vergallo & Gulino (n. 70) 2.

75 *Pretty v. the United Kingdom* (n. 71) para. 65.

76 *Haas v. Switzerland*, Application No. 31322/07, Council of Europe: European Court of Human Rights, January 20, 2011, para. 61.

physical body. In *Beyond the Body: Death and Social Identity*, Elizabeth Hallam, Jenny Hockey, and Glennys Howarth observe that much of social theory has positioned the body as the primary site through which essential truths about the self are revealed.[77] In a similar vein, the control a person exercises over their body, including the ability to make irreversible changes, often serves as a measure of individual agency, continually subject to negotiation. Within this normative framework, agency is closely tied to the control one exerts over the body, and the inability to control a dead body is seen as a breach of that agency—highlighting the vulnerability of the body in death.[78] However, Hallam, Hockey, and Howarth suggest that to fully comprehend human identity and agency, one must look beyond the confines of the physical body, arguing that human experience is not only embodied but also intersubjective, shaped by shared social interactions and relationships.[79] In doing so, it becomes possible to trouble the certainty granted to physical death as the endpoint of the self. As the authors note, "It is the confinement of our gaze to the body alone which produces forms of binaristic thinking within which "life" and "death," as biologically based categories, come to stand in a clear and oppositional relationship to one another."[80] By expanding our gaze beyond the body, we can adopt a more expansive understanding of human sociality, one that encompasses the complexities of agency even in death.[81]

Walter observed that, while death is an individual experience, we also "die as we live, as social beings."[82] This resonates with the idea that agency, particularly in death, cannot be understood purely through an individualistic lens or one that is limited to the site of the physical body of the person experiencing death. The communal aspect of agency is further explored in relational theories of law, which challenge traditional notions of autonomy as fundamentally individualistic. Catriona Mackenzie and Natalie Stoljar, in their influential work *Autonomy Refigured*, use a feminist lens to argue that autonomy is not solely based on rational individualism but can also be relational, shaped by the social dimensions of selfhood.[83] Similarly, Jennifer Nedelsky, in *Law's Relations: A Relational Theory of Self, Autonomy, and Law*, critiques the Anglo-American tendency to equate autonomy with independence.[84] She proposes that respect for autonomy

[77] Elizabeth Hallam, Jenny Hockey, & Glennys Howarth, *Beyond the Body: Death and Social Identity* (Routledge 1999) 166.

[78] Ibid. 168.

[79] Ibid. 170.

[80] Ibid. 171.

[81] Ibid.

[82] Walter (n. 61) 204.

[83] Catriona Mackenzie & Natalie Stoljar, "Introduction: Autonomy Refigured" in Catriona Mackenzie & Natalie Stoljar (eds.) *Relational Autonomy: Feminist Perspectives on Autonomy, Agency, and the Social Self* (Oxford University Press 2000) 3–5.

[84] Jennifer Nedelsky, *Law's Relations: A Relational Theory of Self, Autonomy, and Law* (Oxford University Press 2012) 5.

should focus on the relationships that constitute individuals and make their values meaningful.[85] Relational legal theory offers an alternative understanding of agency as being deeply embedded in social and cultural structures rather than more individualistic conceptions of autonomy.[86] Understandings of suicide attackers' agency is shaped by the posthumous narratives constructed around their deaths. These narratives, grounded in societal and cultural factors, offer agentic meaning to their actions, reinforcing the notion that agency, even in death, is a collective, socially mediated phenomenon.

As Thomas Osborne argues, in the case of suicide, the inherent ambiguity created by the inability of the person who committed suicide to clarify their state of mind amplifies the need for external constructions of agency.[87] Even where suicide notes are present, their legitimacy is questioned based on the assumption that a person committing suicide could not have been in a rational state of mind. The practice of conducting psychological autopsies, which "usually involves the interviewing of surviving relatives and friends as well as consulting public and private documentation (such as medical notes) to seek to determine the 'state of mind' of the deceased prior to their death," also mirrors the creation of socially embedded narratives.[88] Therefore, whether the act of suicide is deemed agentic depends on others' interpretations of it. As Dean Sharpe and Natalia Linos point out, the death of the person committing suicide becomes a point of fascination for others and a mystery in need of an explanation by the broader society and culture.[89]

Similarly, despite the finality presented in the death of the suicide attacker, the public nature of these suicides tends to leave a mark over time and thereby prolong narratives of agency surrounding this act.[90] In this context, the combatant's act becomes intertwined with the larger community and the cultural context that gives it meaning. Therefore, suicide attacks are not merely acts carried out by an individual, but acts imbued with cultural and communal meaning.

85 Ibid. 7.

86 John Christman, "Relational Autonomy, Liberal Individualism, and the Social Constitution of Selves" (2004) 117:1/2 Philosophical Studies: An International Journal for Philosophy in the Analytic Tradition 143, 146: "[T]here is evidence of cultural variations in self-concepts relating to the degree of interdependence and inter-relatedness that figures in self-schemas. Finally, conceptions of the self often fail to adequately distinguish the different localities for the function of a 'self' which the models are meant to capture; these include the self as the seat of agency, the self as object of introspective consciousness, the 'self-schema' which frames reflection and memory, the object of recognition by others and social specification, and so on." See also Andrea C. Westlund, "Rethinking Relational Autonomy" (2009) 24:4 Hypatia 26.

87 Thomas Osborne, "Fascinated Dispossession: Suicide and the Aesthetics of Freedom" (2005) 34:2 Economy and Society 280, 284–285.

88 Marsh (n. 42) 38–39.

89 Dean Sharpe & Natalia Linos, "Dying to Live in Palestine: Steadfastness, Pollution and Embodied Space" in Ludek Broz & Daniel Münster (eds.) *Suicide and Agency: Anthropological Perspectives on Self-Destruction, Personhood, and Power* (Routledge 2016) 127.

90 Osborne (n. 87) 285–286.

2.3.2. Social constructions of combatant deaths and suicide in wartime

Viewing suicide as an individual condition overshadows the possibility that some suicides, including suicide attacks, may carry cultural interpretations of agency that are more collective. Contrary to general suicides, which may occur as purely individual acts, suicide attacks during wartime are almost always organized by an armed group or a military and are carried out by a person belonging to such an armed group or military. Therefore, collective influences on an individual's exercise of agency and communal constructions of agency become particularly relevant to them.[91] Scholarly literature in sociology has challenged the trend of individualizing suicides by attempting to understand their social dimensions. For example, in his seminal work *On Suicide*, Émile Durkheim states that individualized psychological causes cannot fully explain all cases of suicide.[92] He posits that suicide depends on "social causes and constitutes a collective phenomenon."[93] However, his recognition of suicide as a social phenomenon has not necessarily led to appreciating cultural understandings that treat suicide attacks as agentic acts performed for the collective. Implicit in his work are condescending attitudes toward suicides that occur in "inferior societies" regulated by, for example, the laws of Manu or Buddhism, among others, where self-sacrifice is encouraged or becomes obligatory.[94] He also examines suicides that occur in the military, another "inferior society," which promotes self-sacrifice and prevents the individual from acting on his initiative: "He must be trained to attach little value to his own being, since he must be ready to sacrifice it whenever he is ordered to do so."[95] Durkheim thereby not only indicates a bias against cultural understandings that valorize self-sacrifice, but he also implicitly questions the agency that combatants exercise over their deaths while operating in such a context.

Scholarly discussions on suicide attacks have mirrored this tendency to analyze social dimensions of these attacks while questioning the narratives of agency constructed around the deaths of suicide attackers. Mia Bloom notes that specific narratives have been intentionally generated around suicide attackers to encourage and entice others to do the same. For example, the Kamikaze pilots were revered as "god-heroes," with their photos publicized in the newspapers.[96] According to her, such narratives spread across armed groups like a "contagion."[97]

[91] Qirko (n. 2) 293.
[92] See Émile Durkheim, *On Suicide* (Robin Buss trans., Penguin Books 2006) 46.
[93] Ibid. 147.
[94] Ibid. 240.
[95] Ibid. 253.
[96] Bloom (n. 3) 16.
[97] Ibid. 18.

Armed groups that observe successful suicide attacks of other armed groups tend also to adopt such "techniques to suit local circumstances".[98] These factors, arguably, contribute to an environment of social pressure that can adversely impact the capacity of the person carrying out the suicide attack to make a rational decision on their own life or death. Robert Pape too dilutes the agentic nature of the suicide attacker's death by shifting focus toward the strategic and organized apparatus of the armed group, rather than on the narratives constructed around the attacker's death.[99] This scholarship on suicide attacks combines the pathologizing of suicide with the communal dimension of suicide attacks. They thereby conclude that suicide attacks are a pathology at a social level. The term "contagion" used to describe the spread of suicide attacks evokes disease and illness, one that is transmissible from one society to another.

Here, contagion is not depicted as spreading on its own but through the manipulation of combatants' minds by armed groups. This pathologizes suicide attackers' deaths by claiming that command structures within the military or non-State armed groups adversely impact their capacity to exercise agency. However, according to Mary Douglas, what we classify as being dangerous and contagious are acts that are contrary to understandings of "good citizenship" and specific moral values and social rules.[100] Likewise, what we consider a contagion is far from being acultural. It reveals assumptions about which behaviors cultural communities permit. Implicit in the scholarship that compares suicide attacks to a contagion is a prescriptive value judgment that suicide attacks deviate from their cultural understandings of good citizenship. This notion of military structures as being mutually exclusive with the agentic choice of combatants ignores how power is exercised not just through direct commands but also through choices that individuals within these structures make, which influence narratives that define acceptable forms of sacrifice.

Militaristic or militant structures are known to enforce a hierarchical governance structure with minimal scope for disobeying orders. The extent to which agency is attributed to individuals acting within such structures, and the narrative tools that support these attributions of agency, are a focal point of this book. As Laura M. Ahearn argues, "agentive acts may also involve complicity with, accommodation to, or reinforcement of status-quo."[101] Walter echoes this sentiment, observing that idealistic notions of individual choice often clash with reality. Authority over death and dying does not rest solely with the autonomous

[98] Ibid. 122.
[99] Robert Pape, *Dying to Win: The Strategic Logic of Suicide Terrorism* (Random House 2006).
[100] Mary Douglas, *Purity and Danger: An Analysis of Concepts of Pollution and Taboo* (Routledge & Kegan Paul 1966) 3.
[101] Ahearn (n. 5) 13.

individual, nor, as argued in military contexts, with an authoritarian external entity, but is shaped through negotiations with others and the influences of surrounding narratives on how lives and afterlives are communally valued.[102] According to Steven G. Jug, the Red Army maintained troop morale and resilience by creating "symbolic afterlives" for fallen soldiers,[103] reinforcing the idea that individual sacrifices contribute to a larger communal purpose.[104]

In religious understandings, the term "sacrifice" is often associated with acts of self-denial.[105] In Judeo-Christian cultures, sacrificing one's life is closely related to the death of Christ, which acts as a metaphor for martyrdom.[106] According to Stephen Sykes, the European construction of warfare has borrowed language from Christian theology to project a narrative that compares the deaths of soldiers on the battlefield to Christ's sacrifice.[107] This is not merely a narrative of historical relevance. The language of sacrifice, rooted in religion, continues to be central to how combatant deaths are seen.[108] For example, in the United States, "the institutionalization of 'war-culture'" benefits from contextualizing soldiers' deaths in Christian understandings of sacrifice.[109] This is so, as Kelly Denton-Borhaug posits, the "rhetoric of sacrifice . . . legitimates violence by covering the activities of killing with a sacred canopy made up of values such as loyalty and freedom."[110] Both the death of Christ and soldiers' deaths are presented as serving a larger purpose that justifies them.[111] Their deaths go beyond being perceived as deaths of individuals, and are instead seen as serving fellow brothers in arms, their country, and are glorified by their communities.[112] Likewise, our understandings of the deaths of soldiers are shaped by the cultural assumptions that frame their deaths as a sacred sacrifice.[113]

The use of conscript armies also highlights how the narrative of a soldier's sacrifice sits somewhat uneasily within the liberal paradigm. During World War I, mass conscription translated to large numbers of combatants being led to death on the battlefield. Gabriella Blum highlights how the "Napoleonic wars saw mass recruits of poorly armed, poorly trained, and ill-equipped soldiers, who were

[102] Walter (n. 61) 202.
[103] Steven G. Jug, "Mourning Deaths and Constructing Afterlives in the Red Army at War" in Candi K. Cann (ed.) *The Routledge Handbook of Death and the Afterlife* (Routledge 2018) 136.
[104] Ibid. 137.
[105] Stephen Sykes, "Sacrifice and the Ideology of War" in Robert A Hinde (ed.) *The Institution of War* (Palgrave Macmillan 1992) 87, 91, 93.
[106] Ibid. 87, 90.
[107] Ibid. 93–94.
[108] Kelly Denton-Borhaug, "War-Culture and Sacrifice" (2010) 18:2 Feminist Theology 175, 187.
[109] Ibid. 176.
[110] Ibid. 186.
[111] Ibid. 189.
[112] Babak Rahimi, "Sacrifice, Transcendence and the Soldier" (2005) 17:1 Peace Review: A Journal of Social Justice 1, 2.
[113] Denton-Borhaug (n. 108) 190.

sent to charge attacks by constituting a human wave, ultimately earning the label of 'cannon fodder,'"[114] creating "the image of the totally victimized soldier."[115] In "The Paradox of Riskless Warfare," Paul Kahn critiques the use of conscript armies in modern warfare. According to him, conscription challenges the degree of independent choice exercised by soldiers who engage in a battle for survival.[116] In his work *Putting Liberalism in Its Place*, Kahn further contends that the role of the soldier elicits the nature of sacrifice that is needed to maintain the social contract of liberalism by defending the liberal State from "others."[117] Soldiers' sacrifice precedes and provides the conditions for this rational liberal existence. Liberalism, however, fails to fully examine the contradictions presented in this necessary sacrifice, which makes its own existence a possibility.[118] The collectivist approach that militaries take toward their soldiers is at odds with the valorization of individual will and autonomy within the liberal model of thinking.[119] The sacrifice of a combatant presents a contradiction, as their deaths are a necessary component to protect the liberal order while also being seemingly irreconcilable with the liberal idea of a good life.

Legal frameworks inspired by liberal thinking, such as IHRL, often take for granted and exalt a person's individual agency. For example, IHRL jurisprudence on end-of-life decisions deems external influences on a decision relating to death as compromising the individual's agency. However, whether a combatant's death is considered a sacrifice has much to do with how intertwined their death is with a larger social purpose. In other words, the label of sacrifice is reserved for those who die while serving the collective. This collective logic applies to militaries even in otherwise liberal societies. The military ethic holds that a person is driven by their duty to the group.[120] One way in which this conflict is mediated is through narratives of heroic sacrifice that portray these deaths as being agentic. In these narratives, these deaths are presumed to take place within a specific comfort zone shaped by cultural assumptions on the extent, the purpose of this sacrifice, and those who can engage in it. The notion of heroism is central to how agency is attributed to combatant deaths: the stories about fallen soldiers

[114] Gabriella Blum, "The Dispensable Lives of Soldiers" (2010) 2:1 Journal of Legal Analysis 115, 122.

[115] Leonard V. Smith, *Between Mutiny and Obedience: The Case of the French Fifth Infantry Division during World War I* (Princeton University Press 1994) 12.

[116] Paul W. Kahn, "The Paradox of Riskless Warfare" (2002) 22:3 Philosophy and Public Policy Quarterly 2, 2.

[117] Paul W. Kahn, *Putting Liberalism in Its Place* (Princeton University Press 2009) 229.

[118] Ibid. 224.

[119] Patrick Porter, "War and the Religious Will to Sacrifice" (2005) 17:1 Peace Review: A Journal of Social Justice 17, 18.

[120] Samuel P. Huntington, *The Soldier and the State: The Theory and Politics of Civil-Military Relations* (Harvard University Press 1957) 90.

often depict them as having taken deliberate acts for the collective, implying that dying in this process is therefore agentic rather than coercive.

Militaries' collectivist logic is also reflected in IHL's complex relationship with liberal ideals. IHL, having originated in the modern Western legal tradition, while aspiring to treat the individual with humanity and mitigate the harshness of war, projects a universalism that has imperial foundations; therefore, IHL's extension of liberal values has its blind spots, which help maintain its appearance of universality, including its treatment of combatants.[121] IHL functions within a highly collectivized structure: as per IHL, one is either a civilian or a combatant, and obligations or privileges are assigned based on which classification one falls under, as per the law.[122] It classifies persons based on overlapping criteria of nationality, affiliation with a party to a conflict, and profession, designating varying levels of protected status accordingly. Thus, civilians protected by the Fourth Geneva Convention, as defined in Article 4, have to be "in the hands of a Party to the conflict or Occupying Power of which they are not nationals."[123] In these categories, the group that receives the least attention is the treatment of its troops by an armed force. Therefore, the status-based approach adopted by IHL diminishes the soldiers' individuality. In turn, IHL provisions fail to give direct expression to how individual combatants exercise agency on the battlefield.

IHRL has strived to imbue IHL with more respect for individual humanity and dignity, and to clarify the extent to which combatants exercise agency over their deaths.[124] IHRL principles have been slowly trickling into building an individualized approach to ensuring that governments owe duties to its nationals, including their soldiers.[125] Nonbinding instruments of Council of Europe organs, specifically Recommendation 1742 (2006) of the Parliamentary Assembly on the human rights of members of the armed forces of April 11, 2006, emphasize that "members of the armed forces cannot be expected to respect humanitarian law and human rights in their operations unless the army ranks guarantee respect for human rights." Furthermore, the jurisprudence from the UK courts has utilized Article 2 of the ECHR, dealing with the right to life, to regulate the relationship between the commanders and their troops stating that "a finding that in all circumstances deaths or injuries in combat that result from the conduct of operations by the armed forces are outside the scope of article 2

[121] Kahn, *Putting Liberalism in Its Place* (n. 117) 7.

[122] Jeff McMahan, *Killing in War* (Clarendon Press 2009); Blum, "The Dispensable Lives Of Soldiers" (n. 114) 117.

[123] This principle has been expanded through the Tadic judgment, which suggested that in some situations, rather than nationality, allegiance to a party to the conflict should be considered in determining whether or not individuals qualify for the status of "protected persons." *The Prosecutor v. Dusko Tadić (Appeal Decision)*, IT-94-1-AR72, International Criminal Tribunal for Yugoslavia (ICTY), Decision, October 2, 1995.

[124] Blum, "The Individualization of War" (n. 6) 48, 52.

[125] Ibid.

would not be sustainable."[126] In the example of the *Smith case*, the UK military was held accountable for a duty of care for the lives of its soldiers. Requiring States to respect the individual human dignity of their soldiers is a positive development. However, I would be reticent to go as far as Kahn, to argue that "politics of rights" has shifted "the logic of sacrifice."[127] IHRL requires that militaries exercise their power over combatants with due diligence. This confirms that while the military's power over its soldiers is limited, it still carries significant weight in making life-and-death decisions over combatants.

The concept of deviant agency further complicates the understanding of combatants' deaths. Stories of mutinies can be seen as a space where combatants negotiate their agency in a collectivized military structure. Leonard V. Smith provides examples of the gray area that existed between orders of the French military and the extent to which combatants obeyed them.[128] He cites the case of the Fifth Inventory Division of the French Army in World War I, which, having faced some failures in attack, mutinied, refusing to participate in battle in the trenches in May and June 1917.[129] A handful of soldiers out of around a thousand who participated in the mutiny faced execution following court-martial procedures, as a symbolic upholding of the sovereign command structure in wartime.[130] Through their stories of resistance the author attempts to present soldiers as more active agents of history. He, therefore, recognizes that even in collectivized contexts, persons have the agency to negotiate their actions.[131] This is the case even when militaries treat mutinies as punishable insubordination. While mutinies cannot be equated to suicide, it presents a case where even in conscript armies, the soldier makes a choice to risk being punished by death for an act of resistance rather than to die on the battlefield. Mutinies therefore further highlight the complexity of individual agency exercised in collective structures.

Those who commit suicide have historically been seen as exercising deviant agency or as being incapable of making agentic decisions. However, local narratives on suicide attacks do not treat them in this manner. Instead, they often glorify these attackers' deaths as a subversive exercise of agency. Likewise, the agency exercised by suicide attackers is a complex phenomenon, influenced by specific cultural contexts, that sits uneasily with the medicalized universal understandings of suicide that do not accommodate local realities in which suicide attacks occur. For example, Francesca Di Marco traces the history of

126 United Kingdom, *Smith and others (FC) v. The Ministry of Defence* [2013] UKSC 41, para. 58.
127 See Paul W. Kahn, *Sacred Violence: Torture, Terror, and Sovereignty* (University of Michigan Press 2008).
128 Leonard V. Smith, "'War and Politics': The French Army Mutinies of 1917" (1995) 2:2 War in History 180, 197.
129 Ibid.
130 Ibid. 200.
131 Ibid. 184.

Japanese psychiatrists in the Meiji period, a time of political nationalism, and attempts to reconcile the objective scientific approach to suicide with cultural factors that contributed to suicide in Japan.[132] This exercise engendered a clash of Western science and cultural practices, for example, suicides that relate to Samurai culture, such as *seppuku*, not being considered to stem from a pathology.[133] Likewise, historical and cultural contexts cannot be entirely separated from how meaning is given to suicides. Even the universalizing effect of scientific objectivity may not be able to counteract the cultural attitudes toward life and death. Therefore, a critical awareness of the narratives that feed into how suicide is viewed in different contexts is vital. Whether a person decides to engage in a suicide attack is often impacted by the cultural context in which an attacker operates. This is primarily the case as how a particular culture perceives death, and more specifically, its sociopolitical narratives on the deaths of suicide attackers, may influence the suicide attacker's act. While contributing to the decision of the attacker to commit suicide, these external cultural dimensions do not necessarily negate the agency exercised by the attacker in carrying out a suicide attack. The following chapters show how narratives on suicide attackers offer frames of agency that can coexist with cultural influences.

2.4. Conclusion

In this chapter, I set out the approaches to suicide attacks that pathologize or elevate the agency of the individual committing suicide. Through the analysis of these opposing discourses, I argued that it is vital to adopt a more nuanced approach that critically evaluates the role that cultural factors play in the exercise of individual agency by suicide attackers. I highlighted the importance of cultural narratives of heroic sacrifice that lie beneath the surface of IHL's framework. The combatant, as seen in IHL, conforms to attributes found in narratives of sacrifice. This is so the idea of warfare projected by IHL is a cultural construct, although its rules, which are now universally applicable, do not expressly allude to this. I argued that these cultural biases in the Western notions of heroic sacrifice of combatants do not align with how local cultural narratives depict suicide attackers' deaths as agentic acts. I do not attempt to create a singular narrative of agency as it fits IHL's cultural framework, and then apply it to the case of suicide attackers. Rather, suicide attackers' deaths offer avenues to understand combatant deaths as intertwined with culturally specific understandings of agency.

132 Di Marco (n. 35) 357.
133 Ibid. 347.

3
Kamikaze Attacks and the Limits of Risk in Combat

3.1. Introduction

In the late thirteenth century, Kublai Khan, launched a fleet to capture Japan. Japanese legend narrates how these Mongol ships met with typhoons of mythic proportions, which defeated their invasions twice.[1] This reverse wind, which had carried the Mongols off, complemented the valiant defense of the Samurai. Some saw this as a magical rescue. Hence, it was a Divine Wind, also known as "Kamikaze," rescuing Japan from foreign invasion.[2] Many parallels can be drawn between this myth and the pilots who were named after it in World War II. In Japanese narratives, Kamikaze pilots embodied the warrior's way—men who died in the name of the Emperor to prevent Japan from losing the war, like the Divine Wind did.[3] The Japanese military carried out these attacks from October 1944 to August 1945, toward the tail end of World War II. Japanese army and navy pilots intentionally killed themselves while attempting to crash their planes into Allied ships or manned weapons, often successfully. These operations used powered airplanes, gliders, and submarine torpedoes, which were, at times, unequipped to return to base.[4] Accordingly, these missions provided little hope of survival for the pilots executing them.[5] The exact number of Kamikaze flights is not known, but an estimated 7,465 kamikazes flew to their deaths; 120 US ships were sunk, and many more were damaged. Kamikaze attacks killed 3,048 allied sailors, and another 6,025 were wounded.[6]

[1] "Kamikaze typhoons spared Japan from Kublai Khan," *EARTH Mag* (March 2, 2015).
[2] Jonathan Clements, *A Brief History of the Samurai: A New History of the Warrior Elite* (Robinson 2010) 140.
[3] Emiko Ohnuki-Tierney, *Kamikaze, Cherry Blossoms and Nationalisms: The Militarization of Aesthetics in Japanese History* (University of Chicago Press 2002) 158.
[4] Ibid. 3: "The airplanes, best known among these operations, flew close to the water to avoid detection by radar. The underwater torpedoes, called 'human torpedoes,' were carried by submarines close to the target." See also Peter Hill, "Kamikaze" in Diego Gambetta (ed.) *Making Sense of Suicide Missions* (Oxford University Press 2005) 3.
[5] Ibid.
[6] Rosemarie Skaine, *Suicide Warfare* (ABC-CLIO 2013) 128.

Suicide Attacks and International Humanitarian Law. Vishakha V. Wijenayake, Oxford University Press.
 DOI: 10.1093/9780197812174.003.0003

The image of the Kamikaze pilots willfully plummeting to their deaths has evoked shock and awe in the eyes of the West. According to Mia Bloom, Japan resorted to suicide attacks because they perceived it as "a tactic against which the American Navy could not defend itself" while also exerting an immense psychological impact on American troops.[7] The terror of waiting for the attacks sent some men into "insanity" and "breakdown."[8] Unlike suicide attacks that target civilians, Kamikaze attacks usually targeted legitimate military targets and did so without resorting to perfidy. In many ways, the attacks resembled traditional attacks between State armed forces, except for the certainty with which these pilots embraced their deaths.

During and in the aftermath of World War II, the Kamikaze "became synonymous with reckless people, fanatical chauvinists, the inscrutable and untrustworthy 'Other,'"[9] and their image also became settled in popular discourse. Indeed, the Larousse French dictionary uses the term "Kamikaze" as a term generally used for "*auteur d'un attentat suicide*," imbuing Kamikaze pilots with meanings from beyond their cultural and wartime confines. For States that had to oppose them in combat, Kamikaze attacks generated a fear emanating from their embodiment of recklessness. This was seen as a manifestation of cultural norms that challenged their preconceived limits on how far individual agency could go in risking one's life to a shocking new extreme. Therefore, I posit that the shock and fear associated with Kamikaze attacks stem from a conflict of cultural assumptions about ways of dying.

This chapter looks at Kamikaze pilots to understand and, where relevant, challenge the assumptions underlying International Humanitarian Law's (IHL's) portrayal of conduct of hostilities and how it somewhat implicitly dictates the contours of agency regarding the risks that combatants take on the battlefield. The reciprocity principle reverberates through IHL provisions and shapes how the conduct of hostilities is perceived. The principle of reciprocity is a "legal, political, and sociological phenomenon" and "reflects the fact that most agents will agree to be bound by a norm on the basis that they thereby obtain a benefit."[10] This definition of reciprocity acknowledges that, for a reciprocal relationship to exist, two or more actors must exercise agency with a common understanding

[7] Mia Bloom, *Dying to Kill: The Allure of Suicide Terror* (Columbia University Press 2007) 15.

[8] Ibid.

[9] Emiko Ohnuki-Tierney, *Kamikaze Diaries: Reflections of Japanese Student Soldiers* (University of Chicago Press 2006) xiv–xv.

[10] René Provost, "Asymmetrical Reciprocity and Compliance with the Laws of War" in Benjamin Perrin (ed.) *Modern Warfare: Armed Groups, Private Militaries, Humanitarian Organizations, and the Law* (UBC Press 2012) 18; René Provost, *International Human Rights and Humanitarian Law* (Cambridge University Press 2002) 121. He further states that obligations are reciprocal if their creation, execution, and termination depend, in a general manner, on the existence of connected obligations on others.

that would benefit all parties involved. As this chapter will go on to further unpack, this agentic nature of reciprocity on the battlefield is fundamental to how IHL approaches combatant deaths, and therefore, its potential to engage with narratives that depict suicide attacks as agentic acts.

The idea of reciprocity of risk in combat, like IHL itself, is intertwined with the narratives of war historically developed in Europe. IHL is one of the oldest branches of international law and enshrines "a collective (European) *conscience*."[11] Its rules are a product of this mindset containing "cultural and religious norms, social structures" and formal and informal wartime practices common to this European context.[12] Therefore, its idea of warfare is a sociolegal construct,[13] which includes assumptions on how and to what extent combatants exercise agency over their deaths. With regard to reciprocity, in Medieval Europe, the chivalric codes that later became assimilated into the customs and practices of war functioned on mutual trust between knights of warring parties.[14] If a knight treated an enemy knight humanely, there was an expectation that the enemy would reciprocate this behavior. A guarantee of reciprocity was also an essential aspect of formal rules of war that predated the Geneva Conventions. These rules only applied if common understandings existed among warring parties.[15] The *si omnes* clause found in these treaties provided that if one party to a conflict did not subscribe to a treaty, it would not apply to relations between all parties to the conflict.[16] For example, Article 2 of Hague Convention No. IV states that its regulations "do not apply except between Contracting Powers, and then only if all the belligerents are parties to the Convention."[17] In the Rules of Land Warfare of the US Army of 1914[18] and the rules of the French Army at the time,[19] the binding nature of international law was implicitly subordinated to the condition of reciprocity and demanded mutual respect between opposing forces. Accordingly, reciprocity in battle, founded on a common understanding

[11] Martti Koskenniemi, *The Gentle Civilizer of Nations* (Cambridge University Press 2001) 51.

[12] Ibid. 43; Nathaniel Berman, "'The Appeals of the Orient': Colonized Desire and the War of the Riff" in Karen Knop (ed.) *Gender and Human Rights* (Oxford University Press 2004) 202.

[13] Michael Walzer, *Just and Unjust Wars: A Moral Argument with Historical Illustrations* (4th ed., Basic Books 2006) 25.

[14] Bruno Zimmermann et al., *Commentary on the Additional Protocols of 8 June 1977 to the Geneva Conventions of 12 August 1949* (Brill 1987) para. 1498.

[15] Yoshito Kita, "The Japanese Military's Attitude Towards International Law and the Treatment of Prisoners of War" in Ian Gow, Yoichi Hirama, & John Chapman (eds.) *The History of Anglo-Japanese Relations, 1600–2000* (Palgrave Macmillan UK 2003) 255.

[16] Theodor Meron, "The Humanization of Humanitarian Law" (2000) 94:2 The American Journal of International Law 239, 247.

[17] Convention (IV) respecting the Laws and Customs of War on Land and its annex: Regulations concerning the Laws and Customs of War on Land, October 18, 1907, International Peace Conference 1907, The Hague.

[18] US War Department, Office of the Chief of Staff, *Rules of Land Warfare* (US Government Printing Office 1914) 13.

[19] Robert Jacomet, *Les lois de la guerre continentale* (2nd ed., L. Fournier 1913) 26.

of how warriors should treat each other, constituted an important part of the image of warfare constructed by rules of combat.

This image of war, as shared between belligerents, often went hand in hand with, or necessarily extended from, their shared cultural beliefs and practices. Indeed, the role that culture played in realizing reciprocity on the battlefield was formally acknowledged in some legal instruments. For instance, the obligations in the Saint Petersburg Declaration of 1868 applied only to the belligerent relations between contracting "civilized nations," in a context where the term "civilized" meant primarily European or European settler communities. As such, the Declaration implies that mutual respect for wartime rules would only be possible if warring parties shared a European or "civilized" mindset. Similarly, the British military manual of 1914 afforded commanders the discretionary power of deciding whether or not to apply rules of war in colonial contexts, thus predicating the application of humanitarian principles on the commander's charity toward a colonial other rather than being the result of a legal obligation.[20] These examples reveal an assumption that it is only where common European or "civilized" cultural understandings were present and for warriors who belonged to these cultural contexts that rules of war would or could be applied reciprocally. Reciprocity was not necessarily maintained when faced with more heterogeneous cultural practices outside the European cultural context.

Today, the Geneva Conventions of 1949 are universally ratified, and the culturally specific nature of how warriors engage in reciprocal warfare is no longer explicit in IHL provisions. All parties to conflicts are obliged to respect the rules of war set out in IHL, irrespective of the cultural origins of their adversary. The requirement in Common Article 1 for IHL rules to be respected "in all circumstances" means they are nonreciprocal in nature, and "bind each High Contracting Party regardless of whether the other Parties observe their obligations."[21] Moreover, as IHL rules are *erga omnes* obligations, any State can demand another State to respect these rules even when the Party making such a claim is not directly party to a conflict, and therefore "not likely to be acting in the defence of reciprocal interests."[22]

[20] Frédéric Mégret, "From 'Savages' to 'Unlawful Combatants': A Postcolonial Look at International Humanitarian Law's 'Other'" in Ann Orford (ed.) *International Law and Its Others* (Cambridge University Press 2006) 282.

[21] International Committee of the Red Cross (ICRC), *Commentary on the First Geneva Convention: Convention (I) for the Amelioration of the Condition of the Wounded and Sick in Armed Forces in the Field (Commentaries on the 1949 Geneva Conventions)* (Cambridge University Press 2016) para. 188.

[22] Provost, "Asymmetrical Reciprocity and Compliance with the Laws of War" (n. 10) 19, 20; ICRC, *Updated Commentary on the First Geneva Convention* para. 119. Also see Knut Dörmann & Jose Serralvo, "Common Article 1 to the Geneva Conventions and the Obligation to Prevent International Humanitarian Law Violations" (2014) 96:895–896 Int Rev Red Cross 707.

Despite these developments in IHL, notions of reciprocity as rooted in Eurocentric warfare continue to influence today's framework of IHL.[23] For example, René Provost analyzes this point in the context of asymmetrical warfare, showing an instance of how reciprocity becomes vital to belligerents' respect for IHL when combat moves beyond the traditional, symmetrical, and European image of war.[24] In this chapter, I will proceed to unpack this claim regarding the cultural roots of reciprocity as applied in another context of war, specifically with regard to how combatants risk their lives on the battlefield. In doing so, I investigate whether an assumption of cultural homogeneity on the battlefield is crucial to maintaining reciprocity of risk in combat and to what extent cultural heterogeneity, as engendered by internal military ethos such as the no-surrender policy practiced by the Japanese military during World War II, challenged IHL's boundaries regarding combatants' agency to risk their lives in battle.

IHL's approach to the extent to which combatants risk their lives in combat is underscored by a culturally specific assumption embodied in what is known as the "reciprocity of risk in combat," which provides that combatants of parties to a conflict make themselves vulnerable to danger at the hands of their adversaries.[25] This reciprocity of risk in combat is founded on Western notions of chivalry which dictate that belligerency demands shared understandings between belligerents, including the extent of the danger to which they expose themselves mutually. The understanding that, to cause harm to an adversary, a combatant must assume a risk of harm to oneself prevents unlimited violence from taking place.[26] This is so as the corollary of this formulation is that where the adversary does not pose a threat, the legitimacy of targeting the adversary, being founded on the mutual threat existing between them, also fails. European codes of chivalry established this principle as an element of civilized warfare, distinguishing it from "savagery," which was often equated with absolute violence. As Liivoja notes, this idea of warfare as a rule-based endeavor with established limits is one of "the most pervasive, but also the most intangible" influences of chivalry in IHL.[27] Thus, "reciprocity of risk in combat," which stems from chivalric ideals of warfare, becomes foundational to IHL's objective of maintaining restraint in warfare.[28]

23 Provost, "Asymmetrical Reciprocity and Compliance with the Laws of War" (n. 10).

24 Ibid. 19.

25 Paul W. Kahn, "Imagining Warfare" (2013) 24:1 European Journal of International Law 199, 200, 218.

26 Paul Robinson, "'Ready to Kill but Not to Die': NATO Strategy in Kosovo" (1999) 54:4 International Journal 671, 672.

27 Rain Liivoja, "Chivalry without a Horse: Military Honour and the Modern Law of Armed Conflict" in Rain Liivoja & Andres Saumets (eds.) *The Law of Armed Conflict: Historical and Contemporary Perspectives* (Tartu University Press 2012) 93.

28 Ibid. 91; Anna Evangelidi, "Restraint in Bello: Some Thoughts on Reciprocity and Humanity" in Mats Deland et al. (eds.) *International Humanitarian Law and Justice: Historical and Sociological Perspectives* (Routledge 2018) 100.

The unarticulated nature of reciprocal risk can be examined in light of what silent spaces in the law tell us about its cultural assumptions. Silences in the law could stem from an assumption that persons would behave in a predictable manner consistent with dominant cultural narratives when presented with a specific circumstance, wherein it is unnecessary for the law to dictate how they should or should not behave. Lon Fuller similarly argued that meaningful human interaction depends on a paradigm in which persons behave according to a "predictable pattern."[29] Such patterns can be communicated not only through words but also through ritualistic acts with a specific meaning, including consistently practiced reciprocal behavior.[30] Within IHL's image of warfare, one such pattern is the reciprocal way combatants risk their lives, which also provides a degree of predictability to the conduct of hostilities. Within this image of war, when combatants confront each other on the battlefield, they engage in a dialogue on the risk they take on themselves at the hands of the adversary.[31] This "bond of mutual risk" brings a dimension of shared understanding into war[32] and has become internalized within the morality of IHL.[33] However, the presumed predictability of this behavior leads it to be taken for granted, to the extent that IHL deems it unnecessary to include it in its provisions expressly.

The assumption of reciprocity of risk has become ingrained with the categories constructed in IHL. Those in the category of combatants are presumed to risk their lives until they are considered *hors de combat*. IHL makes this category-based assumption despite the threat an individual combatant could pose to the adversary at a different point in time. This rule gives rise to moral debates as exemplified by the case of the naked soldier: Robert Graves in his autobiography *Goodbye to All That* narrates his refusal to kill an enemy soldier bathing naked on the battlefield.[34] The nakedness of the soldier evokes a sense of innocence and humanness that lay beyond the uniform and weaponry that identifies his combatant status. Walzer argues that when a combatant of the adversary is not posing a threat, he becomes

> a fellow creature . . . whose activities have the savor of peace and camaraderie, whose person is as valuable as my own. . . . He alienates himself from me when he tries to kill me, and from our common humanity. But the alienation is temporary, the humanity imminent.[35]

[29] Lon L. Fuller, "Human Interaction and the Law" (1969) 14:1 American Journal of Jurisprudence 1, 2.

[30] Ibid. 6.

[31] Provost, "Asymmetrical Reciprocity and Compliance with the Laws of War" (n. 10) 36.

[32] Frédéric Mégret, "The Humanitarian Problem with Drones" (2013) 2013:5 Utah Law Review 1283, 1310.

[33] Kahn, "Imagining Warfare" (n. 25) 201.

[34] Robert Graves, *Good-Bye to All That: An Autobiography* (2nd rev. ed., Vintage 1958) 176.

[35] Walzer, *Just and Unjust Wars* (n. 13) 142.

IHL finds an easy route to resolve the case of the naked soldier by categorizing soldiers as a class that is trained to fight with weapons on command.[36] By joining the class of combatants, there is a presumption of exposing oneself to mutual risk. Being subsumed into a category to assess whether a combatant poses a risk also takes away the situationality of the human agency in taking on risk to one's life.

The rationale of the nonthreatening or harmless soldier comes through when IHL prevents a combatant from being attacked when they are *hors de combat*.[37] How a combatant becomes *hors de combat*, indicating that he or she no longer poses a threat, is regulated through IHL. Article 41 of Additional Protocol I to the Geneva Conventions establishes that "a person who is recognized or who, in the circumstances, should be recognized to be *hors de combat* shall not be made the object of attack, " and goes on to specify that a combatant is considered *hors de combat* if

(a) "he is in the power of an adverse Party;
(b) he clearly expresses an intention to surrender; or
(c) he has been rendered unconscious or is otherwise incapacitated by wounds or sickness, and therefore is incapable of defending himself;

provided that in any of these cases he abstains from any hostile act and does not attempt to escape."

In both elements (a) and (c) of the provision, being *hors de combat* does not require the combatant to engage in an agentic act to gain their protection. This may be given that they are victims of physical injury or are at the hands of the adversary, thereby limiting their capacity, in the view of the drafters, to act voluntarily. IHL thereby implicitly disregards individual combatant agency, by subsuming them into categories and equating a harmless soldier to one who, at most times, is incapable of exercising agency. Only (b) dealing with surrender considers the intention of the combatant and thereby places an expectation on them to exercise an agentic act toward ceasing to engage in combat. As a result, the principle of surrender becomes a site where combatants are given the space in IHL provisions to negotiate how much risk they are willing to undertake when engaging in combat. As I will show later in this chapter through the analysis of Kamikaze pilots who functioned within a never surrender policy, the cultural ethos of militaries and how they practice reciprocity of risk influences how a combatant exercises their agency on the battlefield.

Implicit in IHL's assumption regarding a combatant's capacity to express their intention to surrender is how IHL deems that combatants exercise agency when

[36] Ibid. 144.
[37] Anthony J. Coates, *The Ethics of War* (1st ed., Manchester University Press 1997) 250.

risking their lives. This is so as IHL subscribes to reciprocal warfare found in narratives of honorable warriors, which are, in turn, influenced by European chivalric codes. As a demonstration of mutual risk in combat, chivalry dictated that knights put their lives at risk by fighting openly. These narratives view war as a regulated competition between consenting parties.[38] The code of chivalry reflected the ethos of warriors as persons freely choosing to fight. Hence, when they risked their lives, it was assumed that this was done as a voluntary act: the deaths of the aristocratic class in the process of a tourney, a quest, or a war were not a cause for moral indignation because they had consented to participate in such activities.[39] Given that "they seek out the excitement of battle, perhaps because they enjoy it," even a harrowing fate was not called unjust.[40] Likewise, "the fundamental characteristic of the profession of arms [was] the willingness to engage in self-sacrifice up to and including death."[41] An assumption of risk to personal safety, taken on as an agentic choice, was key to a warrior's valor.[42]

Underlying these descriptions of how a warrior's honor lies in their willingness to expose themselves to risk is the idea that to be considered honorable, a warrior engaging in combat must exercise agency. Being forced to risk one's life against one's will does not evoke similar feelings of valor. Such oppression would evoke qualities of victimhood rather than those of an agentic hero who sacrifices themselves out of their own volition. This readiness to expose oneself to risk underlies how combat is seen in IHL. Walzer states: "You can't kill unless you are prepared to die."[43] Combatants' right to legally kill other combatants is premised on the ground that such combatants grant their opponents an equal right to target them.[44] When read with the chivalric narratives that undergird IHL, this principle operates on the presumption that combatants are agentic actors willing to risk their safety in battle. This also explains why IHL treats deaths of combatants as legitimate while sparing civilians from direct harm. Combatants consented to bear arms. Therefore, they can be harmed. Civilians do not consent to be harmed because they do not engage in active hostilities.

While there is an understanding that combatants would choose to risk their lives in battle, the extent of this risk varies by the military ethos and the cultural context of the respective armed force. Although, in codes of chivalry that inspire

[38] Walzer, *Just and Unjust Wars* (n. 13) 26.
[39] Ibid. 25.
[40] Ibid. 26.
[41] Jeffrey K. Walker, "Old Laws and New Wars" (2000) 94 Proceedings of the Annual Meeting of the American Society of International Law 312, 313.
[42] Ibid.
[43] Michael Walzer, *Arguing about War* (Yale University Press 2004) 101.
[44] Combatant privilege does not expressly apply in the context of non-international armed conflicts. Scholars debate the impact of this asymmetry in the recognition of combatants on the reciprocal foundations of IHL.

rules of IHL, combatants are expected to risk their lives, this risk is assumed to be a limited one rather than an absolute one. Hersch Lauterpacht states that "it is impossible to visualize the conduct of hostilities in which one side would be bound by rules of warfare without benefiting from them and the other side would benefit from rules of warfare without being bound by them."[45] In this statement, he assumes that warfare where belligerent parties share common understandings of how to engage in combat and excludes all cases where combatants from different parties may experience different realities on the battlefield. At times, such differences in experience may result from the opposing party's lack of respect for reciprocity. Instances where reciprocity in conduct of hostilities may break down include where combatants are not granted similar benefits by their own military structures or due to cultural understandings about risking their lives that differ from those of the opposing party, the never surrender policy of the Japanese, further examined in this chapter, being an example of this. Such heterogeneity in practice among belligerent parties means that parties do not play by the same rules when engaging in combat, thereby breaking down the reciprocity that Lauterpacht seems to take for granted. Therefore, the notion of reciprocity of risk in warfare is linked to how the military ethos in different cultural contexts shapes how combatants exercise agency when risking their lives in battle.

The narrative of combatant deaths projected by IHL rules assumes that all combatants risk their lives in a similar manner. However, this does not consider narratives on how combatants from different cultures choose to assume risk and die in combat. In this case study of Kamikaze pilots, I examine how, contrary to historical cultural narratives on warriors' sacrifice that inspired IHL provisions, the voluntary nature of the Samurai Warriors' deaths was not dependent on an idea of limited risk.[46] For instance, the *Hagakure*, an early eighteenth-century compilation of Samurai clan ethics, dictated that where a choice is presented between life and death, the Samurai must choose the latter.[47] This language of choice frames narratives constructed around the deaths of Kamikaze pilots. This heterogeneity in the amount of risk a combatant takes during battle can challenge the delicate balance of reciprocity of risk that underlines IHL. By looking to the Kamikaze attacks, I will demonstrate how suicide attacks and the never surrender policy of the Japanese reveal assumptions inherent within IHL about the amount of risk a combatant is expected to take in battle. What becomes evident in challenging this assumption is the tenuous relationship IHL has with

[45] Hersch Lauterpacht, "The Limits of the Operation of the Law of War" (1953) 30 British Yearbook of International Law 206, 212.
[46] Clements (n. 2) xviii.
[47] Yamamoto Tsunetomo, *Hagakure: The Book of the Samurai* (William Scott Wilson trans., Kodansha International 2002) 17.

the cultural diversity in how combatants exercise agency when assuming risk to their lives on the battlefield.

In the following sections, I explore how Kamikaze pilots challenged IHL's boundaries built around the notion of reciprocity of risk in combat. In section 3.2, I argue that according to IHL, the risk to which combatants expose themselves on battlefields should neither be overly minimized to the point of riskless warfare nor should it lead to combatants fighting till death, thereby posing that IHL presumes an agentic combatant would assume risk to their lives in a limited manner. I delve further into how IHL tries to ensure that the risk that combatants undertake in combat is limited by studying the principle of surrender. This principle can be practiced meaningfully only through a reciprocal exchange, which requires that parties to a conflict adopt a similar notion of limited risk. The narrative that underlies IHL of agentic sacrifices by honorable warriors, therefore, rests on the assumption that homogeneous parties to a conflict would exercise limited and reciprocal risk in combat. In section 3.3, I question how this notion of limited risk, which depends on homogeneous military practices, can be balanced with culturally diverse ways in which militaries approach risk to combatants' lives. This includes the Kamikaze pilots' practice of fighting till death. I study Kamikaze pilots' deaths considering the Japanese policy prohibiting surrender, the heterogeneity it creates within the battlefield, and what this says about the agentic nature of their deaths. I show how the narratives of agency constructed around the absolute risk taken by Kamikaze attackers challenge the victim-perpetrator binary embedded in how IHL views combatant agency.

3.2. The limited nature of combatants' risk

Despite IHL's assumption that there is reciprocity of risk in how combatants engage in battle, this is not a consistent practice on the battlefield. The main argument forwarded in this section is that IHL's idea of agentic deaths in warfare is premised on "a goldilocks standard" regarding how much risk a combatant takes in combat: not too little, not too much, but a reasonably limited amount of risk to one's life. The differences in the extent of risk that combatants from diverse cultural contexts undertake in battle can upend this delicate balance. To preserve this balance, IHL attempts to regulate how much risk combatants take through treaty and customary rules governing methods of warfare. I examine the principle of surrender to show how IHL strives to maintain a practice of limited risk to the lives of combatants. This notion of limited risk reveals IHL's cultural assumptions on how combatants exercise agency over their deaths during combat.

3.2.1. IHL's attempts to regulate riskless warfare

Chivalric honor does not find direct expression in IHL. This has led scholars to argue that IHL does not impose an express rule that says one ought to "expose oneself to a good fight," and to refrain from killing enemies at no risk to one-self.[48] Mark Osiel theorizes that "it would be perverse, in analyzing twentieth-century wars, to say that soldiers are placed on the battlefield for the purpose of exhibiting chivalry".[49] This is so, as through industrialization and advances in technology, war has moved from being romanticized to being pragmatic, prioritizing efficiency over valor. However, the notion of chivalry is implicit in IHL's attempts to regulate States' measures to expose their combatants to as minimal risk as possible. This expectation for soldiers to assume a certain degree of risk can be gleaned through IHL's view on means or methods of warfare that lead to riskless warfare and therefore have the capacity to ensure that combatants can cause harm to their opponent while exposing themselves to little or no risk. Such attacks have the capacity to challenge the reciprocity of risk in combat and have often been considered dishonorable or unchivalrous within the European cultural narratives undergirding IHL.

That reciprocity of risk in combat provides an honorable foundation for how conduct of hostilities is imagined in IHL can be seen in the rule against perfidy found in Article 37 of Additional Protocol I.[50] It defines perfidy as acts "inviting the confidence of an adversary to lead him to believe that he is entitled to, or is obliged to accord, protection under the rules of international law applicable in armed conflict, with intent to betray that confidence."[51]

In this definition of perfidy, the "confidence" or the trust that exists between combatants of opposing parties is key, as it reflects the understanding that, in the kind of warfare that is imagined in IHL, a combatant should be able to rely on certain basic rules of behavior from the enemy.[52] Reciprocity of risk in combat is one such principle that rests on mutual trust in war. A combatant who engages in a perfidious act unfairly reduces the risk of being attacked by feigning protected status and therefore pretending to pose no threat. Given that reciprocity of risk

[48] Thomas Hurka, "Proportionality in the Morality of War" (2005) 33:1 Philosophy and Public Affairs 34, 63.

[49] Mark J. Osiel, *Obeying Orders: Atrocity, Military Discipline and the Law of War* (Routledge 2001) 15.

[50] 1987 Commentary to the Additional Protocols (n. 14) para 1498; Liivoja, "Chivalry without a Horse" 87; Customary IHL Study, "Customary IHL Rule No. 65: 'Perfidy,'" ICRC—IHL Database, online: https://ihl-databases.icrc.org/customary-ihl/eng/docs/v1_rul_rule65 accessed January 18, 2025.

[51] Protocol Additional to the Geneva Conventions of August 12, 1949, and relating to the Protection of Victims of International Armed Conflicts (Protocol I), June 8, 1977, 1125 U.N.T.S. 3, Art. 37(1).

[52] Morris Greenspan, *The Modern Law of Land Warfare* (University of California Press 1959) 319.

in combat dictates that the license to target another combatant would cease where no mutual threat exists, such a combatant gains an advantage against his adversary. In doing so, he destroys the faith that combatants are entitled to have in one another.[53] Likewise, Geoffrey Best claims that acts of perfidy undermine the very foundation of the IHL framework.[54] Admittedly, a ban on perfidious attacks attempts to prevent diluting the principle of civilian immunity. In addition, the ban on perfidy is evidence that under IHL, when a combatant gains an advantage over the enemy by unduly limiting the risk he faces from his adversary, such combatant goes against the mutual trust embedded in reciprocity of risk in combat.

IHL rules regulating weapons also address situations where a combatant engages in combat while not assuming any risk unto themselves. All weapons are required to comply with principles of IHL,[55] which include principles such as military necessity, discrimination, and proportionality. Sean Watts argues that honor or chivalry is an additional principle that should be considered when deciding whether a weapon is consistent with IHL.[56] These notions of chivalry frown upon weapons that limit risk a combatant assumes.[57] Employing weapons that minimize the risk of harm to combatants has been sanctioned as "treacherous or dishonorable" and in some instances continues to be prohibited within IHL.[58] Using poison as a weapon is a case in point.[59] Poison was banned by ancient Greeks and Romans, as well as by ancient Indians because of its secretive nature.[60] Today, the use of poison is prohibited under customary IHL applicable in both international and non-international armed conflicts.[61] Watts argues that the ban on poison is partly explained by the poisoners' ability to cause damage without being detected and without risking accountability, which goes against the understanding that in war, combatants ordinarily resign themselves to lethal expectations by entering combat.[62] It thereby challenges the reciprocity of risk in combat, stemming from an idea of chivalry and fairness.

[53] Coates (n. 37) 241.

[54] Geoffrey Francis Andrew Best, *War and Law since 1945* (paperback ed., Oxford University Press 1997) 290.

[55] *Legality of the Threat or Use of Nuclear Weapons*, Advisory Opinion, I.C.J. Reports 1996, 226, International Court of Justice (ICJ), July 8, 1996, para. 86.

[56] Sean Watts, "Regulation-Tolerant Weapons, Regulation-Resistant Weapons and the Law of War" (2015) 91 International Law Studies Series US Naval War College 540, 543–544.

[57] Ibid.

[58] Ibid. 555.

[59] Ibid.

[60] Ibid. 563.

[61] Customary IHL Study, "Customary IHL Rule No. 72: 'Poison and Poisoned Weapons,'" ICRC—IHL Database, online: https://ihl-databases.icrc.org/customary-ihl/eng/docs/v1_rul_rule72 accessed January 18, 2025; Hague Convention IV of 1907 United States, Instructions for the Government of Armies in the United States in the Field, prepared by Francis Lieber, promulgated as general order No. 100 by President Abraham Lincoln, Washington, DC, April 24, 1863, Art. 70.

[62] Watts, "Regulation of Weapons" (n. 56) 563.

Despite the influence of chivalry, historically, militaries have always sought to develop means of warfare that lessen the harm to which their combatants are exposed. In turn, such techniques tend to come under criticism for unsettling the code of honor underlying war: "ancient societies often scorned the bow and javelin as inconsistent with honorable warfare and agreed to prohibit their use in some conflicts".[63] Innocent II and the Second Lateran Council of 1139 prohibited the use of the crossbow by militaries, claiming it was a "hateful to God and unfit for Christians".[64] However, members of the Council were unable to prevent its widespread production and use.[65] Medieval criticisms against the crossbow focused on the weapon enabling archers to kill knights from safe cover.[66] For similar reasons, gunpowder was called a "wicked and terrible discovery" which had "destroyed martial glory, left the profession of arms without honor, and reduced valor and virtue to nought."[67] What is common for both the crossbow, gunpowder, and other such weapons is that they can cause harm to the enemy from a distance while exposing combatants to minimal danger. Therefore, they contradict the chivalrous, knightly tradition of fighting face to face, mutually exposing themselves to risk. With respect to various weapons, their effectiveness has been too appealing for States to resist, despite the ethical and moral tensions created by its inconsistency with honor and chivalry.[68]

In this same vein, while not prohibited under IHL, the use of unmanned drones in combat operations raises many moral and ethical concerns. There have been arguments made about the capacity of a drone to carry out attacks that are consistent with IHL (i.e., the principle of proportionality). However, scholars argue that even if the use of drones were taken not to violate any specific rules of IHL expressly, it still would not quite meet the ethical standards of warfare. This is so as drones, being unmanned, render their operators entirely secure,[69] fundamentally affecting the moral core of IHL.[70] Mégret argues that

[63] Ibid. 567.

[64] Eitan Barak, *Deadly Metal Rain: The Legality of Flechette Weapons in International Law: A Reappraisal Following Israel's Use of Flechettes in the Gaza Strip (2001-2009)* (Brill 2011) 83.

[65] W. Robert McFadden, "The Ethical Aspects of Limited War" (1971) 13:1 Journal of Church and State 113, 117.

[66] Shane R. Reeves & William J Johnson, "Autonomous Weapons: Are You Sure Those Are Killer Robots—Can We Talk about It" (2014) 2014:4 Army Lawyer 25, 27: "[T]he crossbow, and its ability to penetrate a noble's armor while being fired by an unskilled conscript, was seen as an unequivocal violation of chivalric code."

[67] David A. Bell, "In Defense of Drones: A Historical Argument" New Republic (January 27, 2012), https://newrepublic.com/article/100113/obama-military-foreign-policy-technology-drones; "Hague Declarations and Wishes Topic VII" (1905) 1905 International Law Studies Series US Naval War College 132, 134: "History shows that it has been customary to put any new means of war under the ban for a time."

[68] Eric Talbot Jensen, "Emerging Technologies and LOAC Signaling" (2015) 91 International Law Studies Series US Naval War College 621, 622.

[69] Mégret, "The Humanitarian Problem with Drones" (n. 32) 1300.

[70] Ibid. 1303.

"the use of drones in a context where only one side has access to that far superior technology renders war essentially meaningless as a concept," depriving war of "all features of the classical duel situation."[71] One way this happens is how drones disrupt the type of reciprocal armed interaction on which normative conditions of IHL are built.

Despite these debates on the ethics of riskless warfare, IHL is not settled on whether there exists a duty to expose one's combatants to at least a minimal level of risk. As mentioned before, the balance of reciprocity of risk rests on combatants exposing themselves to harm while attacking their opponents. On this basis, it is possible to object on moral grounds to the idea that soldiers are "ready to kill but not to die."[72] Likewise, deaths of combatants become an expected consequence of war, and it can be argued that "risking one's life is part of what it means to be a soldier."[73] Peter Margulies highlights this line of scholarly argument as supporting the existence of a "duty to risk: the State has a categorical duty to risk its own forces".[74] The use of technology or weapons of less risk to one's own forces has been referred to by some as a "coward's strategy."[75] In IHL, there is, arguably, a duty on the part of combatants to risk their lives in combat. This is especially the case when such a risk would facilitate the protection of civilian lives. For example, Avishai Margalit and Walzer claim that "it is the capacity to injure that makes combatants legitimate targets in the context of war." Those who enter the legal category of combatants take risks that others are not required to take.[76] They expose themselves to those risks rather than impose them on civilians who have not subscribed to such an undertaking.[77] Furthermore, while the preservation of one's forces is an important consideration for commanders' decisions, it cannot be a relevant military advantage for the principle of proportionality, given that soldiers are lawful targets because of

[71] Ibid. 1311.
[72] Ibid. 1305.
[73] Robinson, "Ready to Kill" (n. 26) 673.
[74] Peter Margulies, "Valor's Vices: Against a State Duty to Risk Forces in Armed Conflict" (2012) 37:2 Vermont Law Review 271, 272: Margulies articulates this duty as one imposed by the State on the combatant. Therefore, his argument differs from the language in narratives on chivalry, where the agency is attributed to the soldier who chooses to risk their life. However, it is possible to marry these two viewpoints, first, that of a duty being imposed on combatants by their militaries, and second, that of the narrative of combatant agency when risking their lives. To view agency as coexisting with duty, it is important to understand how this duty to risk combatant lives in IHL is read within the narratives of agentic sacrifice of a soldier. IHL combines these two ideas by saying that a duty to risk a combatant's life must remain within the purview of Western constructions of agentic actions: this leads to the assumption that in fulfilling their duties to the military, combatants can take limited risks to their lives.
[75] Ibid.
[76] Michael Walzer & Avishai Margalit, "Israel: Civilians & Combatants" The New Yorker (May 14, 2009), online: https://www.nybooks.com/articles/2009/05/14/israel-civilians-combatants/ last accessed January 18, 2025.
[77] Ibid.

their status. Accordingly, combatants are expected to face risks that are inherently associated with engaging in hostilities, and arguably this burden cannot be shifted onto civilians.[78] In this context, the duty to expose one's own combatants to risk is justified on the basis that it facilitates restraint in the violence caused to civilians.[79]

While a soldier is expected to assume risk, military practice demonstrates a trend of not recognizing a duty to take on risk to one's own forces. This is clear in the arguments made in favor of the doctrine of force protection which claims that the protection of one's troops is a priority in war. Australia and New Zealand, for example, made declarations when ratifying Additional Protocol I that "the term 'military advantage' involves a variety of considerations including the security of attacking forces."[80] Scholars argue further that a State *should* attend to minimizing the losses of its own troops.[81] Asa Kasher and Amos Yadlin claim it is immoral to deprioritize the duty to minimize casualties among one's own combatants: "A combatant is a citizen in uniform. In Israel, quite often, he is a conscript or on reserve duty. His state ought to have a compelling reason for jeopardizing his life."[82] Bradley Jay Strawser uses a similar logic to argue that the use of drones is not only permissible but also "ethically obligatory".[83] He bases this argument on the fact that in the military structure where soldiers follow the orders of their commanders, it is immoral to order a combatant to endanger his life unnecessarily.[84] Similarly, commanders are not to waste the lives of their own soldiers in the pursuit of unattainable or relatively unimportant military objectives.[85] These scholars distinguish acceptance of risk from reckless and unnecessary deaths of combatants. To them, the latter falls outside the ambit of the

[78] Laurent Gisel, "International Expert Meeting Report: The Principle of Proportionality," International Expert Meeting June 22–23, 2016, Quebec, International Committee of the Red Cross, 2018, 26. It was also noted that, as per the "courageous restraint" guidance by International Security Assistance Force (ISAF)/United States Forces Afghanistan (USFOR-A) commanders in Afghanistan, actually required troops to accept casualties to their own forces in order to minimize the number of civilian incidental casualties, considering the wider goal of the campaign.

[79] Jeff McMahan, "The Just Distribution of Harm Between Combatants and Noncombatants" (2010) 38:4 Philosophy of Public Affairs 342, 351–353.

[80] Gisel (n. 78) 24; New Zealand, Declaration made at the time of ratification to Protocol Additional to the Geneva Conventions of August 12, 1949, and relating to the Protection of Victims of International Armed Conflicts (Protocol I), June 8, 1977, February 8, 1988, para. 5; Australia, Declaration made at the time of ratification to Protocol Additional to the Geneva Conventions of August 12, 1949, and relating to the Protection of Victims of International Armed Conflicts (Protocol I), June 8, 1977, June 21, 1991.

[81] Kenneth Anderson, "The Case for Drones," Commentary (June 2013) Commentary, online: https://www.commentarymagazine.com/articles/anderson-kenneth/the-case-for-drones/ last accessed January 18, 2025.

[82] Asa Kasher & Amos Yadlin, "Assassination and Preventive Killing" (2005) 25:1 SAIS Review 41, 50.

[83] Bradley Jay Strawser, "Moral Predators: The Duty to Employ Uninhabited Aerial Vehicles" (2010) 9:4 Journal of Military Ethics 342, 344.

[84] Ibid.

[85] Coates (n. 37) 241–242.

agentic narrative of combatant risk. In other words, they concede that a narrative where combatants would want to risk their lives at all costs would be unsustainable and inconsistent with cultural iterations of how people are expected to exercise agency in life and death decisions. In the following section, I analyze the principle of surrender to comment on the cultural assumptions influencing how IHL functions on an understanding of how combatants would use their agency to limit the risk of death in battle.

3.2.2. Cultural assumptions embedded in the idea of limited risk in war

The limited nature of the risk a combatant is expected to undertake during combat is intrinsic to the practice of surrender. Hew Stratchan explains how, for surrender to be successful, a shared understanding must exist between opposing parties of respecting a combatant's exercise of agency to stop fighting: "Just as battle rests on a shared acceptance of the need to engage each other, so surrender rests not on a unilateral decision to stop fighting but on the readiness of the enemy to accept that decision."[86] On the battlefield, a combatant is permitted to target another combatant as long as they cause a risk of harm by virtue of their combatant status. If an opposing combatant were to cease engaging in combat, the risk of harm they pose would also cease to exist.[87] The surrender of a combatant extinguishes the reciprocity of risk, and with it the internal morality that legitimizes the targeting of combatants. Surrendering, therefore, communicates a limit to the risk that a combatant is willing to take in battle.

Surrender as a practice depends on a shared understanding of how one party will be treated by the other if a combatant stops fighting. If combatants cannot expect to be spared when they lay down their arms, they have no rationale or motive to surrender. Correspondingly, if one party did not take prisoners, they could not expect to be taken prisoner: "If you will not surrender or be taken prisoner, and if you will torture or kill those who do surrender to you, your enemies will not allow you to be taken or to surrender".[88] This would lead to fights to the

[86] Hew Strachan, "Introduction: Surrender in Modern Warfare Since the French Revolution" in Holger Afflerbach & Hew Strachan (eds.) *How Fighting Ends: A History of Surrender* (1st ed., Oxford University Press 2012) 219.

[87] Walzer, *Just and Unjust Wars* (n. 13) 46: "A soldier who surrenders enters into an agreement with his captors: he will stop fighting if they will accord him what the legal handbooks call 'benevolent quarantine.' Prisoners of war have a right to try to escape-they cannot be punished for the attempt-but if they kill a guard in order to escape, the killing is not an act of war; it is murder. For they committed themselves to stop fighting, gave up their right to kill, when they surrendered."

[88] Lawrence H. Keely, "Surrender and Prisoners in Prehistoric and Tribal Societies" in Afflerbach & Strachan (n. 86) 7.

death.[89] Accordingly, the practice of surrender in battle, and the limited warfare it entails, rests on the notion of reciprocity.

This dimension of reciprocity is reflected in how the principle of surrender developed as a rule within the law of war. Article 23 of the Hague Convention of 1907 forbids the killing or wounding of an enemy who, "having laid down his arms, or having no longer means of defense, has surrendered at discretion."[90] The Commentary to Additional Protocol I examines the drafting history of this provision and notes that

> its first version presented at the Brussels Conference of 1874 contained the words "à merci," which in English would be "at the mercy" or "at the discretion" of somebody . . . and was later replaced by the term "à discrétion," which expresses the same idea.[91]

The use of the term "at discretion" in the Hague Convention meant that the adverse party could decide whether the surrender was to be accepted or not. In relation to surrender, "at discretion" can be defined as the "judgment of a good man."[92] At the time, IHL considered the rule on surrender to apply depending on the benevolence of the victor. The victor's mercy was meant to indicate their understanding that, in war, combatants should be able to lay down their arms and stop endangering their lives. This practice demanded agentic acts on both parties: first, the surrendering combatant who decides to stop fighting; second, the opposing party who chooses to accept this expression of surrender. This exchange was only feasible if both parties subscribed to the notion that combatants risked their lives in a limited manner in combat.

The expectation of a common understanding between parties in the context of surrender depends on both parties sharing homogeneous cultural understandings of the extent to which a person is deemed capable of exercising agentic choice in risking their lives to the point of death. When this principle was formed in IHL, this shared understanding was based on a European context rooted in Christianity. Accordingly, those who surrendered "at discretion" willingly placed their lives in the hands of the victor, who was obliged to respect that responsibility by acting with "decency, honor, and Christian virtue."[93]

89 Russell Buchan, "The Rule of Surrender in International Humanitarian Law" (2018) 51:1 Israel Law Review 3, 3.

90 Hague Convention IV of 1907 (n. 17) Annex to the Convention: Regulations Respecting the Laws and Customs of War on Land—Section II: Hostilities—Chapter I: Means of Injuring the Enemy, Sieges, and Bombardments, Art. 23 (3).

91 1987 Commentary to the Additional Protocols (n. 14) 480, note 1.

92 John Childs, "Surrender and the Laws of War in Western Europe, c. 1660–1783" in Afflerbach & Strachan (n. 86) 156.

93 Ibid.

The mutual or reciprocal nature of respect to one's opponent at the time rested on the cultural construct of chivalry, a code that was rooted in religion. In Medieval France, the act of surrender was considered to be honorable behavior for knights.[94] Geoffroi de Charny, in the *Livre de Chevalerie*, wrote: "And if you are defeated, does not God show you great mercy if you are taken prisoner honorably, praised by friends and enemies alike?"[95] The mercy shown to the person requesting to surrender is, therefore, seen as stemming from a merciful Christian God. Surrender in Medieval times rested on the convention of parole which conveyed an agreement that a prisoner would not take up arms against the enemy that captured them.[96] Even where the underlying motivations for capture of prisoners seem to be monetary in nature (i.e., where ransom was involved), such practice only existed among parties of the Christian faith.[97] Confronting enemies that did not subscribe to such notions due to cultural differences entailed the potential breakdown of reciprocity.

In its development, IHL has taken measures to minimize this reciprocal nature of the act of surrender by creating obligations on the party receiving a surrender to accept it. For example, the general-participation clause, also known as the *si omnes* clause, was explicitly reversed in the 1929 Prisoners of War Convention and the 1929 Convention for the Amelioration of the Condition of the Wounded and Sick in Armies in the Field.[98] Article 82 of the 1929 Prisoners of War Convention provided that "[i]n time of war if one of the belligerents is not a party to the Convention, its provisions shall, nevertheless, remain binding as between the belligerents who are parties thereto."[99] One way a person can be rendered *hors de combat* is if he clearly expresses an intention to surrender, provided that he abstains from any hostile act and does not attempt to escape. The obligation on the adverse party is to cease fire immediately upon being communicated a clear intention of surrender. The term "at discretion" is not present in the version adopted in Article 41 of Additional Protocol I. Surrender as per Additional Protocol I is unconditional and "no argument of military

[94] John Gillingham, "Surrender in Medieval Europe—An Indirect Approach" in Afflerbach & Hew (n. 86) 58.

[95] Geoffroi de Charny, Richard W. Kaeuper & Elspeth Kennedy, *A Knight's Own Book of Chivalry* (University of Pennsylvania Press 2013) 72.

[96] Major Gary D. Brown, "Prisoner of War Parole: Ancient Concept, Modern Utility" (1998) 16 Military Law Review 200, 200.

[97] Gillingham (n. 94) 62.

[98] Convention relative to the Treatment of Prisoners of War, Geneva, July 27, 1929, Diplomatic Conference convened by The Swiss Federal Council with a view to the revision of the Geneva Convention for the Amelioration of the Condition of the Wounded and Sick in Armies in the Field of July 6, 1906, and the elaboration of a Code relating to the Prisoners of War, Geneva; Convention for the Amelioration of the Condition of the Wounded and Sick in Armies, in the Field, July 27, 1929, Diplomatic Conference convened by The Swiss Federal Council with a view to the revision of the Geneva Convention for the Amelioration of the Condition of the Wounded and Sick in Armies in the Field of July 6, 1906, and the elaboration of a Code relating to the Prisoners of War, Geneva.

[99] 1929 Prisoners of War Convention (n. 98).

necessity may be invoked" to refuse it.[100] In requiring the unconditional acceptance of surrender, IHL embeds the notion that there are limits to the risks a soldier is expected take in combat and extends it to how diverse cultures across geographical contexts are meant to conduct wars. In doing so, it also puts in circulation its own understanding of how combatants exercise their agency in combat.

Through the principle of surrender, which ensures combatants have a choice as to when to stop fighting, IHL portrays combatant deaths as being voluntary even though they may not necessarily engage in combat by their own choice. Given that a combatant has the option to surrender during hostilities, it may seem that if they were to keep fighting, they make a conscious choice to risk their life. This mirrors the practice of certain "primitive" societies, where, although individuals could "not avoid combat without exposing themselves to dishonor and ostracism", running away was often acceptable.[101] Even after the professionalization of militaries, military codes still required certain standards to ensure that the "courtesies of the chivalric age" continued.[102] One such courtesy seems to be that fighting to the death must be a voluntary act. Walzer claims that whenever entering into battle is not voluntary, as in the case of most soldiers in professional armies, combatants are provided the choice to stop fighting without serious sanctions.[103] While in all cases when a combatant is targeted by the enemy, especially in aerial warfare or when using bombs or missiles, there might not be the chance to stop fighting, IHL, in principle, makes provision for fighting to stop, through the principle of surrender.

How combatants exercise their choice to stop fighting cannot be decoupled from the internal culture of a military and the expectations that militaries place on their own combatants. For example, many militaries require combatants to exert a specific degree of effort in battle. In modern legislation, the term "utmost exertion" speaks to the degree of risk a soldier is expected to take prior to being legitimately capable of giving up fighting. The Canadian Defence Act makes it an offense for any military person when ordered to carry out an operation of war, to fail to use his utmost exertion to carry the orders into effect.[104] In the Armed Forces Act of Ghana, combatants are guilty of an offense if, when ordered to carry out an operation of war, a combatant fails to use their utmost exertion to carry out the order.[105] When in contravention of these provisions, such a combatant

[100] 1987 Commentary to the Additional Protocols (n. 14) para. 1619.
[101] Walzer, *Just and Unjust Wars* (n. 13) 26.
[102] Ibid. 35.
[103] Ibid. 25.
[104] Canada, National Defence Act of 1985, section 73.
[105] Ghana, Armed Forces Act of 1962, section 15(c). Section 14 of the Armed Forces Act 1962 of Ghana requires all commanders, when under orders to carry out an operation of war or on coming into contact with an enemy, to use their utmost exertion to bring their officers and the men under their command into action, and encourage them to fight courageously.

may be subject to punishment by death.[106] The term "utmost exertion" can be interpreted in diverse ways depending on the ethos of a given military and how it understands the notions of honor, bravery, or cowardice. Walzer argues that rules that dictate when and how fighting is to end, for example, whether fighting is to always be broken off at sunset, tend to be less universal and more susceptible to being particularized based on local contexts.[107] Similarly, I argue that whether a combatant chooses to obey an order to fight to the death largely depends on the cultural context in which such a combatant operates. Likewise, the next section delves into how Kamikaze pilots' deaths embedded in the Japanese policy of never surrender marked a heterogeneity in the risk assumed by a combatant. It upsets the internal morality of war based on reciprocity of risk, more easily practiced in wars between homogeneous cultures. In turn, it also questions to what extent the agentic narrative of a warrior risking their lives in battle can survive cultural heterogeneity.

3.3. Kamikaze and the heterogeneity of risk in combat

IHL assumes that the risk that combatants take in conducting hostilities is limited. Paul Kahn subscribes to this assumption when he states that "[e]very [S]tate wants to minimize its own losses when it commits itself to the use of force. There is nothing new in this."[108] This statement implies the existence of an interest on the part of a military to accrue minimal damage to its combatants, whether it be for utilitarian, political, or moral reasons. This is an intuitive claim on Kahn's part, which reflects the modern cultural presumption in favor of self-preservation. However, this culture of self-preservation cannot be taken for granted. Restraints that are observed in war are determined by each society. Each cultural context tends to determine "who can fight, what tactics are acceptable, when battle has to be broken off, and what prerogatives go with victory into the idea of war itself."[109] Therefore, whether war tends to be limited, how it is limited, and the extent of its limits vary by time and place.[110] These differences extend to how combatants are expected to risk their lives during hostilities and how narratives around the agency of their deaths are constructed. The Kamikaze pilots' absolute intent to die renders death no longer a risk but a certainty. As

[106] Ibid., section 15. Also see Malaysia, Armed Forces Act of 1972, section 40(b): "In the Armed Forces Act 1972 of Malaysia a combatant who when ordered to carry out an operation of war, fails to use his utmost exertion to carry out the orders into effect is guilty of an offence."
[107] Walzer, *Just and Unjust Wars* (n. 13) 25.
[108] Paul W. Kahn, "War and Sacrifice in Kosovo" (1999) 19:2/3 Philosophy of Public Policy Quarterly 1, 2.
[109] Walzer, *Just and Unjust Wars* (n. 13) 23.
[110] Ibid. 24–25.

Emiko Ohnuki-Tierney argues, "[W]hile German soldiers were trained to kill, Japanese soldiers were trained to die."[111] Likewise, the West's shock at the Kamikaze attacks stemmed partly from the fact that the Japanese soldiers were ever ready to die, which was deemed an irrational characteristic beyond comprehension for non-Japanese.[112] This type of agency that assumes absolute risk that seemingly goes against the grain of self-preservation does not fit well with IHL's vision of warfare where combatants undertake a limited risk and opt to surrender.

3.3.1. Cultural heterogeneity on the battlefield and reciprocity of risk in combat

Reciprocity of risk in combat is inversely proportional to heterogeneity in warfare. Theodor Meron compares the operation of IHL during times of armed conflict to a boxing match: "Pummeling the opponent's upper body is fine; hitting below the belt is proscribed."[113] This image assumes that both opponents are playing the same game and therefore the same rules apply. His vision of IHL regulates aspects of a struggle for life and death between contestants who operate based on formal equality. According to him, this equality is assumed as it derives from the Medieval tradition of chivalry, which he states guarantees a modicum of fair play. Meron's allusion to chivalry depicts warfare as structured battles where both parties follow the same rules.[114] Due to this perception of reciprocal warfare having existed in European history, IHL is structured to operate most reliably between militaries of homogeneous cultures.[115] However, what would be harder to imagine is a match where each player engages in different games: reciprocity becomes a less stable framework for combat behavior in such an instance.

War does not always occur between militaries or armed groups that have shared understandings about how combatants risk their lives. The internal culture of the opponents' military is a crucial factor determining reciprocity on the battlefield. It is particularly pertinent to the practice of surrender. How surrender is practiced on battlefields must be assessed while keeping in mind a military's ethos within specific cultural contexts. This is more so given that the mindset of a combatant is made up of "his or her political circumstances, convictions,

[111] Ohnuki-Tierney, *Kamikaze Diaries* (n. 9) 4.
[112] Ohnuki-Tierney, *Kamikaze, Cherry Blossoms and Nationalisms* (n. 3) 20.
[113] Meron (n. 16) 240.
[114] Ibid.
[115] Mégret, "From 'Savages' to 'Unlawful Combatants'" (n. 20): "The notion that the law of nations did not apply, at least not in its entirety (but often not at all), to non-European peoples, was well accepted in the nineteenth century."

interests, and customs; his or her expectations, unspoken assumptions, and fears; and maybe even the impact of their militant self-images, as well as of the tendencies of their parent societies."[116] Local military practices play a role in how combatants surrender partly because treaties and military manuals lack specificity on the elements of an effective and legal surrender.[117] In the case of surrender, "to repudiate the assumption that [a combatant] represents a threat to military security," "the burden is upon the surrendering party to make his intentions clear, unambiguous, and unequivocal to the capturing unit."[118] As per the Commentary to Additional Protocol I, in land warfare, a combatant who seeks to "indicate that he is no longer capable of engaging in combat, or that he intends to cease combat, lays down his arms and raises his hands."[119] Furthermore, a combatant may "cease fire, wave a white flag and emerge from a shelter with hands raised, . . . or if surprised, raise his arms to indicate that he is surrendering, even though he may still be carrying weapons."[120] However, such practices are not legally binding and therefore may or may not be used by parties to a conflict in engaging in surrender. Specific conditions indicating a surrender are open to interpretation by States and armed groups. When IHL is interpreted by actors on the ground in this way, they become part of "an interpretive community."[121] Provost argues that, in this process of interpretation, the local culture of interpreters becomes significant.[122]

This cultural diversity in practice can impact the predictability of interactions on the battlefield. Interactions and rituals surrounding surrender are built around the common understanding that soldiers can and/or would wish to, under certain circumstances, give up fighting by engaging in predictable patterns of action. This can result in "an interactional expectancy" on the battlefield, generating a sense of obligation to accept a surrender where

116 Holger Afflerbach & Hew Strachan, "Introduction" in Afflerbach & Strachan (n. 86) 4: the authors suggest that the first of these issues concern "the culture, religion, and ideology; psychological factors, such as emotion, hatred, vengeance, hope, and feelings of honor; the male self-image of the warrior; the mood and convictions of the parent societies, and the resulting 'good-boy orientation' of the soldier produced by a parent society. The second issue has to do with command and leadership; morale, discipline, and the efficiency of punishment by military authorities; the parent societies, and whether they stigmatize surrendering soldiers; the practical possibilities of surrendering; the attitude of the victor and the probable fate of the soldier who has surrendered in captivity; and the rules and norms regulating these and many other points."

117 Buchan (n. 89).

118 Ibid.

119 1987 Commentary to the Additional Protocols (n. 14) para. 1618.

120 Ibid.

121 René Provost, "Interpretation in International Law as a Transcultural Project" in Andrea Bianchi, Daniel Peat & Matthew Windsor (eds.) *Interpretation in International Law* (Oxford University Press 2015) 290, 296. He further argues that meaning is derived from the converging interpretations given to a text by actors who thereby become members of an interpretive community.

122 Ibid. 291.

indications of commonly understood signs of surrender are demonstrated. However, Fuller states that any analysis in terms of "interactional expectancies" must acknowledge those who are outsiders to such expectancies.[123] Likewise, cultural heterogeneity can be antithetical to the formation of interactional expectancies, given that the way life is organized may differ drastically from one culture to another. World War II Japan stands as the "other" who falls outside this interactional expectancy. This is so as the policy of never surrender which was an integral part of Japanese military ethos during World War II meant that their combatants did not conform to the commonly accepted rituals of surrender.

During World War II, Western militaries became aware of how the Japanese military operated under a military ethos not shared by them. This becomes clear in reading the *US Handbook on Japanese Military Forces of 1944*.[124] The handbook recognizes the determination of the Japanese soldier "to fight to the last or commit suicide rather than be taken prisoner". It alludes to motivations intrinsic to Japanese culture that shape the behavior of Japanese soldiers, noting that their suicidal combat methods are likely "motivated by the disgrace which a combatant realizes would be brought on his family should he fall into the enemy's hands".[125] This handbook provides insights into a specific Western narrative in which Japanese soldiers did not share the same military ethos as their Western counterparts due to cultural differences. This Western gaze zeros in on whether the practice of surrender was a plausible option for Japanese soldiers given their military's beliefs about honor and disgrace.[126] I take these insights under advisement, to examine the Kamikaze pilots' deaths, considering the cultural ethos within the Japanese military. In doing so, I consider how agency in relation to death can be understood in this cultural context as compared to the self-preservationist bias that is embedded in IHL.

The Japanese forces were ordered never to surrender. Historically, a non-victorious Samurai was not expected to return alive from the battlefield.[127] The Bushido code set out the values of the warrior and can be compared as a Japanese counterpoint to European codes of chivalry,[128] and they did not permit retreat.

[123] Fuller (n. 29) 9.
[124] United States, *TM E 30-480 Handbook on Japanese Military Forces, 1944* (US Government Printing Office, 1944).
[125] Ibid. 9.
[126] Ross Hassig, "How Fighting Ended in the Aztec Empire and Its Surrender to the Europeans" in Afflerbach & Strachan (n. 86) 114.
[127] Kita (n. 15) 259.
[128] Samuel P. Huntington, *The Soldier and the State: The Theory and Politics of Civil-Military Relations* (Harvard University Press 1957) 125.

These values were transferred to the military ethics of World War II Japan. In the words of General Araki:

> Retreat and surrender are not permissible in our Army . . . To become a captive of the enemy by surrendering after doing their best is regarded by foreign soldiers as acceptable conduct. But according to our traditional Bushido, retreat and surrender constitute the greatest disgrace and are actions unbecoming to a Japanese soldier.[129]

The Kamikaze fighters, engaging in suicidal missions, in most cases with no room for return, epitomized this military ethic. In this manner, the Japanese military culture in World War II eschewed the homogeneity of practice on which reciprocity in risk is based. In lieu, it demonstrates that the amount of risk that a combatant is expected to take is determined by the culture and ethos internal to a military.

The suicidal practices of the Japanese military were intertwined with their combatants' refusal to surrender in battle: "The Japanese fought past a point of tactical hopelessness. A point where Western counterparts would have been expected to lower their flags and lay down their arms."[130] The military code for the imperial navy of 1872 prohibited surrender or escape, a policy that arguably led to mass suicides (*gyokusai*).[131] The Japanese military ethos during World War II also demanded utmost loyalty.[132] It claimed that "the spirit of the soldier is best exemplified by those who silently do their duty, joyfully braving death in obedience to command given at a time when they are undergoing great hardships."[133] The Japanese Senjinkun Military Code at the time of World War II demanded soldiers "to keep fighting vigorously and stubbornly"[134] and to "never give up a position but rather die."[135] This attitude challenges the IHL principles that are built on the notion of reciprocity of risk in battle. IHL recognizes that combatants can be rendered *hors de combat* and among the ways in which this may occur is when a combatant falls into the power of an adverse party or by clearly expressing an intention to surrender.[136] Both these avenues were made unavailable for Japanese soldiers by their military.

[129] Ibid. 129.
[130] Mordecai G. Sheftall, "Kamikaze Warfare in Imperial Japan's Existential Crisis, 1944–5" in Afflerbach & Strachan, *How Fighting Ends* (n. 86) 384–385.
[131] Ohnuki-Tierney, *Kamikaze Diaries* (n. 9) 4.
[132] Japan, Senjinkun Military Code of 1941, Chapter I.3: "Essential to victory and requisite for maintaining peace is the condition wherein the entire Army, united in the bonds of absolute loyalty, moves as one in response to a command"; Ohnuki-Tierney, *Kamikaze, Cherry Blossoms and Nationalisms* (n. 3) 79: "This was a pocket-sized military code issued to soldiers in the Imperial Japanese forces on 8 January 1941 in the name of then War Minister Hideki Tojo."
[133] Senjinkun Military Code (n. 132).
[134] Ibid.
[135] Ibid. chapter 1.6.
[136] Customary IHL Study, "Customary IHL Rule No. 47: "Attacks against Persons Hors de Combat," ICRC—IHL Database, online: https://ihl-databases.icrc.org/customary-ihl/eng/docs/v1_rul_rule47 accessed January 18, 2025.

In IHL, those who surrender are given the right to be treated as prisoners of war.[137] However, in order to maintain honor, Japanese soldiers were required not to be taken prisoner: "If alive, do not suffer the disgrace of becoming a prisoner."[138] Student soldiers were taught to commit suicide using their own weapons, rather than be captured alive.[139] Hence, there was no place in the Japanese military code for prisoners.[140] The Japanese soldier had been taught that he who surrenders to the enemy is a coward and not worth consideration. These values on surrender and capture also had a spillover effect on how they valued the lives of others and the reciprocal nature of how IHL imagines warfare.[141] Yoshito Kita argues that their belief that surrender was a shameful act made Japanese soldiers repugnant to enemy prisoners who claimed their international legal rights or "who asked that their families at home be notified of their survival".[142] This shows that the expectations of risk within a military can have an impact on how each party views the exercise of agency on the part of enemy combatants.

Prohibitions against surrender were not a practice unique to the Japanese. Codes of honor in early human societies "forbade warriors to surrender: they had to win or die, with no mercy."[143] Ancient Romans were no more accepting of surrender than the Japanese. It was a soldier's to sacrifice his life meaning that they were to die rather than surrender.[144] Today's legislation governing military discipline does not contain stringent prohibitions against surrender. However, remnants of historical practices that frowned upon surrender remain. This is seen in the fact that current laws try to ensure that surrender is only used as a last resort. For example, commanding officers of the Canadian Forces who, when capable of making a successful defense, surrender to the enemy are guilty of an offense.[145] Similar provisions can also be seen in Ireland's Defense Act, Armed Forces Acts of Ghana, Gambia, Kenya, and the Military Penal Code of Iraq.[146]

137 1987 Commentary to the Additional Protocols (n. 14) para. 1619.

138 Senjinkun Military Code (n. 132) chapter II.8.

139 Ohnuki-Tierney, *Kamikaze Diaries* (n. 9) 7.

140 Edwin P. Hoyt, *Warlord: Tojo against the World* (Cooper Square Press 2001) 43.

141 Ibid. 83.

142 Kita (n. 15) 260.

143 Jean Pictet, *Development and Principles of International Humanitarian Law* (Brill Nijhoff 1985) 6.

144 Hans-Henning Kortüm, "Surrender in Medieval Times" in Afflerbach & Strachan, *How Fighting Ends* (n. 86) 43.

145 Canada, National Defence Act, 1985 (n. 104) section 73.

146 Ireland, Defence Act of 1954, section 124(b); Ghana, Armed Forces Act of 1962, (n. 105) Section 15(c), Section 14: Section 14 of the Armed Forces Act 1962 of Ghana requires all commanders when under orders to carry out an operation of war or on coming into contact with an enemy, to use his utmost exertion to bring his officers and his men under his command into action, and encourage them to fight courageously; Gambia, Armed Forces Act of 1985, Section 37(c). Also see Iraq, Military Penal Code, No. 13 of 1940, Section 55: In Iraqi law, the penalty of death will be imposed on a commander who surrenders his post to the enemy without the exhaustion of all the available means of defence, or who negotiates with the enemy for an agreement stipulating the surrender of his military

In all these cases, surrender is only permitted if exercised in situations where successful defense is not possible. Therefore, such laws indicate to commanders that a decision to surrender can only be exercised as a last resort and cannot be made lightly, even when one's forces are at great risk.

Such regulation of surrender also extends to all combatants within the military. The Singapore Armed Forces Act states that "every person subject to military law who, knowingly and without lawful excuse surrenders himself to the enemy or leaves the battle shall be guilty of an offence and shall be liable on conviction by a subordinate military court to suffer death or any less punishment authorized by this Act."[147] It is unclear in this instance what would amount to a lawful excuse. In Afghanistan, surrendering to the enemy because of fear is punishable by confinement from one to five years.[148] Again, the legislation is vague regarding the type of fear this refers to. However, one possibility is that a combatant surrendering to the enemy does so due to fear of death, prioritizing their self-preservation. Furthermore, certain provisions in national legislation make it an offense to engage in acts that could be indicative of surrender. In the US Rules of Land Warfare of 1914, a flag of truce was considered to be a white flag used for the purpose of surrender.[149] According to these Rules, the white flag, when used by troops, indicates a desire to communicate to the enemy an armistice or a surrender.[150] The Army Act of Sri Lanka makes it an offense for any military person to send a flag of truce to the enemy.[151] These are a legislative negation of the agency of the combatant to use a white flag, thereby putting into question their capacity to exercise the principle of surrender available to them under IHL.

Domestic legislation also dictates that soldiers are not to allow themselves to be captured by the enemy. The Armed Forces Act of Malta[152] and the Armed Forces Act of Malaysia[153] feature provisions making it an offense to be captured

forces. Kenya, Armed Forces Act of 1968 (Revised 2009), section 15(d): "any commander who in the course of any action by or against the enemy, improperly withdraws from the action or from his station, shall be guilty of an offence and liable, on conviction by court martial, to suffer death or any other punishment provided by this Act."

[147] Singapore, Armed Forces Act of 1972, section 12(f).

[148] Afghanistan, Military Crimes Code of 2005, section 14.

[149] United States, War Department: Office of the Chief of Staff, *Rules of Land Warfare* (Government Printing Office 1914) 72.

[150] Ibid.

[151] Sri Lanka, Army Act of 1949. Also see Ireland, Defence Act (n. 146) section 125 (b) and (c): in Ireland, "every person subject to military law who treacherously or without due authority sends a flag of truce to the enemy, is guilty of an offence against military law and shall, on conviction by court-martial, be liable to suffer death or any less punishment awardable by a court-martial. This provision however envisages a situation where a white flag can be used to surrender where it is done as per due authority"; India, Army Act of 1950, section 34(f): The Army Act of India makes it an offense to treacherously or through cowardice send a flag of truce to the enemy.

[152] Malta, Armed Forces Act of 1970, section 41(1).

[153] Malaysia, Armed Forces Act (n. 106) section 43(1).

by the enemy against orders. Similarly, as per the Armed Forces Act of Singapore, every person subject to military law whom the enemy captures through his negligence or disobedience is guilty of an offense.[154] The Defence Force Act of Botswana makes it an offense for a person in the military, through disobedience of orders or willful neglect of his duty, to be captured by the enemy.[155] The Armed Forces Act of Kenya makes it an offense for any person subject to the Act to be captured by the enemy through disobedience of orders or willful neglect of his duty.[156] This can be contrasted with militaries where a soldier surrendering to his enemy despite his best efforts does "not shame himself as a soldier or as a citizen".[157] These provisions bar individual soldiers from exercising their agency in availing themselves of the right, as it were, to surrender as provided for them under IHL. Therefore, while IHL may dictate that once an intention to surrender is expressed, the adversary is obligated to respect such a request, these provisions penalize the combatant who makes such an offer. This shows that heterogeneous laws dictating military practice influence how combatants exercise their agency when they surrender on the battlefield.

While drafters of IHL principles recognized that some parties would not allow their troops to surrender, this was seen as a problem that could be remedied through a solution that required enemy soldiers to be more lenient in terms of defining what a valid surrender means. Accordingly, the delegates negotiating the Additional Protocols to the Geneva Convention accepted that "a formal surrender is not always realistically possible, as the rules of some armies purely and simply prohibit any form of surrender, even when all means of defense have been exhausted."[158] Their response to this issue was to establish that a defenseless adversary is *hors de combat* whether or not he has laid down arms.[159] This interpretation seems to conflate surrender with Article 41(2)(c) of Additional Protocol I, which states that a person should be recognized as being *hors de combat* if "he has been rendered unconscious or is otherwise incapacitated by wounds or sickness, and therefore is incapable of defending himself." It thereby equates the agentic act of surrendering (i.e., where a combatant chooses to stop fighting) with an instance when a combatant is rendered helpless and defenseless. This proposed solution further fails to capture the cultural norms internal to a military that influences a combatant's choice to surrender. It indicates that the drafters may have evaded questions of how and whether a combatant exercises

[154] Singapore, Armed Forces Act (n. 147).
[155] Botswana, Defence Force Act at 31(1).
[156] Kenya, Armed Forces Act of 1968 (n. 146) section 21(1).
[157] Kita (n. 15) 256.
[158] 1987 Commentary to the Additional Protocols (n. 14) para. 1612.
[159] Ibid.

agency when deciding to surrender and how this agency can be shaped by the internal ethos of a military.

It is possible to reconcile this heterogeneity of risk through a reading of IHL that renders it illegal for armed forces to deny their own troops the ability to surrender. Common Article 1 to the Geneva Conventions enshrines the duty to ensure respect for IHL which applies to States, including their armed forces.[160] Accordingly, State Parties must ensure that their armed forces are protected by the principles of the Geneva Conventions. Indeed, in the case of *Ntaganda*, the ICC determined that war crimes would extend to the acts of armed groups in relation to their own troops.[161] While in this case, such protection applied in the context of child soldiers, the ICRC's Updated Commentary to Common Article 3 to the Geneva Conventions seems to argue that this provision could also extend protection to all combatants.[162] These developments in IHL make it possible to argue that IHL principles also regulate how militaries or armed groups treat their own troops.

The principle of surrender can also be extended to one's troops when read with the prohibition against no-quarter orders, which not only applies to the adversary but is of general application. Under Article 40 of Additional Protocol I, "it is prohibited to order that there shall be no survivors, to threaten an adversary therewith or to conduct hostilities on this basis." Separating this provision from Article 41 was one way of underlining the fundamental importance of the principle that "combatants who went on defending themselves to the limit of their strength and finally surrendered and laid down their arms, should not be exterminated."[163] Article 40 is equally concerned with persons who are already in the power of the adverse Party, as with all those who are defenseless on the battlefield, or on the point of surrender. Therefore, it would impose obligations on parties to a conflict in relation to one's own troops, preventing them from requiring their combatants to conduct hostilities on the basis that there cannot be any survivors. When reading the rule prohibiting no quarter in conjunction with the principle of surrender, IHL makes express provision for ensuring that the risks that combatants undertake in warfare are limited not through the acts of the adversary but through the internal military culture to which they belong. While this approach would regulate military rules applying to their troops to the detriment of suicidal warfare, it is also based on the assumption that a combatant's decision to fight till death is purely based on military orders.

[160] Updated Commentary to the First Geneva Convention (n. 21) para. 118.

[161] *Prosecutor v. Bosco Ntaganda*, Decision Pursuant to Article 61(7) (a) and (b)of the Rome Statute on the Charges, ICC-01/04-02/06, PTC II, June 9, 2014, paras. 76–82.

[162] Updated Commentary to the First Geneva Convention (n. 21) para. 547.

[163] 1987 Commentary to the Additional Protocols (n. 14) para. 1589.

In military law, it is the duty of all subordinates to obey orders. Failing to do so is often a punishable offense.[164] However, historical experiences of mass atrocities have enlightened international law to the fact that there must be a balance between the need to maintain discipline on the field and deterring soldiers from engaging in war crimes.[165] Accordingly, the duty to disobey manifestly unlawful orders reflects the developments that occurred post-World War II in the Nuremberg and Tokyo trials which established that a superior order cannot at all times be used as a defense for engaging in acts that are manifestly unlawful in nature.[166] Today, the duty to disobey a manifestly unlawful order is a rule of customary international law which is intrinsic to combatants respecting principles of IHL, regardless of their superior orders. Orders amounting to war crimes would necessarily have to be disobeyed. Developments in International Human Rights Law (IHRL) have also laid restrictions on the types of orders that can be made. This jurisprudence has utilized Article 2 of the European Convention of Human Rights to regulate the relationship between the commanders and their troops, stating that "a finding that in all circumstances deaths or injuries in combat that result from the conduct of operations by the armed forces are outside the scope of article 2 would not be sustainable."[167] Likewise, commanders have an obligation to protect the right to life of their own troops, and orders that are in contravention of this right under specific circumstances would violate IHRL.

What customary law on the duty to disobey manifestly illegal orders reveals is IHL's recognition that combatants have the power to exercise agency even in military contexts. This is consistent with Walzer's claim that "even the pawns of war have rights and obligations."[168] However, while an order to fight to death goes against IHL's moral underpinnings of reciprocity of risk in warfare, and despite the advancements in IHRL, whether such an order can be considered manifestly unlawful remains unsettled, questioning whether combatants are deemed obliged to disobey an order to fight to the death. When faced with such hard cases, where the law's requirements are not obvious (as where the illegality of a superior's order is not fully manifest), combatants are more likely to ask themselves: "What is required of honorable soldiers?" rather than "What does international law require?"[169] The principal role of martial honor is to help the soldier

[164] Customary IHL study, "Customary IHL Rule No. 154: Obedience to Superior Orders" ICRC—IHL Database, online: https://ihl-databases.icrc.org/customary-ihl/eng/docindex/v1_rul_rule154 accessed January 18, 2025; United Kingdom, Armed Forces Act of 2006, section 2(3).

[165] Bohrer Ziv, "The Superior Orders Defense: A Principal-Agent Analysis" (2014) 41:1 Georgia Journal of International Comparative Law 1, 20. Also see Eric Posner & Alan Sykes, "An Economic Analysis of State and Individual Responsibility Under International Law" (2007) 9 American Law and Economics Review 72, 129.

[166] Osiel (n. 49) 42.

[167] United Kingdom, *Smith and others (FC) v. The Ministry of Defence* [2013] UKSC 41, para. 58.

[168] Walzer, *Just and Unjust Wars* (n. 13) 40.

[169] Osiel (n. 49) 23–24.

identify the proper course of action where "bright-line rules do not provide clear guidance".[170]

The appeal to something other than merely the law in war can be seen in the adoption of the Martens Clause. The Martens Clause in the preamble to the 1899 Hague Convention (II) appeals to "public conscience" as a safety net where principles of international law provide no cover.[171] The notion of public conscience can be disputed subjectively by combatants. In Hannah Arendt's account, to Adolf Eichmann, "[t]he most potent factor in the soothing of his own conscience was the simple fact that he could see no one, no one at all, who actually was against the Final Solution."[172] Hence, the notion of public conscience is not a monolith, and a combatant's choice to act is influenced by how the ethical principles of the public to which he is most related. Similarly, culturally varied notions of agency influenced how Kamikaze pilots engaged in suicide attacks. The exercise of limited risk in combat is based on a culturally homogeneous image of warfare. IHL's image of limited risk in combat rests on the assumption that when ordered to fight till death, combatants would exercise their agency in favor of self-preservation. In the next section, I will show how this bias in favor of self-preservation tends to delegitimize narratives that depict fighting till death as agentic acts.

3.3.2. Choosing to fight to death?

The West's shock at suicide attacks partly stems from the presumption that individual survival is an "ultimate rational end", which exposes a bias against the notion that self-destruction can be as agentic or heroic a choice as self-preservation.[173] Walzer embodies this presumption in his claim that there is a limit to the risks that we require combatants to accept.[174] Even Carl von Clausewitz who advocated for absolute warfare, concedes that

> no matter how highly rated the qualities of courage and steadfastness may be in war, no matter how small the chance of victory may be for the leader who

[170] Ibid. 37.

[171] "Until a more complete code of the laws of war is issued, the High Contracting Parties think it right to declare that in cases not included in the Regulations adopted by them, populations and belligerents remain under the protection and empire of the principles of international law, as they result from the usages established between civilized nations, from the laws of humanity and the requirements of the public conscience."

[172] Hannah Arendt, *Eichmann in Jerusalem: A Report on the Banality of Evil* (1st ed., Penguin Classics 2006) 62.

[173] K. M. Fierke, "Agents of Death: The Structural Logic of Suicide Terrorism and Martyrdom" (2009) 1:1 International Theory 155, 156.

[174] Walzer, *Just and Unjust Wars* (n. 13) 156.

> hesitates to go for it with all the power at his disposal, there is a point beyond which persistence becomes desperate folly, and can therefore never be condoned.[175]

It may be argued that von Clausewitz thought that to stop fighting was only the result of a linear, rational decision-making process, of cost-benefit analysis.[176] Rationality, in this case as applied to decisions of life and death, is not a mathematical construct based on strict logic but is embedded in social values of different cultures.

Even in the Western context, as dictated by the reciprocity of risk in combat, the military constitutes a subculture where combatants compromise self-preservation by having to expose themselves to some degree of danger in battle. Where combatants failed to do so, there are instances in which they faced punishment. The early modern Austrian army executed twenty officers for cowardice following the battle of Lützen in 1632.[177] A regiment that retreated during the second battle of Breitenfeld in 1642 was punished by hanging its every tenth man.[178] As per the law of Ireland, a member of the military "who misbehaves or induces others to misbehave before the enemy in such a way as to show cowardice" is guilty of an offense punishable by death.[179] Therefore, self-preservation in military contexts is not absolute. However, this requirement to expose oneself to danger is also balanced by the image of the chivalrous warrior who did not fight in a manner that went beyond the contours of agency as was recognized as reasonable. For example, in the Western Medieval hero system, there was no cultural pressure on the leading warrior classes to compel knights to accept a norm that obliged them to die for their country or nation.[180] These cultural narratives influence how combatants behave in combat.

In the modern world wars, while soldiers in countries other than Japan, too, may have been ordered to fight to the death, such orders were rarely followed in practice: "By 1942 fighting to the last man had become for the British, French, and Italian armies, to name the most obvious, nonsensical rather than honorable."[181] These men tended to fight up to a certain point and then either surrender, run away, or withdraw, and in some cases, with honor intact and without incurring the penalty of a court-martial for doing so.[182] This behavior may

[175] Carl von Clausewitz, *On War* (Princeton University Press 1984) 251.
[176] Afflerbach & Strachan, "Introduction" (n. 116).
[177] Childs (n. 92) 158.
[178] Ibid.
[179] Ireland, Defence Act (n. 146) section 125(h).
[180] Childs (n. 92) 148.
[181] Hassig (n. 126) 119.
[182] Ibid.: "For example, in spite of Hitler's view that the German 6th Army should 'have closed ranks, formed a hedgehog, and shot themselves with their last bullet,' they surrendered at Stalingrad. Len Smith observes that the generals of the French army in World War I frequently urged their men on to fight to the death, but that their men did not."

reflect how Western cultural ideas on agency in death influenced them. For example, the biblical story of Abraham and Isaac demonstrates that the duty to obey is not absolute. "God must be obeyed, but He observes certain limits beyond which He will not ask His subjects to go. By implication, an authority that does not accept limits is not entitled to unquestioning obedience."[183] Similarly, in *Leviathan*, Thomas Hobbes outlines the limits of sovereign power by stating that "[if] the Soveraign command a man (though justly condemned,) to kill, wound, or mayme himselfe; or not to resist those that assault him; . . . yet hath that man the Liberty to disobey."[184] This is so as "the right men have by Nature to protect themselves, when none else can protect them, can by no Covenant be relinquished."[185] Accordingly, where a person is taken as prisoner during war, he must have the liberty to accept such status given that he has no other way to preserve his life.[186] As cultural learnings seep into how one views the world, it is fair to presume that these narratives in the West shape how combatants in militaries behave in combat and how they make choices regarding life and death on the battlefield.

As was pointed out through the analysis of the limited nature of reciprocal risk that undergirds IHL and the agency it grants to combatants to surrender during hostilities, IHL's image of limited warfare depends on the assumption that combatants would generally make choices in accordance with self-preservation, to cease fighting where risk to their lives goes beyond a certain limit. On the contrary, in Japan, suicide earned one social prestige.[187] The Japanese, who fought to the last man, present a clash of culture and ideology pertaining to how combatants exercise agency over how they risk their lives in combat, which meant their conduct was not treated as agentic acts of heroism but as fanatical and even "sub-human."[188] Treating them as "fanatics" strips them of their agency based on the influence their culture had on their actions. The Kamikaze pilots were, therefore, seen as being unable to exercise agency due to the pressures of cultural narratives considering suicides as something glorious.[189] This implies that the Kamikaze pilots were brainwashed through narratives that glorify suicide, so much so that when ordered to engage in a suicide attack, there was hardly any counteracting value system that urged him to disobey such order in favor of the agentic choice of self-preservation.

[183] V. Lee Hamilton & Herbert Kelman, *Crimes of Obedience: Toward a Social Psychology of Authority and Responsibility* (revised ed., Yale University Press 1990) 53, 60.

[184] Thomas Hobbes & Henry Morley, *Leviathan: Or, The Matter, Form, And Power of a Commonwealth Ecclesiastical and Civil* (4th ed., G. Routledge and Sons 1894) 105.

[185] Ibid. 100.

[186] Ibid. 107.

[187] Fierke (n. 173) 159.

[188] Huntington (n. 128) 220.

[189] Sheftall (n. 130) 393.

Glorification of suicide which goes against self-preservation was integrated as early as school education.[190] The Imperial Rescript on Education, the study of which was mandatory in every school, required students to always respect the Constitution and observe the laws: "should emergency arise, offer yourselves courageously to the State."[191] The Japanese school textbooks at the time incorporated the duty "to die for the emperor/country."[192] In addition to these influences from childhood that valued self-sacrifice for the nation, Kamikaze pilots were also given incentives to perform this type of sacrifice through "fan mail and handmade dolls they received from schoolgirls to take on their missions".[193] These factors challenge the Western characterization of Kamikaze fighters as victims, granted the influence of cultural narratives that deified their sacrifice may be undeniable. What is often at play here is the notion that when cultural narratives influence one's actions, the fighters would not have been able to make an agentic decision, considering their individual interests.

This approach to Kamikaze attackers' deaths reveals an assumption that overwhelming cultural influences can rob a person of their agentic capacity. William B. Swann, Jr. and Jolanda Jetten challenge the idea that individuals can only operate as agentic actors when situational pressures do not influence them.[194] They argue that current research on agency minimizes the extent to which persons are capable of standing up to authority, leading to a bias that when confronted with external pressures persons are more likely to lose their agency.[195] However, there is sufficient evidence to show that combatants are not always victims devoid of agency when they operate in militaries or armed groups. As noted in chapter 2, mutinies carried out by combatants in diverse military contexts provide evidence of disobedience. Examples of such mutinies come not only from the French garrisons in World War I but also in Uganda where African soldiers mutinied against British officers in 1963.[196] Combatants' agency also comes into question when their responses to their environment are conformist. For example, Milgram presents persons who conform to authority as being more likely to engage in harmful behavior.[197] In wartime, when such conformism leads to combatants taking actions that are manifestly unlawful in IHL, deviant agency is attributed to them, and such combatants are treated as perpetrators. Similarly,

[190] Huntington (n. 128) 128.

[191] Kenneth G. Henshall, *Historical Dictionary of Japan to 1945* (Scarecrow Press 2014) 515.

[192] Ohnuki-Tierney, *Kamikaze, Cherry Blossoms and Nationalisms* (n. 3) 127.

[193] Bloom, *Dying to Kill* (n. 7) 16.

[194] William B. Swann Jr. & Jolanda Jetten, "Restoring Agency to the Human Actor" (2017) 12:3 Perspectives on Psychological Science 382, 382.

[195] Ibid. 383.

[196] Amii Omara-Otunnu, *Politics and the Military in Uganda, 1890–1985* (Palgrave Macmillan 1987) 55.

[197] See Stanley Milgram, "Behavioral Study of Obedience" (1963) 67:4 Journal of Abnormal and Social Psychology 371–378.

when conformism leads to the violation of cultural assumptions that undergird IHL, such as the bias in favor of self-preservation, they can be seen as deviant actors. In the case of the Kamikaze, this narrative of deviant agency applies to conforming with orders harmful to their own lives.

IHL's views on agency perceive that when combatants operate in military structures, their actions are only agentic if they promote self-preservation, even if it requires nonconformity with orders. This reflects a limited way of viewing how persons exercise agency when confronted with external influences. Swann and Jetten posit that "exercising agency requires being responsive to a situation rather than being in competition" with it.[198] They urge researchers to be open to diverse ways in which individuals show responsiveness to their situations. This includes accepting that when individuals conform to authority, they may still perceive themselves as making an agentic decision. As in the case of Kamikaze attackers, a conformist agentic decision made within a military environment may not always prioritize individualist notions of life and death but instead value the needs of the community.[199]

The understanding of agency as being socially embedded is more prevalent in specific cultures, including Japan. Hazel R. Markus and Shinobu Kitayama have adopted this critical lens toward agency, considering how many Asian cultures tend to construe individuality as intertwined with the "fundamental relatedness" of one another.[200] They posit that the Japanese cultural context values an interrelated notion of the self. The notion of self-preservation can be reconsidered in light of how the idea of self is seen as embedded with one's community in the Japanese context. The Japanese notion of agency translates to a person's efforts to harmonize their personal goals and emotions with those of the collective.[201] Based on these understandings of the self as culturally constructed, Markus and Kitayama offer different models of agency: "different histories, religions, ontologies, and ideologies, as well as different institutional and interpersonal practices, give rise to different understandings of the nature and source of agency or of being-in-action."[202] A study of Asian and in particular the Japanese culture provides a model of conjoint agency as opposed to the disjoint model of agency observed in American and Western cultures. Conjoint agents do not experience themselves as free from others.[203]

198 Swann & Jetten (n. 194) 383.

199 Ibid. 387.

200 Hazel R. Markus & Shinobu Kitayama, "Culture and the Self: Implications for Cognition, Emotion, and Motivation" (1991) 98:2 Psychological Review 224, 224.

201 Ibid. 228.

202 Hazel Rose Markus et al., "Going for the Gold Models of Agency in Japanese and American Contexts" (2006) 17:2 Psychological Science 103, 104.

203 Hazel R. Markus & Shinobu Kitayama, *Cross-Cultural Differences in Perspectives on the Self* (University of Nebraska Press 2003) 10.

The idea that a socially embedded self can make agentic choices that are contrary to Western ideals of self-preservation are also found in historical narratives on the Samurai. The ideologies of the Samurai Code were reproduced and integrated into the Japanese military ethos during World War II. The Japanese never surrender policy can be linked back to a defining characteristic of Samurai warriors: an "ethos of suicidal constancy."[204] This policy was meant to promote a sense of spiritual strength in the Japanese military.[205] Renouncing self-interest, even interest in one's own survival, was fundamental to the Samurai.[206] Therefore, combatants who fight till death may do so, going beyond a narrow, individualist idea of self-preservation, to encompass the intention of preserving one's community or culture. Kusunoki Masashige, renowned Samurai who later became an unofficial emblem of the Kamikaze pilots, epitomizes this culture of valuing honor, bravery, and prowess above life itself. Ordered into a battle he knew he could not win, he still led the charge and died proclaiming that he wished he had seven lives to give for his country.[207] Flowing from this historical narrative, the headbands of the suicide pilots often bore the slogan "seven lives for the fatherland." Major General Nara Takeji, the Chief of Military Affairs Department, alluded to Samurai tradition to emphasize the differences between Japanese and Western service members: "From ancient times, *samurai* did not expect to return alive from battle-fields. The only choice for these warriors was either to annihilate the enemy or to sacrifice their lives. Even when a soldier loses his combat ability, there is no excuse for surrendering to his enemy."[208] This Samurai ethic presents death in the language of choice, as a selfless agentic act done on behalf of a community. In this manner, the undertones of Samurai culture became a part of the lives of those who would go into battle in World War II.

Narratives coming from within the Japanese military depict Kamikaze pilots as choosing to die when engaging in suicidal missions. This volition on the part of the combatant becomes particularly pertinent in suicidal missions, given that suicide is expected to be a voluntary act.[209] Ohnuki-Tierney notes that because the Kamikaze operation was a guarantee of death, rather than issuing orders in the name of the emperor, the Japanese military made a show of voluntariness on the part of the pilots.[210] She writes:

[204] Clements (n. 2) xix.
[205] Kita (n. 15) 256.
[206] Tsunetomo (n. 47) 20.
[207] Clements (n. 2) xix.
[208] Kita (n. 15) 259.
[209] Michael J. Kral, "Suicide as Social Logic" (1994) 24:3 Suicide and Life-Threatening Behavior 245, 248.
[210] Ohnuki-Tierney, *Kamikaze Diaries* (n. 9) 7.

> In most instances, all the members of a military corps were summoned to a hall. After a lecture on the virtues of patriotism and sacrifice for the emperor and Japan, they were told to step forward if they were willing to volunteer to be tokko'tai pilots. Sometimes this process was done in reverse: men were told to step forward if they did *not* want to be pilots. It would have been extremely difficult, if not impossible, for any soldier to stay behind or to step forward when all or most of his comrades were "volunteering." Sometimes the officer in charge went through a ritual of blindfolding the young men—a gesture ostensibly intended to minimize peer pressure—and asking them to raise their hands to volunteer.[211]

Such elaborate measures to paint a perception of voluntariness was necessary because there is an underlying assumption in warfare that a sacrifice by a combatant to give up his life is only just if such action was a voluntary one. Even in a culture which is often portrayed as built on blind obedience, an element of agency and voluntariness was attached to the combatant.

In preparing themselves for death, the combatants were portrayed as making an agentic choice. Edwin P. Hoyt writes that Japanese soldiers comport themselves for death every day, and this provided them with the attitude needed to fight and to avoid being taken prisoner.[212] In doing so, these soldiers can be seen as responding to their environment by aligning themselves with the needs of the group. An excerpt of the last entry of Ensign Heiichi Okabe's diary demonstrates the extent to which the policy demanding fighting till death was internalized by combatants:

> *What is the duty today? It is to fight.*
> *What is the duty tomorrow? It is to win.*
> *What is the daily duty? It is to die.*
> *We die in battle without complaint.*[213]

The word "duty" is repeated here. However, the invocation of duty does not necessarily negate agency.

The cultural narratives from Japan also present an idea of death that is not mutually exclusive with the preservation of an embodied self. In Samurai ethics, victory and defeat were temporary and circumstantial. According to the Japanese notion of courage, "life itself was thought cheap if honor and fame could be attained therewith: hence, whenever a cause presented itself which

[211] Ibid.
[212] Hoyt (n. 140).
[213] Skaine (n. 6) 136.

was considered dearer than life, with utmost serenity and celerity was life laid down."[214] Accordingly, "to an ambitious Samurai a natural departure from life seemed a rather tame affair and a consummation not devoutly to be wished for."[215] Japanese narratives depicted fulfilling one's duty as a soldier as worthy of Heaven's blessings.[216] All soldiers who died in battle were deified and their names inscribed in a national shrine.[217] Among these, the Yasukuni Shrine received special status derived from the fact that the emperor himself paid tribute there to the souls of the war dead. A parting remark supposedly made by soldiers going into battle was "see you in Yasukuni Shrine."[218] These cultural practices show how the Kamikaze pilots' "selves" continue to be preserved long after their biological deaths. This is possible because their idea of the "self," rather than being purely rooted in a physical embodied form, is socially embedded.

This Japanese policy challenges the intuitive assumption that agentic combatants risk their lives within some limits of self-preservation. This cultural assumption, favoring self-preservation rather than an intent to die with certainty, makes the former more acceptable within the agentic narrative of a warrior. Applying IHL's frame of agency to Kamikaze attackers could lead them to being depicted as helpless victims of their military. In the same manner, those who follow military orders that are contrary to IHL's cultural assumptions are likely to be seen as perpetrators exercising deviant agency. This challenge of boxing the agency of Kamikaze pilots' deaths into a victim/perpetrator binary complicates IHL's engagement with them. Instead, IHL could be more open to how agency in warriors' deaths is seen in narratives from the Japanese military during World War II. These narratives view the self as being socially embedded. The relationship between death, self-preservation, and agency is understood differently in this context than it is in IHL.

3.4. Conclusion

In this chapter, I argued that the extent of risk that IHL expects a combatant to take as an occupational hazard of war is limited. IHL provides the opportunity for a combatant to surrender, dictating that it would be accepted unconditionally. IHL assumes a homogeneous image of warfare, which I established is necessary for limited risk in combat to function smoothly. However, as seen through

[214] Inazo Nitobe, *Bushido: The Soul of Japan* (12th ed., Teibi Publishing Company 1907) 74; Peter R. Mansoor, "The Evolution of Military Ethos over the Ages" (2014) 94:2 Phi Kappa Phi Forum 10–12.
[215] Skaine (n. 6) 131–132.
[216] Henshall (n. 191) 505.
[217] Huntington (n. 128) 129.
[218] Hill (n. 4) 15.

the Kamikaze attacks, the level of risk that combatants are expected to take in the battlefield varies from culture to culture. If a soldier were to sacrifice one's life, IHL assumes that it is done so voluntarily. IHL recognizes that combatants can make voluntary decisions as long as they have the choice to preserve their lives in battle. IHL assumes that given the choice to obey or disobey an order to fight to death, a combatant would disobey it and hence preserve the image of limited warfare that it strives to sustain. This fits well with the Western assumption that it is rational to take actions in favor of self-preservation. However, the way the never surrender policy was obeyed by Kamikaze pilots carrying out suicide attacks demonstrates that combatants making the choice to limit risk in combat based on self-preservation cannot be taken for granted by IHL. Their suicidal acts may seem deviant given that they go against the bias in favor of self-preservation in IHL. However, I proposed that IHL can view these deaths as a socially embedded expression of agency in a cultural context where self-preservation is understood as going beyond biological death.

4
LTTE Female Suicide Attackers and Gendered Agency in Combat

4.1. Introduction

Former Prime Minister of India Rajiv Gandhi was killed in a suicide attack on May 21, 1991, in the southern Indian state of Tamil Nadu. A Tamil woman named "Danu," dressed in a shalwar kameez,[1] a bulge near her belly indicating pregnancy, bent before him to show obeisance at his feet.[2] Her appearance was deceptive. While at Gandhi's feet, she detonated the explosive device fitted to her body, killing herself, Gandhi, and many others on the spot.[3] Danu was a combatant of the Liberation Tigers of the Tamil Eelam (LTTE), a non-State armed group that was active in Sri Lanka.[4] An ethnically diverse country, Sri Lanka witnessed a three-decade-long protracted internal armed conflict between the Sri Lankan government and armed groups primarily representing the Tamil people. Of its twenty million population, the majority are Sinhalese (74.9 percent), followed by Tamils (15.3 percent) and Sri Lanka Moor (9.3 percent); other ethnic groups, namely, Burgher, Malay, Sri Lanka Chetty, and Bharatha, comprise 0.5 percent.[5]

[1] The traditional Hindu tunic worn over baggy pants.

[2] Sharika Thiranagama & Gananath Obeyesekere, *In My Mother's House: Civil War in Sri Lanka* (University of Pennsylvania Press 2013) 25: "It is believed that the LTTE attack against Rajiv Gandhi was due to the latter's decision to send Indian Peacekeeping Forces into the Northern part of Sri Lanka"; Mia Bloom, *Bombshell: Women and Terrorism* (University of Pennsylvania Press 2011) 151: "On July 29, 1987, Indian prime minister Rajiv Gandhi and Sri Lankan president J.R. Jayewardene signed the Indo–Sri Lankan Accord. The Indian Peace Keeping Force (IPKF) arrived on the island with ten thousand troops on July 30 to help protect the Tamil population. However, they eventually turned their forces loose on the civilian population. At the peak of the intervention, India deployed four divisions (almost 80,000 men), including three infantry divisions as well as paramilitary and special forces."

[3] It must be noted however that this incident would not have been governed by International Humanitarian Law (IHL) given that it took place outside the territory of Sri Lanka. However, I use this example given that it is emblematic of the type of suicide attacks that the LTTE conducted within Sri Lanka, which fall within the ambit of IHL.

[4] Swati Parashar, "Feminist International Relations and Women Militants: Case Studies from Sri Lanka and Kashmir" (2009) 22:2 Cambridge Review of International Affairs 235, 240, note 5.

[5] Census of Population and Housing, (2012) Department of Census and Statistics of Sri Lanka, 3.3. For more insight into the plural nature of the Tamil identity, see Daniel Bass, "Making Sense of the Census in Sri Lanka: Up-Country Tamils and Sri Lankan Tamil Nationalism" in R. Cherana (ed.) *Pathways of Dissent: Tamil Nationalism in Sri Lanka* (Sage 2009) 141: "Tamil ethnicity in Sri Lanka remains plural and multifaceted, despite dominant portrayals of a united Sri Lankan Tamil identity. . . . Cultural and linguistic variations once politically split Low-country Sinhalas from

Suicide Attacks and International Humanitarian Law. Vishakha V. Wijenayake, Oxford University Press.
 DOI: 10.1093/9780197812174.003.0004

The Sinhalese population is predominantly Buddhist, albeit with a Christian minority; Tamils are predominantly Hindu, also with a Christian minority.[6] Tamils reside primarily in the northern and eastern provinces, which separatist groups claim deserve to be an independent Tamil nation.[7]

Following independence from Britain in 1948, government policies favoring the Sinhalese alienated the Tamil minority, resulting in communal violence and radicalization of some sections of the Tamil community. While Tamil parties continued parliamentary politics, by the mid-1970s, militarized groups demanded a separate State, the "Tamil Eelam."[8] There have been several militant Tamil separatist groups, including the Tamil Eelam Liberation Organization, the Eelam Revolutionary Organization of Students, the Eelam People's Revolutionary Liberation Front, and the People's Liberation Organization of Tamil Eelam.[9] These groups generally have not agreed with each other on their demands and have frequently fought among themselves. The LTTE, "organized around the cult of its leader Vellupillai Prabhakaran," gradually attained hegemony in the mid-1980s as the self-proclaimed "sole and legitimate representative" of the Tamil people.[10]

The LTTE was formed in 1972 as the Tamil New Tigers, transforming intothe Liberation Tigers of Tamil Eelam in 1976.[11] In 1990, the LTTE assumed control of critical areas of the north, as well as parts of the east.[12] The LTTE's military wing "consisted of a regular force and a reserve force": the former had "land, air, and sea components; an intelligence branch; and a Special Forces unit."[13]

Up-country Sinhalas and they were counted separately in the census through 1971. Although these differences have abated over time, similar divisions among Tamils in Sri Lanka, possibly because of their minority status, have continued to be socially and politically salient. For example, many East coast Tamils resent the hegemony of northern Jaffna Tamils. Despite these internal differences, the Sri Lankan government has consistently lumped together East coast and Jaffna Tamils under the category of 'Sri Lankan Tamils' since the late 19th century. However, the government has always considered Up-country Tamils to be a distinct group, although they were not counted separately in the census until 1911. Sri Lankan Tamils formed 12.7 per cent of the island's population in the last reliable, island-wide census in 1981, and Up-country Tamils were 5.5 per cent."

6 Miranda Alison, "Cogs in the Wheel? Women in the Liberation Tigers of Tamil Eelam" (2003) 6:4 Civil Wars 37, 38.

7 Thiranagama & Obeyesekere (n. 2) 13.

8 Report of the OHCHR Investigation on Sri Lanka (OISL), Human Rights Council, 30th Sess. Agenda Item 2, U.N. Doc. A/HRC/30/CRP.2 (September 16, 2015), para. 47.

9 Ibid. para. 150.

10 Alison, "Cogs in the Wheel?" (n. 6) 38; OISL Report (n. 8) para. 150; Parashar (n. 4) 240; Thiranagama & Obeyesekere (n. 2) 24: "The secretive, highly disciplined, and militarily effective LTTE emerged as the self-declared 'sole representative of the Tamil people' in 1986, when it proscribed or absorbed other militant groups (e.g., TELO, the Tamil Eelam Liberation Organization, and EPRLF, the Eelam People's Revolutionary Liberation Front) and families associated with them in a year of intense fratricidal conflict."

11 OISL Report (n. 8) para. 49.

12 Thiranagama & Obeyesekere (n. 2) 25.

13 OISL Report (n. 8) para. 158.

The LTTE also had a suicide squad referred to as the Black Tigers.[14] Its suicide attacks took place in the context of conventional military engagements as well as in the form of clandestine operations, at times targeting civilians, in various parts of the country.[15] The first recorded suicide mission by the LTTE took place on July 5, 1987. Captain Miller, a volunteer cadre from the Black Tigers, drove a lorry loaded with explosives to a State military camp and detonated it along with himself. One hundred and twenty soldiers died, and over another hundred were seriously injured as a result.[16] Suicide attacks became a hallmark tactic of the LTTE, frequently used prior to the ceasefire period, resuming in late 2005 until 2009.[17] Some of these suicide attacks targeted political leaders and civilians, therefore, making them *prima facie* illegal under the rules of distinction in IHL.[18] When the LTTE cadres feigned civilian status to conduct suicide attacks, for example as pregnant women, these attacks became perfidious, and again, illegal under IHL.[19]

As demonstrated by the example of Captain Miller, suicide attacks in the LTTE were not carried out by women exclusively. Nor was their participation as combatants in the LTTE restricted to being suicide bombers, carrying out approximately one-third of LTTE's suicide attacks.[20] While women's participation as combatants was not common within the LTTE in the 1970s, from the mid-1980s, the LTTE recruited women into their fighting ranks,[21] and became a significant part of its strength.[22] While women's involvement was initially mostly limited to supporting roles, outside or in the periphery of combat missions, soon they were given military training and participated in combat.[23] The special section for women—*Vituthalai Pulikal Munani* (Women's Front of the Liberation

14 Adele Ann Balasingham, *Women Fighters of Liberation Tigers* (Thasan Printers 1993) 12; OISL Report (n. 8) para. 162.

15 OISL Report (n. 8) para. 153; Thiranagama & Obeyesekere (n. 2) 187.

16 Balasingham (n. 14).

17 OISL Report (n. 8) para. 224.

18 The principle of distinction is codified in Articles 48, 51(2), and 52(2) of Additional Protocol I to the Geneva Conventions of 1949.

19 Prohibition against perfidy found in Article 37 of Additional Protocol I.

20 Parashar (n. 4) 250.

21 Alison, "Cogs in the Wheel?" (n. 6) 38: Although Alison writes that in the 1980s appeals were made by the different groups for women to join the struggle, it is not clear what prompted the LTTE to shift to a policy of recruiting women; Nimmi Gowrinathan, "The Committed Female Fighter: The Political Identities of Tamil Women in the Liberation Tigers of Tamil Eelam" (2017) 19:3 International Feminist Journal of Politics 327, 330: "As the movement encountered more complicated enemies, such as the Indian Peace Keeping Force in the late 1990s, the LTTE began the practice of forced recruitment, which ranged from 'one-person-per-family' requirements (male or female) to the abduction of young men and women to be forcibly conscripted."

22 OISL Report (n. 8) para. 158: "However, the LTTE was not unique among Tamil armed groups in this respect." Thiranagama & Obeyesekere (n. 2) 203: "On 12 December the EPRLF women launched a large women's protest march appealing for unity and an end to all political killings. The march comprised of women within the EPRLF as well as women from outside the movement of all ages. The march would be the last action the EPRLF women's wing would ever organize."

23 Alison, "Cogs in the Wheel?" (n. 6) 38–39.

Tigers) was established in 1983; were trained for combat in first in Tamil Nadu, India in 1985; battled the Sri Lankan army in July 1986; and shortly afterward, "in October 1987, Velupillai Prabhakaran set up the first all-women training camp in Jaffna", which later acquired its own leadership structure.[24] As of the early 2000s, around one-third of the LTTE cadres were female.[25] Testimonies also indicate that the suicide bombing squad—the Black Tigers—had a division for female cadres called Freedom Birds.[26] As LTTE fighters, females wore a cyanide capsule around their necks to be taken upon capture. Adele Balasigham, the wife of LTTE chief political strategist Anton Balasigham, referred to the LTTE female fighters as "the most fierce, extremely disciplined and courageous women combatants in the world."[27]

The LTTE's female fighters are examples of women participating in political violence during wartime. International law has become increasingly attentive to how women experience war.[28] However, these developments have primarily focused on the victimization of women,[29] resulting in a narrative that depicts males as agents of conflict while females are their victims, particularly of sexual violence. I do not dismiss the relevance of and the need to investigate violence against women. However, in comparison, women's participation in violence, and particularly their role as combatants, has received less attention by IHL scholars. Studying female suicide attackers is useful in understanding how their participation in the LTTE's ethnonationalist liberation struggle challenges IHL's gendered notions of who can exercise agency in combat and death.

In section 4.2. of this chapter, I argue that embedded within IHL are patriarchal foundations stemming from law's public/private divide, the State-centricity of international law, and the military's hypermasculinity. Set in this gendered backdrop, IHL rules present women as helpless victims of war, thereby questioning their capacity to exercise agency during conduct of hostilities. IHL's

[24] Kim Jordan & Myriam Denov, "Birds of Freedom? Perspectives on Female Emancipation and Sri Lanka's Liberation Tigers of Tamil Eelam" (2007) 9:1 Journal of International Women's Studies 42, 46; ibid. 38.

[25] Alison, "Cogs in the Wheel?" (n. 6) 38–39; Jonathan Matusitz, "Symbolism in Female Terrorism: Five Overarching Themes" (2019) 23:4 Sexuality & Culture—An Interdisciplinary Quarterly 1332, 1337; ibid. 46: "female soldiers comprise approximately one-third of the fighting forces and are inducted in all units of the movement including its naval force (the Sea Tigers), and its suicide squad."

[26] Bloom, *Bombshell* (n. 2) 158.

[27] Balasingham (n. 14) 1.

[28] *Beijing Declaration and Platform of Action, adopted at the Fourth World Conference on Women*, United Nations, October 27, 1995: this document recognized that the vulnerability of women during armed conflict is a direct consequence of their status in society. "The various and systematic forms of violence that civilian women experience at the hands of armed combatants, whether state armies or paramilitary personnel, in situations of armed conflict have been extensively documented and highlighted in the former Yugoslavia, Rwanda and other parts of Africa and Asia."

[29] Michelle Burgis-Kasthala, "Scholarship as Dialogue: TWAIL and the Politics of Methodology" (2016) 14:4 Journal of International Criminal Justice 921, 930.

gender tropes place women within a victim perpetrator binary that does not facilitate a nuanced assessment of the agency exercised by women who engage in political violence. In section 4.3, I show how ethnonationalist armed groups challenge these gender biases in IHL with a relatively higher degree of participation of female combatants and by generating narratives of female liberation through combatancy. I argue that narratives of agency constructed around female combatancy in the LTTE reveal how agency can be relational, ambivalent, and accommodative of diverse values. Female suicide attackers' deaths within the LTTE present a complex exercise of agency that is hard to fit into the overly simple gendered victim perpetrator binary in IHL.

4.2. IHL's gendered framework

Gender biases permeate the law, its depiction of Statehood, and the militarist understandings of warfare. Being a State-centric legal regime that governs warfare, IHL is gendered on all three counts. This gendered nature of IHL rules impacts narratives of agency exercised by female combatants in non-State armed groups like the LTTE.

4.2.1. IHL as State-centric, militarized, and patriarchal

The Western liberal understanding of law often portrays rules as applying equally to all members of society.[30] The main thrust of feminist jurisprudence is that "law is a force in society created by men, practiced by men, applied by men—for the (not necessarily conscious) purpose of maintaining traditional patriarchal dominance."[31] For feminist legal scholar Catharine MacKinnon, assuming that law is objective denies how sex inequality "participates in constructing reality from the dominant point of view" in tacit but profound ways.[32] Granting women "'equal' opportunity to live up to standards designed around men" is an example of how perceived objectivity of legal rules perpetuates discrimination against

[30] Anna Grear, "'Sexing the Matrix': Embodiment, Disembodiment and Law: Towards the Regendering of Legal Rationality?" in Jackie Jones et al. (eds.) *Gender, Sexualities and Law* (Routledge 2011) 39, 44: "[The] paradigmatic liberal legal subject [is] a socially decontextualized, hyperrational, wilful individual systematically stripped of embodied particularities in order to appear neutral and of course, theoretically genderless, serving the mediation of power linked to property and capital accumulation."

[31] Hilaire Barnett, *Sourcebook on Feminist Jurisprudence* (Taylor and Francis 2012) 60.

[32] Catharine A. MacKinnon, "Feminism, Marxism, Method, and the State: Toward Feminist Jurisprudence" in Katharine T. Bartlett & Rosanne Kennedy (eds.) *Feminist Legal Theory: Readings in Law and Gender* (Westview Press 1991) 181.

and disadvantages the lived realities of women.[33] The law's creation of public and private spheres of life is another such example. In this dichotomy, women's role traditionally relates to the private sphere of the home and the family.[34] The nonintervention by law into private life often results in the State creating a power vacuum that the husband or the father fills.[35] First, by making the family a private domain the law creates a normative framework of State non-intervention which exacerbates power hierarchies within families, and prevents the State from regulating harm to women, such as domestic violence and marital rape, thereby tacitly approving the continuation of gendered power relations within the family.[36] Second, by shifting women's role to the private sphere, the law undermines women's contribution to matters deemed public. It thereby creates gendered binaries, which perpetuate a system that favors men.

International law not only embodies the gender biases inherent in this legal culture but also plays an important part in constructing gendered realities in how States interact with one another and how they regulate matters within their borders.[37] Likewise, international law mirrors patriarchal dichotomies prevalent in domestic law. Cynthia Enloe articulates this by transforming the phrase "the personal is political" to "the personal is international" and "the international is personal."[38] In domestic law, the issues that arise in the domestic sphere which disproportionately affect women are not given sufficient attention through the law. Similarly, by focusing on how States interact with each other, international law fails to fully recognize how persons within those States experience and contribute to international legal rules. This private sphere within State boundaries permits legal nonintervention implying that universal norms do not, in fact, apply equally in all domains.[39] In this manner, international legal rules merge State-centricism with patriarchy's public/private divide. As shown in chapter 1,

[33] Joan Williams, "Market Work and Family Work in the 21st Century" (1999) 44 Villanova Law Review 305, 318.

[34] Barnett (n. 31) 135. As a result, women are consequently disentitled to participate in the public sphere.

[35] Katherine O'Donovan, *Sexual Divisions in Law* (Weidenfeld & Nicolson 1985) 6–7.

[36] Rosemary Hunter, "Contesting the Dominant Paradigm: Feminist Critiques of Liberal Legalism" in Vanessa E. Munro & Margaret Davies (eds.) *The Ashgate Research Companion to Feminist Legal Theory* (Taylor & Francis 2013) 13, 19.

[37] Ibid. 17. This liberal legalism's account of the legal person does not merely function as a representation of reality but actively contributes to the construction of gender as a binary system.

[38] Cynthia Enloe, *Bananas, Beaches and Bases: Making Feminist Sense of International Politics* (2nd ed., University of California Press 2014) 256; Caron E. Gentry & Laura Sjoberg, *Beyond Mothers, Monsters, Whores: Thinking about Women's Violence in Global Politics* (Bloomsbury 2015) 18.

[39] Hilary Charlesworth, "Worlds Apart: Public/Private Distinctions in International Law" in Margaret Thornton (ed.) *Public and Private: Feminist Legal Debates* (Oxford University Press 1995) 243, 250; Henri Meyrowitz, "Les guerres de libération et les conventions de Genève" (1974) 39:6 Politique étrangère 607, 611: "Dans les conflits internes, *l'inégalité* des parties est le principe fondamental." Also see Hilary Charlesworth, Christine Chinkin, & Shelley Wright, "Feminist Approaches to International Law" (1991) 85:4 American Journal of International Law 613.

when knowledge structures create binaries to assign some issues as irrelevant to their scope, these issues are silenced, ignored, or made invisible.[40] Hilary Charlesworth argues that international law claims to be gender-blind while maintaining silence on different ways in which women experience the world.[41] Such silences within international law can reveal how the invisibility of women constitutes "an integral part" of the international legal order, rather than merely being a gap that can be easily filled.[42] Patriarchal ways of viewing the world are, therefore, embedded in the central tenets of international law and shape its silences.

In addition to international law's gender bias, the notion of the State, which is arguably the central tenet of the international legal system, is also gendered.[43] In this manner institutionsand even States can take on qualities that perpetuate gendered ways of framing the world.[44] Feminist scholar Laura Sjoberg thereby attributes masculine qualities to States not purely because they are governed primarily by men but also due to the gendered nature of how States' organizational practices are structured.[45] One such organizational practice imbuing masculinity is warfare, which falls squarely within the public sphere of life reserved for men. Judith Gardam asserts that when law relegates women's voices to the private sphere, it blocks their "involvement in the decision making in that most public and powerful function of the [S]tate: the making of foreign policy and decisions as to the use of force in international relations."[46] This robs them of the opportunity to be full participants in military contexts.

IHL, as a body of law that regulates armed conflicts, embodies patriarchal roots inherent in the State-centric structure of warfare. It classifies armed conflicts through a State-centric lens into international and non-international armed conflicts, which mirrors the gendered public and private dichotomy in general legal frameworks. The degree of protection granted to each type of conflict varies greatly. Most articles in the four Geneva Conventions regulate international armed conflicts. Protocol I, which deals with international armed conflicts, contains more provisions, regulations, and protections than Protocol II governing non-international armed conflicts. Granted, Common Article 3 to the four Geneva Conventions contains a provision dictating that persons taking no active part in the hostilities must in all circumstances be treated humanely,

[40] Gentry & Sjoberg (n. 38) 28.

[41] Hilary Charlesworth, "Feminist Methods in International Law" (1999) 93:2 American Journal of International Law 379, 381.

[42] Ibid.

[43] Ibid.; Gentry & Sjoberg (n. 38) 40.

[44] Laura Sjoberg, "Introduction," in Laura Sjoberg (ed.) *Gender and International Security: Feminist Perspectives* (Routledge 2009) 4–5.

[45] Ibid. 3.

[46] Judith Gardam, "A Feminist Analysis of Certain Aspects of International Humanitarian Law" (1992) 12:1 Australian Yearbook of International Law 265, 277.

without any adverse distinction founded on sex, among other criteria.[47] In the same vein, Additional Protocol II prohibits rape, enforced prostitution, and any form of indecent assault, and requires the separation of women and men in detention.[48] These provisions recognize gendered experiences of non-international armed conflicts. However, violating these provisions does not constitute a grave breach of IHL, a category reserved for violations of rules applicable in international armed conflicts.

To be accepted within the public sphere of international law, entities that are not States are expected to conform to the State structure, mirroring how the patriarchal structure sets social norms based on masculine standards to which women are expected to conform to be accepted as equals in certain public domains. Likewise, IHL only regulates violence that is classified as armed conflict. For violence within a State to be classified as an armed conflict, the non-State entity engaging in violence must achieve a specific level of organization.[49] Indicators that demonstrate a high level of organization require non-State armed groups to emulate, at least to some extent, the organizational structures seen in State armed forces. To be governed under the higher degree of regulation and scrutiny warranted by the public sphere of IHL, such an armed conflict should fall within Article 1(4) of Additional Protocol I. This provision applies "to armed conflicts in which peoples are fighting against colonial domination and alien occupation and against racist régimes in the exercise of their right of self-determination."[50] As such, non-State armed groups

[47] International Committee of the Red Cross (ICRC), Geneva Convention for the Amelioration of the Condition of the Wounded and Sick in Armed Forces in the Field (First Geneva Convention), August 12, 1949, 75 U.N.T.S. 31, Article 3(1); International Committee of the Red Cross (ICRC), Geneva Convention for the Amelioration of the Condition of Wounded, Sick and Shipwrecked Members of Armed Forces at Sea (Second Geneva Convention), August 12, 1949, 75 U.N.T.S. 85, Article 3(1); International Committee of the Red Cross (ICRC), Geneva Convention Relative to the Treatment of Prisoners of War (Third Geneva Convention), August 12, 1949, 75 U.N.T.S. 135 Article 3(1); International Committee of the Red Cross (ICRC), Geneva Convention Relative to the Protection of Civilian Persons in Time of War (Fourth Geneva Convention), August 12, 1949, 75 U.N.T.S. 287, Article 3(1).

[48] Protocol Additional to the Geneva Conventions of August 12, 1949, and relating to the Protection of Victims of Non-International Armed Conflicts (Protocol II), June 8, 1977, Geneva, Articles 4 & 5.

[49] *Prosecutor v. Haradinaj et al. (Trial Judgment)*, IT-04-84-T, International Criminal Tribunal for the former Yugoslavia (ICTY), April 3, 2008, para. 60; *Prosecutor v. Boskoski and Tarculovski (Trial Judgment)*, IT-04-82-T, International Criminal Tribunal for the former Yugoslavia (ICTY), July 10, 2008, paras. 199–203; and *Prosecutor v. Limaj et al. (Trial Judgment)*, IT-03-66-T, International Criminal Tribunal for the former Yugoslavia (ICTY), November 30, 2005, paras. 94–134. The ICC has also applied some of these elements; see *Situation in the Democratic Republic of the Congo, in the case of the Prosecutor v. Thomas Lubanga Dyilo*, ICC-01/04-01/06, International Criminal Court (ICC), March 14, 2012, para. 537; and *The Prosecutor v. Germain Katanga and Mathieu Ngudjolo Chui*, ICC-01/04-01/07 OA 8, International Criminal Court (ICC), September 25, 2009, para. 1186.

[50] As enshrined in the Charter of the United Nations and the Declaration on Principles of International Law concerning Friendly Relations and Co-operation among States in accordance with the Charter of the United Nations.

must, to avail themselves of a higher level of recognition, aspire to the ideal of the State.[51]

The focus on the inter-State level makes IHL blind to many aspects of violence that operate within the private sphere of the State. It thereby grants the State more liberty to exercise violence against its citizens with minimal regulation.[52] An example of this differential treatment is how the degree of violence that triggers an armed conflict varies in international and non-international armed conflicts. In inter-State warfare, there is no requirement that the use of armed force between the Parties reach a specific level of intensity for an armed conflict to commence.[53] Any military operations by one State in the territory of another State that has not consented to such operations would be interpreted as an armed interference in the latter's sphere of sovereignty and would constitute an international armed conflict under Article 2(1).[54] In comparison, the level of violence in a non-international armed conflict must reach a high level of intensity and be protracted. IHL would not regulate violence below this threshold.[55] Much like how the lack of consent becomes a non-issue where there is no legal recognition of marital rape, most unconsented-to violence by States does not yield legal scrutiny by IHL where it occurs within the "private" sphere of the State.

Recent developments in International Criminal Law (ICL) have attempted to ensure that violence against women remains within the sphere of international accountability even when it occurs in the context of non-international armed conflicts.[56] Article 8 of the Rome Statute makes rape a war crime in the context of non-international armed conflicts. International Criminal Court's (ICC)

[51] Gardam, "A Feminist Analysis of Certain Aspects of IHL" (n. 46) 269: "The concept of self-determination of peoples has as its aim the achievement of the Western patriarchal state."

[52] Note, however, that International Human Rights Law (IHRL) regulates how a State treats its own citizens. While the distinction between IHL and IHRL is becoming less rigid, IHL remains the *lex specialis* during periods of armed conflict and occupation.

[53] International Committee of the Red Cross, *Commentary on the First Geneva Convention: Convention (I) for the Amelioration of the Condition of the Wounded and Sick in Armed Forces in the Field (Commentaries on the 1949 Geneva Conventions)* (Cambridge University Press 2016) para. 236.

[54] Ibid. para. 237.

[55] Ibid. para. 431: "[T]he requisite degree of intensity may be met 'when hostilities are of a collective character or when the government is obliged to use military force against the insurgents, instead of mere police forces.' In this light, it is understood that Article 1(2) of Additional Protocol II, which provides that the 'Protocol shall not apply to situations of internal disturbances and tensions, such as riots, isolated and sporadic acts of violence and other acts of a similar nature, as not being armed conflicts,' also defines the lower threshold of common Article 3. This understanding has been confirmed by State practice in that, for other treaties applicable to non-international armed conflict, States have chosen to refer to a combination of common Article 3 and Article 1(2) of Additional Protocol II."

[56] International Committee of the Red Cross, *Commentary on the Third Geneva Convention: Convention (III) Relative to the Treatment of Prisoners of War (Commentaries on the 1949 Geneva Conventions)* (Cambridge University Press 2020), paras. 737–743: For more on how Common Article 3 has been interpreted to include a prohibition on sexual violence in light of recent developments in ICL.

Elements of Crimes document notes that if the invasion of a body is accompanied by the threat of force or coercion, "such as that caused by fear of violence, duress, detention, psychological oppression or abuse of power, against such person or another person, or by taking advantage of a coercive environment" among other things, such invasion can constitute a war crime.[57] In doing so, ICL recognizes gendered impacts of war. It also acknowledges the contextual elements that can influence a person's capacity to make decisions about their body when operating within an oppressive or coercive environment. Proximity of combat has been considered in assessing the existence of a coercive environment in ICL jurisprudence.[58] These ICL rules that question a person's capacity to give genuine consent in wartime contexts can facilitate justice for victims of sexual violence.

Broad and multifaceted measures characterize IHRL treatment of situations involving women and armed conflict.[59] For example, General Recommendation 30 of the Committee on the Elimination of Discrimination against Women acknowledges that women take leadership roles during conflict as combatants, among other things.[60] It further recommends that State parties should ensure women's equal representation at all decision-making levels in armed forces.[61] U.N. Security Council Resolution 1325 (2000), dealing with women in peace and security, also incorporates human rights principles on gender equality into the conflict resolution paradigm.[62] However, given its focus on conflict resolution and peacebuilding, it does not directly discuss the participation of women in combat. Much of the scholarly literature that examines the application of IHRL to women in armed conflicts tends to similarly speak of women's involvement in resolving conflicts, as well as in preventing sexual violence of women and girls, and the violation of their reproductive rights and health.[63] Ensuring that women are physically safe during conflict can indeed enhance their freedom and autonomy, especially, as I will show later, when done in the language of agentic participation rather than that of victimhood. However, the focus seen in both

[57] *Elements of Crimes*, International Criminal Court (ICC), 2011, ISBN No. 92-9227-232-2, 8.

[58] *The Prosecutor v. Mikaeli Muhimana (Judgement and Sentence)*, ICTR- 95-1B-T, International Criminal Tribunal for Rwanda (ICTR), April 8, 2005, paras. 552–553.

[59] Judith Gardam, "More of the Same—Feminist Interactions with IHL" (paper presented at Center for International Governance Justice Workshop: Recent Developments in Feminist Thinking in International Law and International Rights, Australian National University, December 3, 2014) [unpublished].

[60] General Recommendation No. 30 on women in conflict prevention, conflict and postconflict situations, November 1, 2013, UN Committee on the Elimination of Discrimination Against Women (CEDAW), CEDAW/C/GC/30, para. 42.

[61] Ibid. para. 46(a).

[62] Security Council resolution 1325 (2000) [on women and peace and security], U.N. Security Council, October 31, 2000, S/RES/1325 (2000). Also see Golie G. Jansen, "Gender and War: The Effects of Armed Conflict on Women's Health and Mental Health" (2006) 21:2 Affilia 134.

[63] For example, see Gloria Gaggioli, "Sexual Violence in Armed Conflicts: A Violation of International Humanitarian Law and Human Rights Law" (2014) 96:894 International Review of the Red Cross 503.

ICL and IHRL on protecting women during conflict and ensuring their participation in conflict resolution processes means that IHL's gendered assumptions on women who participate in violence remain relatively unchallenged by developments in these branches of international law.[64]

Gender stereotypes of women in IHL cannot be decoupled from the role that militaries have played in forming IHL treaties and customary rules.[65] Militaries function alongside societal gender norms.[66] This is true, even though militaries can be seen to identify their own paradigms for lawful behavior that are distinct from those of civilian life.[67] The principles that establish the worldview of a community, including the military, mirror the cultural constructs of the larger society in which the community resides.[68] Gender is one such cultural construct.[69] Given how military practices largely influence the formation of IHL rules, it is highly susceptible to be influenced by the patriarchal structures prevalent within the military.[70] Likewise, the normativity in IHL, as applicable to the treatment of combatants, is male.[71] The architecture of IHL reflects this

[64] Catherine O'Rourke, *Women's Rights in Armed Conflict under International Law* (Cambridge University Press 2020) 36: "[A] regime's underpinning legal sources is an important factor in determining the nature and degree of feminist engagement with the regime. Therefore, stagnant treaty development under IHL contrasts with the considerable dynamism of ICL, in particular surrounding the adoption of the Rome Statute in 1998."

[65] This distinction between IHL and ICL remains relevant given that not all countries are subject to the jurisdiction of the ICC or ad hoc tribunals. The obligation to prevent and punish war crimes, particularly in internal armed conflicts, still stems from core treaties of IHL.

[66] Within the term "militaries," I also include non-State armed groups. The different ways in which state militaries and ethnonationalist non-State armed groups relate to gender will be discussed in later sections of the chapter.

[67] Robert Cover, "Foreword: Nomos and Narrative" (1983) 97:1 Harvard Law Review 4, 33.

[68] Ibid.

[69] This is reflected in UN definitions of gender, which emphasize the fact that "gender" is a social construct and therefore is a learned rather than innate category. For example, Integrating the Human Rights of Women Throughout the United Nations System. Report of the Secretary General, U.N. ESCOR, 53d Sess., U.N. Doc. E/CN.4/1997/40 (1996), para. 10, states: "As sex refers to biologically determined differences between men and women that are universal, so gender refers to the social differences between men and women that are learned, changeable over time and have wide variations both within and between cultures." Rome Statute of the International Criminal Court, UN General Assembly, July 17, 1998, Article 7(3): For this statute, it is understood that the term "gender" refers to the two sexes, male and female, within the context of society.

[70] Chris Jochnick & Roger Normand, "The Legitimation of Violence: A Critical History of the Laws of War" (1994) 35:1 Harvard International Law Journal 49, 57: "[L]aw helps condition people to accept the prevailing distribution of social and political power, which in turn reinscribes its hierarchies into the law. These effects are by their nature hidden; the contingent, malleable power relations that produce law are made to seem natural, neutral, and inevitable." However, it must be noted that there are other political, economic, and cultural influences that also influenced IHL. For example, see Eyal Benvenisti & Doreen Lustig, "Monopolizing War: Codifying the Laws of War to Reassert Governmental Authority, 1856–1874" (2020) 31:1 European Journal of International Law 127.

[71] Judith Gail Gardam & Michelle J. Jarvis, *Women, Armed Conflict, and International Law* (Kluwer Law International 2001) 93; Patricia Smith, "Four Themes in Feminist Legal Theory: Difference, Dominance, Domesticity, and Denial" in Martin P. Golding & William A. Edmundsom (eds.) *The Blackwell Guide to the Philosophy of Law and Legal Theory* (John Wiley & Sons 2008) 91: "If women

historical background. IHL's roots in chivalric codes from Medieval Europe have led to creating an image of a combatant that is inescapably male.[72] The Geneva Conventions are informed by a vision of IHL "that takes as its core actors, male 'warriors' competing for domination over land".[73]

Historically, one of the primary duties of citizenship in Western States has been participation in the State's military. For example, societies in ancient Greece provided the model of the male citizen who took up arms on their behalf.[74] Similarly, Frédéric Mégret claims that "because war in the Western tradition is conceived of as a form of public violence, participation therein can be considered the highest form of (masculine) citizen duty."[75] This idea of a dutiful male citizen fighting for one's country reinforces the gendered public/private, leaving no room for women in military service. The image of the masculine warrior is embedded within many States' military structures. This hypermasculinity of the military fits well within the patriarchal State system. The patriarchal vision of the State considers that the State's duty is to protect its citizens, particularly its most vulnerable, as a *paterfamilias* would protect their family. This means that the State takes on a patronizing duty to protect its women. Women, in turn, are viewed as nurturers who give birth to and raise the ultimate protectors of the State, male combatants. Within this framework, women have long been viewed as those whom the male citizen fights to protect.[76] Their role has been relegated to that of a victim of war who is rendered helpless by the "oppressive and coercive environment" of war, rather than being taken as agentic actors who are capable of being full participants in the military.

Refusing to recognize women as agentic actors in wartime contexts has persisted, despite women's efforts to be included within militaries since ancient

appear to present 'special' issues in the workplace, it is only because the norm from which they are being judged has been formulated by and for men."

[72] Gardam, "A Feminist Analysis of Certain Aspects of IHL" (n. 46) 265; Judith Gardam, "Women and the Law of Armed Conflict: Why the Silence?" (1997) 46:1 International Comparative Law Quarterly 55, 68; Helen Kinsella, *The Image Before the Weapon: A Critical History of the Distinction between Combatant and Civilian* (Cornell University Press 2016) 8; Christine Chinkin & Mary Kaldor, *International Law and New Wars* (Cambridge University Press 2017) 90; Frédéric Mégret, "The Laws of War and the Structure of Masculine Power" (2018) 19:1 Melbourne Journal of International Law 200, 207.

[73] Anna Crowe, "'All the Regard Due to Their Sex': Women in the Geneva Conventions of 1949" Research Working Paper Series (December 2016) 17.

[74] Miranda H. Alison, *Women and Political Violence: Female Combatants in Ethno-National Conflict* (Routledge 2009) 96.

[75] Mégret, "The Laws of War and the Structure of Masculine Power" (n. 72) 205.

[76] Alison, *Women and Political Violence* (n. 74) 97; Gardam & Jarvis (n. 71) 117: "The essence of what it is to be male can be found in the warrior who defends the security of the State. This gendered version of the male is sustained through comparison with other devalued forms of masculinity and femininity. To date, scant regard has been paid to the role that IHL plays in reinforcing these constructions of masculinity and femininity."

times. In the introductory chapter, I referred to the female commander from India, Kuyuli, who sacrificed her life in the name of her queen, fighting against British colonialism.[77] When compared to the current image of male-dominated State militaries, this story of female leadership and militancy seems surreal and mythical. Other notable examples of women include Eleanor of Aquitaine and Joan of Arc, who defied the gendered codes of the day by directly engaging in wartime combat. The latter faced contempt by the knightly classes and was burned at the stake for her unfeminine behavior. While in the nineteenth century, "women participated in the Austrian and Italian armies, some receiving prestigious military honors", they were still the exceptions to the rule.[78]

In recent years, militaries have been more inclusive of women within their ranks. For example, women have served in the Israeli army ever since its establishment in 1948. The Israel Defense Forces (IDF) is one of the only armies in the Western world where women are drafted to military service by law. The United States deployed female soldiers to a war zone for the first time in the 1991 Gulf War. The combat exclusion of women in the United States was repealed only in 2013. In China, the People's Liberation Army (PLA) sends female soldiers on escort missions in the Gulf of Aden, where they are assigned to operate signal, telegraph, radar, steering, and sail-and-cordage posts; to operate submarines and pilot fighter jets; and to fly space missions. As of August 2014, the PLA Navy had its first spokeswoman.[79] In February 2020, the Supreme Court of India ruled that women can serve in command appointments of the armed forces.[80] Despite these numerous advances made by women to break the glass ceiling within military contexts, the military continues to be a male-dominated domain.[81] In today's discourse on international security, the role of securing the State belongs to the "courageous and strong male leadership and macho soldiers who are willing to lay down their lives in the defence of civilized societies and states."[82] Contrary to men, who here are viewed as capable of making the agentic choice to lay down their lives for the State, international law tenets reflect hypermasculinist and

[77] Priya S. Lekshmi, "Velu Nachiyar & Kuyili: The Women Who Took Down the British 85 Yrs before 1857!" The Better India (28 August 2018) online: https://www.thebetterindia.com/157316/news-india-independence-women-fighters-british-raj/ accessed January 5, 2025.

[78] Gardam & Jarvis (n. 71) 48.

[79] Lana Obradovic, "Comparative Analysis of Women's Military Participation in East Asia" (2015) 1 Res Militaris 1, 6.

[80] India, *The Secretary to the Ministry of Defence v. Babita Puniya & Ors*, Civil Appeal Nos. 9367-9369 of 2011, February 17, 2020, para. 68.

[81] Reed M. Wood, *Female Fighters: Why Rebel Groups Recruit Women for War* (Columbia University Press 2019) 45; Michael J. Hughes, *Forging Napoleon's Grande Armée: Motivation, Military Culture, and Masculinity in the French Army, 1800-1808* (NYU Press 2012); Joane Nagel, "Masculinity and Nationalism: Gender and Sexuality in the Making of Nations" (1998) 21:2 Ethnic and Racial Studies 242, 248.

[82] Parashar (n. 4) 236.

militaristic rhetoric that views women as lacking the capacity to be agentic in armed conflicts.

The inclusion of women within militaries has often resulted from women challenging their respective military structures. Militaries have, at times, been compelled by judicial decisions or State policies to integrate women into their ranks. Patriarchal narratives have often opposed these changes. In the IDF, women's participation in the military has generated debates about the "real" role and value of women in society.[83] Here, the "real" role of women, as defined by society and not through the actions of women themselves, would be to dedicate their lives and bodies to the private, domestic, and often reproductive sphere. In *Rostker v. Goldberg*, the US Supreme Court noted that the US Congress in 1980 specifically recognized and endorsed the exclusion of women from combat in exempting women from registration, a move universally supported by military leaders.[84] The US Senate also noted in a report that even merely registering women for combat operations would "leave the actual performance of sexually mixed units as an experiment to be conducted in war with unknown risk—a risk that the committee finds militarily unwarranted and dangerous."[85] This statement made only four decades ago shows the extent to which the vision of a male combatant as the ultimate protector of the State is entrenched into narratives on national security even in liberal democracies. Similarly, the Indian Supreme Court while extending permanent service in 2020, which had only applied to men until then, to all women officers and allowing women to command entire military units, still did not venture into the women's capacity to serve in combat duties. Therefore, the rationale of protecting women from the "inherent risks" posed by combat activities remains undisputed by the Indian Supreme Court.[86] This tacitly confirms the cultural narrative that perceives women as not possessing the agency to subject their bodies and lives to the same risks as men. Through these continued practices of exclusion, the military "reinforces gender constraints" based on the binary of masculinity and femininity.[87] Likewise, while women are increasingly being included as capable members of the military, the masculinized nature of the institution and its challenge to women's agency to engage in combat prevail.

[83] Idit Shafran Gittleman, "Female Service in the IDF: The Challenge of an 'Integrated' Army," Lawfare (February 28, 2018), online: https://www.lawfareblog.com/female-service-idf-challenge-integrated-army last accessed January 19, 2025.
[84] *Rostker v. Goldberg*, 453 U.S. 57 (1981). Gentry & Sjoberg, *Beyond Mothers, Monsters, Whores* (n. 38) 7: "When the United States repealed the combat exclusion of women in 2013, it reopened the debate about women's physical and emotional ability to withstand battle conditions. But the coverage of this decision tended to be highly gendered."
[85] *Rostker v. Goldberg* (n. 84) 92.
[86] India, *Babita Puniya* (n. 80) 29.
[87] Gardam & Jarvis (n. 71) 50.

Male-centric normativity is present even in IHL provisions that attempt to prevent sex-based discrimination. For example, Article 14(2) of the Third Geneva Convention emphasizes the fundamental prohibition of adverse distinction based on sex.[88] This rule sets a requirement of equal treatment of women who are members of the armed forces during captivity.[89] It obliges that women prisoners of war benefit in all cases by treatment as favorable as that granted to men. That the minimum standard of treatment for how female combatants are to be treated is measured by treatment provided to male prisoners indicates that the norm in IHL is biased toward men. In a context where a majority of prisoners of war were men, one may argue that it is reasonable for men to be the reference point of rules governing how prisoners of war are to be treated. In this view, IHL can be understood as merely reflecting a reality in wartime. Yet, even where laws are descriptive, these rules can have a normative power. Judith Butler says that such legal categories can *create* facts on the ground and that every juridical form of power has its productive effect:[90]

> It is not enough to inquire into how women might become more fully represented in language and politics. Feminist critique ought also to understand how the category of "women," the subject of feminism, is produced and restrained by the very structures of power through which emancipation is sought.[91]

The male standard of combatancy in IHL is not merely descriptive but has the effect of extending a male-centric wartime experience to female combatants, thereby perpetuating their "othering" by the legal framework.

This male normativity is furthered by classifying women as special or requiring differential treatment. This makes the woman, the "other," for whom separate rules need to be fashioned. As Judith G. Gardam and Michelle J. Jarvis note, the special provisions in relation to women in IHL "take the male perception of not only what it is to be a woman, but also what it is about women that warrants protection."[92] According to Jean Pictet, "special injunction" is required for the purposes of protecting women.[93] This assumes that every civilized

[88] Updated Commentary to the Third Geneva Convention (n. 56) para. 1688.
[89] Ibid. para. 1689.
[90] Judith Butler, *Gender Trouble: Tenth Anniversary Edition* (Routledge 2002) 4. Also see Judith Butler, *Undoing Gender* (Routledge 2004).
[91] Butler, *Gender Trouble* (n. 90) 5.
[92] Gardam & Jarvis (n. 71) 10.
[93] Jean S. Pictet (ed.), *The Geneva Conventions of 12 August 1949, Commentary, Volume I, First Geneva Convention for the Amelioration of the Condition of the Wounded in Armies in the Field* (ICRC 1952) 140; Jean S. Pictet (ed.), *The Geneva Conventions of 12 August 1949, Commentary, Volume II, Second Geneva Convention for the Amelioration of the Condition of Wounded, Sick and Shipwrecked Members of Armed Forces at Sea* (ICRC 1960) 92.

country affords protection to its weaker beings and their honor and modesty call for respect.[94] This principle treating women as a special category of persons "was designed with a paternalistic view of women in mind".[95] While more recent interpretations to the Geneva Conventions have attempted to move away from these archaic notions of women,[96] IHL's inherent structure that labels women into special categories continues to project a male gaze on women. It shapes how IHL views women's agency in engaging in combat and risking their lives during wartime.

4.2.2. Gendered victims and perpetrators in IHL

The notion of "victim" is socially constructed, with each culture adopting varying frameworks to identify specific qualities as being crucial to establish that a person or a group of persons are worthy of being granted victim status. Nils Christie provides one framework, among many, to deconstruct how some societies may identify victims.[97] According to him, the victim is often seen as being weak and blameless: the victim, therefore, becomes a pure but helpless entity who suffers at the hands of an offender or a perpetrator to whom malicious intention is attributed.[98] This characterization of victimhood requires two mutually exclusive parties: a victim who is wronged and a perpetrator who engages in wrongdoing.[99] The victim is blameless and passive, while the perpetrator is deviant and agentic.[100] Christie also notes that tropes and stereotypes attached to some social groups enable them to appeal to victimhood status more easily.[101] These groups can trigger more empathy because they are perceived

[94] Ibid.

[95] Karima Bennoune, "Do We Need New International Law to Protect Women in Armed Conflict" (2007) 38 Case Western Reserve Journal of International Law 363, 374. Updated Commentary to the Third Geneva Convention (n. 56) para. 1682: It, however, alludes to recent developments on how "women, men, girls and boys may have specific needs, capacities and perspectives linked to the different ways armed conflict and detention may affect them." Accordingly, the commentary states that "the specific mention of the protection of women in Article 14(2) is not to be understood as implying that women have less resilience, agency or capacity within the armed forces, but rather as an acknowledgement that women have a distinct set of needs and may face particular physical and psychological risks."

[96] Updated Commentary to the Third Geneva Convention (n. 56) para. 1682, note 49.

[97] Nils Christie "The Ideal Victim" in E. A. Fattah (ed.) *From Crime Policy to Victim Policy* (Macmillan 1986) 17.

[98] Ibid. 19.

[99] Alice Bosma, Eva Mulder, & Antony Pemberton, "The Ideal Victim through Other(s') Eyes" in Marian Duggan (ed.) *Developments in Critical Victimology* (Bristol University Press 2018) 27, 30.

[100] Joris van Wijk, "Who Is the 'Little Old Lady' of International Crimes? Nils Christie's Concept of the Ideal Victim Reinterpreted" (2013) 19:2 International Review of Victimology 159, 164.

[101] Christie (n. 97).

as blameless, innocent, or pure, due to the roles allocated to them by their culture.[102]

By depicting women as weak beings whose honor and modesty need protection, IHL builds a narrative that facilitates lumping them into the category of victims. Jean Pictet's Commentary to Article 14 of the Third Geneva Convention states:

> It is difficult to give any general definition of the "regard" due to women. Certain points should, however, be borne in mind . . . These points are the following: (a) weakness; (b) honour and modesty; (c) pregnancy and child-birth. These three considerations must be taken into account in the application of provisions of the Convention.[103]

Despite the efforts made by a later version of the Commentary to reflect a more enlightened approach toward how women operate in war,[104] these tropes about women are still relevant, given how deeply entrenched they are within the framework of IHL. These tropes can reinforce existing cultural stereotypes that deny women their agency. At the same time, women who engage in political and public acts of violence are seen as exceptional. There is a dearth of research that depicts violent women as rational actors, even though scholars often characterize violent men as rationally or logically motivated.[105] These women are dehumanized and classified as monsters for acting outside the confines of victimhood assigned to them.

One overly simplified way in which IHL presents women is to treat them as being weak, passive, and helpless. This can be traced back to IHL's Eurocentric roots where a warrior was defined by his prowess in contradistinction to women's fragility. Physical strength was "the essential chivalric trait" which was necessary for the warrior to achieve honor.[106] Warriors used their strength to fight and for the noble cause of protecting the weak. According to these chivalric ideals, women and children were not to be directly targeted.[107] Gardam and Jarvis posit that IHL's principle of distinction, "was drawn in the chivalric tradition between the enemy and the innocents: the enemy were those who carried arms, the innocents did not. This differentiation created a class of persons requiring protection

102 Sarah Federman, "The 'ideal perpetrator': The French National Railways and the social construction of accountability" (2018) 49:5 Security Dialogue 327, 330.

103 Jean S. Pictet (ed.), *The Geneva Conventions of 12 August 1949, Commentary, Volume III, Third Geneva Convention relative to the Treatment of Prisoners of War* (ICRC 1960) 147.

104 Updated Commentary to the Third Geneva Convention (n. 56) para. 1682.

105 Gentry & Sjoberg, *Beyond Mothers, Monsters, Whores* (n. 38) 13.

106 Geoffroi de Charny, Richard W. Kaeuper, & Elspeth Kennedy, *A Knight's Own Book of Chivalry* (University of Pennsylvania Press 2013) 22.

107 Gardam & Jarvis (n. 71) 21.

and thus reinforcing the heroic narrative of knightly men".[108] Likewise, honorable knights were expected to take risks "to protect defenseless young women, widows, or orphans."[109] This portrayal of knights as the natural protectors of "weak, modest, and docile women incapable of looking after themselves" resonates in current IHL provisions.[110]

The degree of protection provided by IHL tends to be directly proportional to how weak the individuals belonging to a group are. Combatants are not considered weak and are not provided protection unless they are no longer engaging in hostilities. Under the same logic, they are afforded significantly more protection when weakened due to being wounded, sick, or shipwrecked by Geneva Conventions I and II or when they are captured by the hostile party and treated as Prisoners of War as per Geneva Convention III. Combatants oscillate from being protected for their temporary states of vulnerability to regaining a status that gives them power over others. On the other hand, as per Sophie Kinsella, in IHL the notion of civilian is imbued with innocence to the extent that the notion of a "guilty civilian appears oxymoronic."[111] Among civilians, weakness is a quality often attributed to groups that are characterized within IHL as deserving special protection. This special protection afforded to women is based almost exclusively on "their perceived weakness, both physical and psychological, and their sexual and reproductive functions".[112] Likewise, women were presented primarily as victims of sexual violence or infantilized, as is seen in the false equivalence made between women and children, and thereby seen aspersons needing protection.[113] Stemming from these historical rules, IHL texts reflect the gendered nature of how the victim–perpetrator binary is conceived in war.[114] Helen Durham and Katie O'Byrne posit that the production of binary categories placing men in the role of violators or protectors, and women as victims can hinder a more critical examination of their roles in times

[108] Ibid. 111.
[109] Charny, Kaeuper, & Kenne (n. 106) 35.
[110] Gardam & Jarvis (n. 71) 108.
[111] Kinsella (n. 72) 8.
[112] Gardam & Jarvis (n. 71) 95.
[113] Griffin Ferry, "Oppression through 'Protection': A Survey of Femininity in Foundational Humanitarian Law Texts" (2017) 35:1 Law & Inequality 57, 74.
[114] Some feminists argue that the process of pursuing justice for sexual violence against women through ICL has further entrenched the vision of women as victims in need of protection. One example for this is how the Rome Statute deals with women's capacity to consent to sexual activities in times of war. By redefining what genuine consent means, ICL attempts to make the prosecution of sexual violence more viable. However, in doing so, it also questions the capacity of women to exercise sexual agency during times of conflict. Providing extensive attention to gender-based violence also obscures the fact that women serve as combatants in armed conflict and, therefore, agents engaging in political violence. Gardam, "More of the Same" (n. 59) 4–5: "[B]y the tendency in so many of the legal initiatives and the ensuing jurisprudence of the ICTY and the ICTR to reinforce a stereotypical vision of women as vulnerable, innocent and lacking in agency."

of armed conflict.[115] It represses nuanced roles that women occupy during armed conflicts.

The essentialized view of women as being weak is compounded by IHL consistently placing women in the same category as children. Article 19 of the Lieber Code sets out that "[c]ommanders, whenever admissible, inform the enemy of their intention to bombard a place, so that the noncombatants, and *especially the women and children*, may be removed before the bombardment commences" (emphasis added). The intent of the Article seems protective, if not patronizing. Similarly, current political dialogue often expresses concern for protecting women and children from wartime violence.[116] But coupling women with children diminishes women's agency and participation in conflict.[117] This women-and-children dilemma is prevalent in the Geneva Conventions, which not only at times equates women to children but also views women primarily in their role of bearing and raising children. Article 38 of the Fourth Geneva Convention states: "Children under fifteen years, pregnant women and mothers of children under seven years shall benefit by any preferential treatment."[118] Chapter II of Additional Protocol I is titled "measures in favor of women and children." This false equivalency and constant entanglement between women and children in IHL signal its view of women's agency.

IHL's tendency to present women and children as quintessential victims in armed conflicts makes it difficult for its rules to grapple with the agency they express when participating in combat. The scholarly literature on how child soldiers skew the victim–perpetrator binary in warfare is instructive on similar tropes surrounding women in combat. The issue of child soldiers, much like wartime violence against women, has received attention in IHRL and ICL, among other branches of international law. Despite IHRL's advances to recognize the evolving capacity and autonomy of children, these regulations are predicated on treating child soldiers as victims. ICL, too, paints persons with broad strokes and boxes them into categories of victims and perpetrators. Mark Drumbl takes the example of Dominic Ongwen, a former child soldier who carried out mass atrocities and was tried at the ICC.[119] Through this example, Drumbl argues that victims can themselves victimize others and that the categories of victim and perpetrator are not as mutually exclusive as ICL would like them to be. The case of

[115] Helen Durham & Katie O'Byrne, "The Dialogue of Difference: Gender Perspectives on International Humanitarian Law" (2010) 92:877 International Review of the Red Cross 31, 34.

[116] Gentry & Sjoberg, *Beyond Mothers, Monsters, Whores* (n. 38) 1.

[117] Ferry (n. 113) 64; Bennoune (n. 95) 377: Bennoune indicates that there is concern that the strong focus on pregnant women and mothers with young children within IHL may infantilize women by equating women with children.

[118] For similar provisions, also see Article 132 of Fourth Geneva Convention.

[119] Mark A. Drumbl, "Victims Who Victimise" (2016) 4:2 London Review of International Law 217, 236–240.

Ongwen shows that the victim–perpetrator relationship can also be circulatory, one begetting the other.[120] The adversarial performances of ICL proceedings depend on the reductionist construction of victim–perpetrator binaries. In legal processes, victim and perpetrator categories become interdependent. A victim is defined relationally to a corresponding offender: to heighten the innocence and vulnerability of the victim, the offender's deviance must be magnified, and vice versa.[121] Scholars further argue that treating child soldiers purely as victims can be counterproductive, given that it fails to recognize their self-constructions and local understandings of agency. This failure to relate to their understanding of agency can prevent their successful reintegration into communities after wars.[122] These efforts can benefit from acknowledging the complicated ways in which child soldiers occupy the spaces of both victim and perpetrator. In using the example of child soldiers' contested agency to understand female combatants better, I do not claim that children's exercise of agency equates to that of women. Instead, the stereotypes of vulnerability and lack of agency constructed around both women and children depict them as perpetual victims, thereby making it difficult for legal rules to appreciate their capacity for agentic violence.

Stereotypical tropes on women do not facilitate engagement with the complex agentic narratives built around women's participation in political violence. Sjoberg and Caron Gentry, in their work *Beyond Mothers, Monsters, Whores: Thinking about Women's Violence in Global Politics*, unpack the filters often employed to depict women who engage in political violence.[123] They argue that these women are often portrayed as "mothers: women who are fulfilling their biological destinies; as monsters: women who are pathologically damaged and are therefore drawn to violence; and/or as whores: women whose violence is inspired by sexual dependence and depravity."[124] These tropes are also entrenched in IHL's provisions on women. IHL rules tend to define women primarily through motherhood. Of the forty-two specific provisions relating to women within the Geneva Conventions and their 1977 Additional Protocols, almost half deal with women in their roles as expectant or nursing mothers.[125] For example, Articles 38 and 50 of the Fourth Geneva Convention provide preferential treatment to pregnant women and mothers of children under seven years of age.[126]

[120] Ibid. 24.

[121] Bosma (n. 99) 31: "The less morally agentic a 'big bad' offender becomes in the eyes of the beholder, the less a victim is perceived as a moral patient."

[122] Ilse Derluyn et al. "Victims and/or Perpetrators? Towards an Interdisciplinary Dialogue on Child Soldiers" (2015) 15:28 BMC International Health and Human Rights 1, 2.

[123] Gentry & Sjoberg, *Beyond Mothers, Monsters, Whores* (n. 38) 11.

[124] Ibid. 12. Also see Lisa Downing, "'(S)extremism': Imagining Violent Women in the Twenty-First Century with Navine G. Khan-Dossos and Julia Kristeva" (2020) 43:2 Paragraph 212.

[125] Gardam & Jarvis (n. 71) 96.

[126] Also see Article 89 requires that interned pregnant and nursing mothers be given additional food "in proportion to their physiological needs." According to Article 76 of Additional Protocol I, arrested, detained, or interned civilian pregnant women and mothers of dependent infants must

These articles accord women visibility solely for their reproductive capacity.[127] The importance attached to pregnancy and motherhood in IHL demonstrates that it views women as more worthy of protection when they partake in motherhood. This is consistent with how to qualify as an ideal victim, one must be carrying out a respectable project.[128] In this case, the respectable project is that of motherhood. It also advances the image of a helpless victim, as when women are seen solely through the lens of reproduction, their bodies are seen as instruments rather than persons with plural identities and with the capacity to participate in the public sphere of warfare.

A second dimension of how IHL views women is through the need to protect their sexual purity and honor. The few express references to sexual violence contained within IHL demonstrate how women's sexual purity is characterized as crucial to their honor. Article 27 of the Fourth Geneva Convention states that "women shall be especially protected against any attack on their honor, in particular against rape, enforced prostitution, or any form of indecent assault." Article 75 of Additional Protocol I prohibits "outrages upon personal dignity, in particular humiliating and degrading treatment, enforced prostitution and any form of indecent assault."[129] These articles assume that sexual attributes of women are characterizing features of their chastity and modesty.[130] A man's honor in wartime contexts is attached to his bravery and fortitude, thereby facilitating narratives that depict them him as an agentic warrior. The honorable man's role is to protect the honor of his territory, including the purity of the women and children who reside within it.[131] Britain during the world wars, subjected women

have their cases considered with the utmost priority, and the death penalty shall not be executed for these women.

[127] Ferry (n. 113) 70; Valerie Oosterveld, "Feminist Debates on Civilian Women and International Humanitarian Law" (2009) 27 Windsor Year Book of Access to Justice 385, 397: Oosterveld argues that feminists are concerned that this characterization identifies "women only in connection with an 'other'—an unborn child or young children—rather than providing rights or protections in civilian women's own right. They further describe how the protection of the unborn child and small children was the rationale for the inclusion of these provisions, which is why women are referred to in their reproductive and mothering roles"; Bennoune (n. 95) 377–378: "The focus on protecting future generations through rules about pregnant women may inadvertently 'instrumentalize' women and their bodies."

[128] Wijk (n. 100) 160.

[129] Also see Article 76 states that "women shall be the object of special respect and shall be protected in particular against rape, forced prostitution and any other form of indecent assault." Similarly, Additional Protocol II adopts language prohibiting, with respect to non-international armed conflicts, "outrages upon personal dignity, in particular humiliating and degrading treatment, rape, enforced prostitution and any form of indecent assault."

[130] Oosterveld (n. 127) 393. Bennoune (n. 95) 378 notes that the Commentary to the Fourth Geneva Convention takes a somewhat enlightened approach to honor, defining it as a moral and social quality invested in individuals, but that this approach "did not supersede the discriminatory social norms at the time of drafting" and grounded the rights of women to maintain bodily integrity in now "outdated notions of chastity and virtue."

[131] Gardam & Jarvis (n. 71) 108.

to curfews to protect their morality; French women suspected of "fraternizing" with German soldiers during World War II and Somali women seen talking to American soldiers during Operation Restore Hope were publicly humiliated including by having their heads shaved, orstripped and beaten in public.[132] The focus in IHL on a woman's modesty and sexual purity mirrors "narratives that blame women's violence on the evils of female sexuality", and many societies seek to strictly control the virtue of women.[133] In this manner, during times of war in particular, women's agency over their bodies is subsumed by narratives that depict their bodies and sexuality as sites where power is negotiated.

These IHL provisions create a stereotypical image of women as inherently "good, innocent, and incapable of committing atrocities",[134] thus dehumanizing women who engage in violence and undermining their agency. Durham and O'Byrne argue that putting women primarily in the category of civilians in war is a result of not only societal concerns about women "not being good enough to fight (in a physical/biological sense), but also that women are too good (morally/ethically) to be exposed to the horrors of war."[135] Women who demonstrate agencies deemed transgressive are thereby considered deviant for daring to embody violence that is typically reserved only for men.[136] Similarly, Nicole Hogg argues that

> the "evil woman theory" enunciated by Western feminist criminologists, whereby some women are deemed to have acted so far beyond society's norms they are no longer deserving of the chivalry of men and are either de-gendered and treated as "non-women," since "real women" do not commit crimes, or dehumanized and treated as "monsters," that is, even worse than male offenders.[137]

She notes how nuns who were complicit in the killing of civilians were compared during their trial to monsters and vultures.[138] Statements from survivors of the Holocaust stress their shock at the violence carried out by female SS guards.[139]

[132] Ibid. 36.
[133] Gentry & Sjoberg, *Beyond Mothers, Monsters, Whores* (n. 38) 12.
[134] Durham & O'Byrne (n. 115) 42.
[135] Ibid. 43.
[136] Julie Rajan, *Women Suicide Bombers: Narratives of violence* (Routledge 2011) 54–55; Gentry & Sjoberg, *Beyond Mothers, Monsters, Whores* (n. 38) 12.
[137] Nicole Hogg, "Women's Participation in the Rwandan Genocide: Mothers or Monsters?" (2010) 92:877 International Review of the Red Cross 69, 100.
[138] Ibid. 99.
[139] Mailänder Elissa, "The Violence of Female Guards in Nazi Concentration Camps (1939-1945): Reflections on the Dynamics and Logics of Power | Sciences Po Mass Violence and Resistance—Research Network" (December 3, 2015), online: violence-female-guards-nazi-concentration-camps-1939-1945-reflections-dynamics-and-logics-p.html last accessed January 19, 2025.

In the Rwandan genocide, Pauline Nyiramasuhuko, who was tried by the International Criminal Tribunal for Rwanda, was described as not being a woman: "She always acted like a man."[140] As Gentry and Sjoberg note: "Their violence makes them bad at being women."[141] The comparison of violent women to monsters builds a narrative that denies female combatants' human or rational agency when they participate in hostilities.

In the following section, I posit that the LTTE, as an ethnonationalist non-State armed group, generated narratives of empowerment around its female combatants. These narratives reveal a complex understanding of agency as it relates to female combatants. Specifically, I analyze how the agentic narratives surrounding the deaths of female suicide attackers subvert the gendered victim–perpetrator binary in IHL. Their suicide attacks demand a more culturally attuned way of viewing how women may exercise in agency while operating within stringent patriarchal structures.

4.3. The contested agency of LTTE's female suicide attackers

In fighting against a State and claiming the right of self-determination themselves, non-State armed groups share a complicated relationship with Statehood in international law. This complexity stems from the fact that, on the one hand, they resist an oppressive State while, on the other hand, aspiring to achieve independent Statehood themselves. Some feminists argue that national identity and gender are inextricably linked, women becoming the symbols of the reproduction of State and/or national identity.[142] The female body came to signify a locus of ownership over which States and non-State militant groups wage their wars and construct national narratives.[143] The non-State armed groups' engagement with Statehood translates to a nuanced relationship with female agency within such armed groups. In grappling with this contested female agency, I challenge the portrayal of women as embodying victimhood within their patriarchal culture in wartime contexts.[144] One manifestation of the gendered nature of

[140] Hogg (n. 137) 100.

[141] Gentry & Sjoberg, *Beyond Mothers, Monsters, Whores* (n. 38) 3.

[142] Ambika Satkunanathan, "Whose Nation? Power, Agency, Gender and Tamil Nationalism" in Asanga Welikala (ed.) *Sri Lankan Republic at 40: Reflections on Constitutional History, Theory and Practice* (Centre for Policy Alternatives 2012).

[143] Rajan (n. 136) 191. Also see Neloufer De Mel, *Militarizing Sri Lanka: Popular Culture, Memory and Narrative in the Armed Conflict* (SAGE 2007).

[144] Darini Rajasingham-Senanayake, "Between Reality and Representation: Women's Agency in War and Post-Conflict Sri Lanka" (2004) 16:2/3 Cultural Dynamics 141, 151–153: "The troubling figure of the LTTE woman soldier—the armed virgin—stands as one of the few highly problematic exceptions to the representation of Tamil women as victims. LTTE women have been portrayed by the wife of an LTTE spokesman as enlightened functionaries of the male leadership of the LTTE. The reality of LTTE women is probably somewhere in between. For while they may have broken out

ethnonationalist struggles is the gender composition of their fighters. Narratives around female suicide attackers in the LTTE challenged the idea that their self-harm stems from helpless victimization at the hands of an oppressive non-State armed group.[145] Through their deaths, female suicide attackers subvert the gendered victim–perpetrator binary that depicts women as blameless victims lacking in agency to engage in political violence.

4.3.1. Female combatants in non-State armed groups

Ethnonationalist armed groups tend to have a higher number of female combatants than State armed forces. This discrepancy exists even with States considered liberal concerning women's rights. For example, in the United States and Canada, women make up around 20 percent of the active-duty military.[146] In comparison, more than 30 percent of combatants in non-State armed groups are women.[147] Studies also indicate that anti-State separatist nationalisms can potentially provide more space for women to participate as combatants than pro-State nationalisms.[148] For example, Chechen women have been visible within the Chechen rebel movement as a whole.[149] The YPJ, an all-female militia battling against Daesh in Rojava, also received public and scholarly attention, particularly after their 2015 defeat of Daesh in Kobane.[150] Indeed, the high casualties and the corresponding need for more combatants inherent to

of the confines of their allotted domesticity and taken on new roles as fighters, it is indeed arguable that they are captive both to the patriarchal nationalist project of the LTTE leader Prabhakaran and the history and experience of oppression by the Sri Lankan military. However, to deny these Tamil nationalist women their agency because they are nationalist is to once again position them within the 'victim' complex, where the militant woman is denied her agency and perceived to be acting out a patriarchal plot."

145 Rajan (n. 136) 143, 148.

146 Lauren Katzenberg, "40 Stories from Women about Life in the Military" New York Times (March 8, 2019), online: https://www.nytimes.com/2019/03/08/magazine/women-military-stories.html last accessed January 19, 2025; National Defence, "Statistics of Women in the Canadian Armed Forces" online: https://www.canada.ca/en/department-national-defence/services/women-in-the-forces/statistics.html last accessed January 19, 2025.

147 Christopher C. Harmon, *Terrorism Today* (Routledge2000) 212.

148 Wood (n. 81) 46; Alison, *Women and Political Violence* (n. 74) 107.

149 Rajan (n. 136) 72: "They detonated explosives virtually every month from 2008 to 2010, and carried out the most deadly of those attacks. In August 2004, Chechen women coordinated attacks on two Russian planes, killing 90, and just recently, in March 2010, they killed 40 in attacks on Moscow's subways. Pape notes that between 1980 and 2003, Chechen rebels employed 14 women bombers, comprising 60 percent of its suicide missions.151 Other research reveals that between 2000 and 2006, women were involved in 70 percent of suicide missions and managed 50 percent of those without men."

150 Bahar Şimşek & Joost Jongerden, "Gender Revolution in Rojava: The Voices beyond Tabloid Geopolitics" (2018) 26:4 Geopolitics 1023, 1024.

conducting asymmetrical warfare would be one way of explaining higher female recruits in non-State armed groups. However, such reasoning would barely scratch the surface of such groups' political workings and the narratives they construct around their female combatants. Ethnonationalist armed groups often couple their secessionist movements with a message for women's liberation. These movements, by challenging the patriarchal construct of the State, also promote a curious tipping of the scales on gender dynamics. Therefore, national liberation movements and women's liberation find common ground in their resistance to the patriarchal State. Karen Knop suggests that by rejecting the centrality of the State, women can work through non-State groups to influence the development, interpretation, and implementation of international law by States. This allows women's interests and concerns not to be exclusively defined by State borders. Challenging State authority offers space for women to identify themselves through their gender in combination with factors such as religion or ethnicity, extraneous to the State.[151] In this manner, ethnonationalist movements provide a space for engaging with how these multiple identities shape women's agency in combat situations. National liberation movements become an avenue, albeit an imperfect one, for women to liberate themselves from patriarchal constraints.[152]

In some wartime contexts, female combatants in non-State armed groups are depicted as enjoying agency in their status "as fighters that they had never previously enjoyed".[153] For instance, the LTTE has often projected female liberation ascritical to their national liberation movement, encouraging them to fight against the state.[154] Adele Balasingham describes the female LTTE cadres known as the Birds of Freedom:

> Women in combat belong to a totally new world, a world outside a normal woman's life. And that is what makes these women fighters so interesting and admirable. They have taken up a life that bears little resemblance at all to the ordinary existence of women. They have literally flourished under such conditions and created for themselves, not only a new women's military structure, but also a legend of fighting capability and bravery.[155]

[151] Karen Knop, "Re/Statements: Feminism and State Sovereignty in International Law Symposium: Feminist Inquiries into International Law" (1993) 3:2 Transnational Law & Contemporary Problems 293, 308–309. Her argument on networks outside the state structure, however, is limited to civil society and to nongovernmental organizations (NGOs).

[152] Satkunanathan (n. 142): as she argues, this is not to say that this is the only way that women can become active participants in wartime political contexts.

[153] Gardam & Jarvis (n. 71) 50.

[154] Parashar (n. 4) 240.

[155] Balasingham (n. 14); De Mel (n. 143) 204; N. Malathy & Radha d'Souza, *A Fleeting Moment in My Country: The Last Years of the LTTE De-Facto State* (Clarity Press 2012) 105.

The allusion in this statement to a "normal woman's life" is an implicit rejection of the male normativity the State embeds in its law, as well as the patriarchal elements of the culture in which Tamil women grow up.[156] To further the overhauling of this ordinary existence of women, the LTTE is also stated to have introduced anti-dowry legislation, and been strict on domestic violence and rape.[157] Therefore, the LTTE can be seen as having created an alternate legal framework that competes with the State law, which offers a new imagination of women and their capacity to contribute to a project that upends traditional structures.

Consistent with its narrative of female empowerment, the LTTE portrayed female fighters as "the ultimate symbol of women's liberation."[158] In this narrative, the female fighter of the LTTE is considered to be necessarily more attuned to the cause of women's liberation as a result of their role as a combatant.[159] These female cadres were uniformed in trousers and shirts, an outfit that civilian Tamil women would not have worn traditionally.[160] Women participated in combat operations equally to male combatants. Balasingham writes, "[W]hen young Tamil women join the LTTE, they are trained for combat. There is no doubt that the women cadres will be deployed in battle": women fighters were "exposed to rural and urban guerrilla warfare, face to face battles," and commando raids.[161] Anthropologist Margaret Trawick was initially "skeptical that a woman might attain liberation by joining the LTTE." However, a female combatant she interviewed seemed to have convinced her that a woman can feel liberated with a gun in her hands. Trawick records the combatant stating:

> As soon as you get married, you have to look after children. We will raise our children and grow old. When we grow old, we will die. There is a difference between that kind of death and the death of a fighter. Rather than that kind of death, I would prefer this kind of death. It is a heroic death. A historic death. A sacrificial death.[162]

156 Satkunanathan (n. 142).

157 Parashar (n. 4) 243. Rajasingham-Senanayake (n. 144) 154: "[W]omen who suffer domestic violence and are physically abused by their spouses now complain to the LTTE cadres who take appropriate action. At the first complaint, the abusive spouse is given a warning, on the second he is fined and if there is a third complaint, he might end up in the LTTE jail. There are also reports that women now sit at LTTE local courts and arbitrate local disputes in the 'uncleared areas.'"

158 Miranda Alison, "'In the War Front, We Never Think that We Are Women': Women, Gender, and the Liberation Tamil Tigers of Eelam" in Laura Sjoberg & Caron E. Gentry (eds.) *Women, Gender, and Terrorism* (University of Georgia Press 2011) 131, 137.

159 Malathy & d'Souza (n. 155).

160 Margaret Trawick, "Reasons for Violence: A Preliminary Ethnographic Account of the LTTE" (1997) 20:1 South Asia Journal of South Asian Studies 153, 161.

161 Balasingham (n. 14).

162 Trawick (n. 160) 172.

She contrasts her combatancy to a life where one is merely subject to social conventions with no apparent agency to carve one's own path. Her reference to the term "sacrifice" taps into narratives, as elaborated in chapter 2, where deaths are seen as agentic. Rather than being victimized by her potential death, she identifies as a hero, the agentic protagonist who rescues helpless victims. The avenue offered by the LTTE allows a female fighter to imagine a narrative of her life that is given meaning through an agentic death. This agency manifests in a "privileged degree of physical power and mobility . . . freeing her from some of the constraints of a mortal, gendered body."[163] These women perhaps did not enjoy multiple avenues from which to choose. Yet their narratives indicate that they felt a sense of control over their own destiny in fighting for a nationalist cause.

The use of female combatants was, moreover, a tactic through which the LTTE ridiculed the State that oppressed it: "[N]othing feminizes masculinity like being beat by a girl."[164] A female combatant of the LTTE recounts the story of how a group of all-female fighters attacked and chased male soldiers of the State armed forces: "We were only girls, no boys. We chased and chased and fought."[165] Trawick notes that these female combatants were gratified in the knowledge that they could "send a crowd of armed men fleeing for their lives and humiliating themselves in fear of 'girls' ".[166] However, this ridicule stems from the patriarchal misconception that women are weaker beings, and therefore, it is shameful to be physically overpowered by them. This feeds into the indoctrination within masculine institutions such as the military which derides the"feminine" or the "effeminate".[167] This type of resistance to patriarchy does not challenge the foundational bias that being successful in military endeavors is a masculine trait and reveals that non-State armed groups can use female combatants to further entrench systemic gender biases.

The LTTE's incorporation of female combatants into their troops was to some extent accompanied by an effort to erase aspects of their gendered identity. Through their intensive military training, they were de-sexualized to become "armed virgins" or "birds of freedom", thus denying them their sexuality and enforcing androgyny.[168] As Caron E. Gentry and Sojberg point out,

> Women who have "men's jobs" do not enter them on a gender-equal or gender-neutral playing field. A woman in a man's job is a "woman who can make it as a man," not because the masculine values required to do that job have been

163 Ibid. 169.
164 Gentry & Sjoberg, *Beyond Mothers, Monsters, Whores* (n. 38) 19.
165 Trawick (n. 160) 173.
166 Ibid. 177.
167 Alison, *Women and Political Violence* (n. 74) 97.
168 Alison, " 'In the War Front We Never Think That We Are Women' " (n. 158) 140.

> questioned or changed, but because she adopts those values, qualifying as masculine despite her womanhood.[169]

Thus, historically, women who joined militaries have often disguised themselves as men.[170] In the LTTE, female combatants were subsumed into a male normativity. Their combatants have frequently been called "the boys" or "our boys," in spite of the prominent role of women in the LTTE since the 1990s.[171] Arguably, for female cadres not to be stigmatized, they have been trained and prepared like men.[172] This leads to women having to "exchange aspects of their gender identity for the masculine version."[173] Integrating women into existing power structures without changing the gender biases inherent within them can make female fighters be seen as props of a male-dominated military structure, instead of transforming it.[174] Therefore, an approach that integrates women into militaries alone does not solve problems stemming from patriarchy ingrained in the military. This argument carries merit and is important to combat the structural nature of patriarchal values. However, its merits can be appreciated without implying that female combatants integrated into these structures lack agency. Implying so can disregard the agentic narratives that are both self-constructed and socially generated around female combatants' lives and deaths.

Despite their narratives of female liberation, ethnonationalist movements, such as the LTTE, are products of the culture in which they are formed. They are, therefore, not impervious to promoting patriarchal systems. Enloe highlights this tension between female agency and imposition of patriarchy in nationalist non-State armed groups: "thousands of women have discovered in nationalist movements a new public persona and an opening for new political participation"; simultaneously, "they often have been treated by male nationalist leaders and intellectuals chiefly as symbols—patriarchally sculpted symbols—of the nation."[175] Her statement evokes how crossing from the private to the public sphere allows female fighters to become active political agents. However, even while being political actors, they risk being pigeonholed as symbols serving a masculinist military agenda. Likewise, when women engage in violence, it is still seen as a need to belong and nurture; "a way of taking care of and being loyal to men".[176]

[169] Gentry & Sjoberg, *Beyond Mothers, Monsters, Whores* (n. 38) 9.

[170] Rajan (n. 136) 62: "as exemplified by Joan of Arc." See also Susan Crane, "Clothing and Gender Definition: Joan of Arc" (1996) 26:2 Journal of Medieval and Early Modern Studies 297.

[171] Alison, "Cogs in the Wheel?" (n. 25) 37.

[172] Mia Bloom, *Dying to Kill: The Allure of Suicide Terror* (Columbia University Press 2007) 158.

[173] Gentry & Sjoberg, *Beyond Mothers, Monsters, Whores* (n. 38) 9.

[174] Joshua S. Goldstein, *War and Gender: How Gender Shapes the War System and Vice Versa* (Cambridge University Press 2001) 41.

[175] Enloe, *Bananas, Beaches and Bases* (n. 38) 87. Also see Cynthia H. Enloe, *Maneuvers: The International Politics of Militarizing Women's Lives* (University of California Press 2000).

[176] Gentry & Sjoberg, *Beyond Mothers, Monsters, Whores* (n. 38) 12.

This is exemplified by the image of the woman holding a rifle and a baby as is found in liberation movements across the world.[177] A "mother-warrior" construction of womanhood emerged in late 1990s about Tamil women, resulting in "gun-and-baby representations".[178] Seen in light of the wider Tamil cultural context, attached to this image of motherhood is a life-giving and self-sacrificing element.

The complex nature of female combatants' agency becomes apparent in how the LTTE has attempted to "straddle Tamil cultural puritanism with a radical disregard for traditional caste and gender hierarchies".[179] Swati Parashar claims that while it seems evident that the LTTE's female combatants have shifted from their private and domestic sphere, whether their status within the LTTE demonstratescollective or individual empowerment, remains contested.[180] Some scholars argue that the LTTE reproduced within their ranks "the inferior status of women within the patriarchal and conservative Tamil society".[181] It explicitly condemned any form of physical contact between its members, including premarital sexual contact: "A senior LTTE woman combatant called Urmila formed a relationship with Uma Maheswaran, one of Prabhakaran's closest associates. The liaison was frowned upon and resulted in the expulsion of the couple from the LTTE causing factionalism within the group."[182] The restrictions on marriage between combatants changed with Prabhakaran's marriage on October 1, 1984. A marriage committee was initiated within the LTTE movement, where an assembly of elders was responsible for arranging marriages between members, which can be seen as an extension of traditional Tamil customs.[183] In propagating such values, it can be argued that the LTTE reinforced existing patterns of Tamil gender constructions on female sexuality.[184] However, Tamara Herath argues that a notable difference between Tamil marriage practices and that of the LTTE was that LTTE women had a say in the choice of the proposed marital partner and was not constrained within a class or caste: "By being able to contribute their

[177] Goldstein (n. 174) 81.
[178] Alison, "'In the War Front We Never Think That We Are Women'" (n. 158) 139.
[179] Rajasingham-Senanayake (n. 144) 156.
[180] Parashar (n. 4) 242.
[181] Ibid. 241.
[182] Neloufer De Mel, "Body Politics: (Re)cognising the Female Suicide Bomber in Sri Lanka": (2016) 11:1 Indian Journal of Gender Studies 75, 83: "The fear of sexual intimacy is grounded in the strict disciplinarian codes decreed by Prabhakaran for his LTTE cadres. Others who were found having illicit love affairs were executed on Prabhakaran's orders. A couple who were guards at Prabhakaran's heavily fortified Base One Four Camp in the Mullative jungle was caught by the leader. The woman was pregnant. Despite the pleas for their lives, both male and pregnant female guards were executed. In 2002 an LTTE female cadre who became pregnant following an affair with an LTTE male combatant at the Rupaskulam LTTE camp in the eastern Amparai district committed suicide by biting on her cyanide capsule. Following this incident, the LTTE transferred all its female cadre out of this camp to Batticoloa."
[183] Bloom, *Bombshell* (n. 2) 156.
[184] Jordan & Denov (n. 24) 51.

own view about whom they wish to marry, the women combatants control if they wish to accept the proposal that was brought to them."[185] In any event, the onus of maintaining discipline in the organization was placed on the women, by upholding women combatants for their sexual morality and overall good behavior with regard to the opposite sex.

Another contested space for female combatants' agency is how national liberation was prioritized within the LTTE, as opposed to female empowerment. Narratives of female LTTE combatants subordinates their gender vis-à-vis the goal of national liberation.[186] The LTTE projected female cadres' self-sacrifice as being central to their value for their movement.[187] Kim Jordan and Myriam Denov argue that the public respect for female soldiers depends on how they are perceived to be acting as "saviors" of the Tamil culture, making the well-being of the nation reliant on women's "traditional caregiving role".[188] Ethnonationalist movements can also fail to serve the women who participate in them, given that women's liberation is often seen as secondary to the achievement of Statehood. Once Statehood is achieved, the nationalist movement becomes the oppressive entity it strove to defeat. According to LTTE ideology, the only way for women to gain equality was through the nationalist movement.[189] Prabhakaran himself has stated that while the women's liberation movement is an integral part of the greater Tamil struggle, only women who are involved with the Tamil nationalist struggle can achieve liberation for women.[190] This statement demonstrates how inadequately the LTTE was committed to the cause of female liberation, perhaps instrumentalizing its message to keep up female combatants' morale. Some female cadres, too, considered feminist goals of emancipation a secondary matter: "The liberation of the whole nation is the priority, and personal [female] empowerment will come later."[191] It is debatable that female combatants' exercise of agency on the battlefield is faulty because they prioritized national liberation over female empowerment. To do so would be to judge what types of decisions are agentic and what others are less so.

Scholarship on the relational theory of autonomy has debated whether the substance of a woman's actions should factor in the construction of narratives of agency around her. Marina Oshana has defended a substantive relational theory of autonomy.[192] According to her, a strongly substantive conception requires

[185] Tamara Herath, "Women Identity in Contemporary Conflicts: The Case of the LTTE" (Ann Arbor: UMI Dissertation Publishing 2011) 137: "When a man (either from civic society or from the ranks of the LITE) is interested in marrying a combatant woman or vice versa, a proposal of marriage is sent to the leader of the woman combatant's unit, seeking the woman's views."

[186] Rajasingham-Senanayake (n. 144) 163.

[187] Rajan (n. 136) 245.

[188] Jordan & Denov (n. 24) 57.

[189] Alison, "Cogs in the Wheel?" (n. 25) 43.

[190] Ibid. 46.

[191] Jordan & Denov (n. 24) 55.

[192] See Marina Oshana, *Personal Autonomy in Society* (Routledge 2006).

an agentic person to subscribe to values consistent with the ideal of autonomy. Therefore, this concept "incorporates content-laden, normative specifications about the social situation of the autonomous person or about the values and commitments she embraces."[193] This approach would view the LTTE female cadre who took first interest in national liberation rather than in female empowerment as needing to embody the ideal values required for her agency to be recognized. John Christman has critiqued this substantive view of agency as being excessively demanding.[194] He argues that adopting a relational theory of autonomy should not result in the denial of variability in self-conception and the multiplicities of identity of the self across time and context.[195] Autonomy is not inimical to communal and social structures. Instead, they shape human identities.[196] There is merit to Christman's critique of Oshana's substantive relational theory. Treating autonomy as accommodating of diverse values, separates one's own cultural biases from interfering with the assessment of how women with plural identities, including female combatants of the LTTE, exercise their agency. Feminist scholars have struggled to come to terms with the complex agency presented in these narratives of female combatants.[197] Darini Rajasingham-Senanayake thus notes that rather than depicting women who navigate patriarchal cultures to find new spaces of autonomy as victims, it is important to acknowledge that their exercise of agency is ambivalent and thus defies neat boxes.[198]

Deaths of female suicide attackers are often seen through a substantive relational lens of agency, which subjects their actions to value judgments. Julie Rajan claims that women could be more susceptible to engaging in suicide attacks than men, given their socialization in patriarchal Asian cultures, where women are more often than not taught to put themselves second and their family, community, and honor first.[199] These narratives depict female suicide attackers as promoting expectations of reproduction and self-sacrifice in patriarchal societies by transforming the womb into a weapon, "as suicide bombers detonate the explosive belts around their waists."[200] How these narratives are presented tend to dilute the agentic nature of their deaths. Insights from a inclusive and relational understanding of agency, however, caution us not to dismiss an act

[193] Marina Oshana, "Is Social-Relational Autonomy a Plausible Ideal?" in Marina Oshana (ed.) *Personal Autonomy and Social Oppression* (Routledge 2014) 3.

[194] John Christman, "Relational Autonomy, Liberal Individualism, and the Social Constitution of Selves" (2004) 117:1/2 Philosophical Studies: An International Journal for Philosophy in the Analytic Tradition 143.

[195] Ibid. 145.

[196] Ibid. 146.

[197] Rajasingham-Senanayake (n. 144) 142.

[198] Ibid. 148.

[199] Rajan (n. 136) 242.

[200] Parashar (n. 4) 239.

as non-agentic simply because its meaning is found in how the actor relates to other persons and values in her culture. The contested nature of agency in female combatants within the LTTE has a direct impact on how IHL relates to its female suicide attackers. In the section that follows, I will show how, through their deaths, female suicide attackers present a subversive agency that challenges the gendered victim–perpetrator binary in IHL.

4.3.2. Female suicide attackers' death as subverting binaries

Not only does IHL view victims and perpetrators as falling into mutually exclusive categories, but within its framework, these categories are also subject to gender biases. This means that women, who, as a class, are considered helpless victims in wartime, are deemed incapable of occupying the place of perpetrators with deviant agency. The complexity with which cultural narratives portray female suicide attackers' agency challenges this dichotomy. Charli Carpenter notes that an overly complicated issue can "create a cognitive dissonance" and draw attention away from issues that do not fit its established framework.[201] One factor that increases the likelihood of such dissonance is the extent to which "a problem requires a complex understanding of political victimization and vulnerability."[202] The female suicide attacker in the LTTE holds qualities of both the perpetrator and the victim, and therefore, generates dissonance in how IHL assesses agency in combatant deaths.

First, suicide attackers, regardless of their gender, tend to be characterized by a sense of vulnerability and weakness that is not employed in narratives on the ordinary combatant. Kamikaze pilots, for example, were compared to cherry blossoms, connoting a sense of fragility.[203] This may be explained by the fact that a suicide attacker is defined by the certainty of their vulnerability to death. It would seem then that in the case of female suicide bombers, this perceived weakness is compounded. Added to the stereotypical image of the fragile woman is the intense fragility of her life. For example, Matthew D. Kirk argues that the Western media's portrayal of female Palestinian suicide attackers focused on their gendered and vulnerable bodies, with the effect of diluting their political agency.[204] The female suicide attacker's use of

[201] Charli Carpenter, *Forgetting Children Born of War: Setting the Human Rights Agenda in Bosnia and Beyond* (Columbia University Press 2010) 43.

[202] Ibid. Also see Erica Bouris, *Complex Political Victims* (Kumarian Press 2007).

[203] Emiko Ohnuki-Tierney, *Kamikaze, Cherry Blossoms and Nationalisms: The Militarization of Aesthetics in Japanese History* (University of Chicago Press 2002) 23.

[204] Matthew D. Kirk, "Islam, Veiling & Political Agency: The Visual Performativity of Palestinian Female Suicide Bombers in Broadcast News Media" (2022) 30:3 Atlantic Journal of Communication 278, 284.

her body as a weapon is treated as an embodiment of the destructive power of patriarchy's control over the female body. In these narratives that question women's agency when they engage in political violence, they are treated as victims of an oppressive culture.

However, narratives arising from within the LTTE add ambiguity to its female suicide attackers' status as victims. In a Black Tiger Day speech, LTTE leader Prabakaran stated:

> I have groomed my weak brethren into a strong weapon called Black Tigers. They possess an iron will, yet their hearts are so very soft. They have deep human characteristics of perceiving the advancement of the interest of the people through their own annihilation.[205]

This statement juxtaposes the opposing notions of weakness and strength. The Black Tigers are weak with soft hearts, making them perceptive to their own people's interests. Evocation of emotionality, weakness, their ability to empathize with others, and devotion to the well-being of others aligns these fighters with the gender normative narratives that put women in a care-giving role. While many such narratives may also classify women as victims, Prabakaran evokes a language of agency in relation to the Black Tigers. Their weakness makes them a "strong weapon." Their emotions are presented as being complementary to an "iron will." They exercise this unwavering intention to accomplish their annihilation. Therefore, this statement does not depict them as being victims of self-harm. It refuses to subscribe to the mutually exclusive binary of victim and perpetrator status. Rather, they are presented as agentic actors who use features of victimhood to strengthen them as agentic actors.

Testimonies from female suicide bombers of the LTTE also evoke multifaceted images of female agency.[206] As Black Tigers, they would be told how and when they would die. Female suicide attackers saw this certainty over their death as a form of empowerment:[207]

> Menake, like other women in the organization, believed that death was sanctified in some way. For her, the main difference between Black Tigers and regular Tamil Tigers was that the regular Tigers didn't know when they would be killed. Black Tigers knew precisely when they would achieve their ultimate destiny.[208]

205 Bloom, *Dying to Kill* (n. 172) 64.
206 Parashar (n. 4) 243.
207 Bloom, *Dying to Kill* (n. 172) 160.
208 Ibid. 168.

This sense of agency and empowerment that female fighters seem to achieve through their death makes their narrative a complex one. Their death makes them powerful agents of violence, seemingly in control of their destiny and that of others. Their tendency to find strength in the certainty of death contrasts with narratives that speak of survivors' agency. What I point to here is the shift in the discourse on violence against women, from referring to women who suffered violence as helpless victims to treating them as agentic survivors.[209] However, embedded in this idea of survival is the fact that they are alive. Suicide attackers, while eschewing victimhood, do not also fit into the label of a survivor in its traditional sense. Their act of death is what gives them agency. Therefore, they are survived by narratives of agency constructed around their death.

Second, women who carry out violent political acts are villainized as perpetrators for deviating from their expected gender roles. Miranda Alison notes that the female fighters in the LTTE have often been represented in "the media and discussed among ordinary people (Tamil and Sinhalese) as being more violent and more terrifying" than male combatants: young men described themselves as "absolutely terrified of the women cadres of the LTTE."[210] These claims contribute to narratives portraying political violent women as monsters .[211] First, specific narratives on women suicide bombers have represented them in ways that question their mental condition and political consciousness.[212] These narratives of madness and irrationality deny them rational agency. However, this denial of agency should be juxtaposed with the scholarly approaches to the act of suicide itself. Michael J. Kral argues that suicide is a conscious and active choice that can occur only when an individual has the intention to stop their own life.[213] Therefore, this focus on the thoughts and intentionality of the suicide attacker separates her from the narrative of irrationality that often surrounds women who engage in political violence. The voluntary nature of the act of suicide grants the female suicide attacker agency and humanizes her.

In addition to narratives that attribute madness to female suicide attackers, some others associate deviance and immorality with their actions. An example of this moral deviance is the case where female suicide attackers feign pregnancy

[209] See Kaitlin M. Boyle & Kimberly B. Rogers, "Beyond the Rape 'Victim'–'Survivor' Binary: How Race, Gender, and Identity Processes Interact to Shape Distress" (2020) 35:2 Sociological Forum 323; Michael Papendick & Gerd Bohner, "Passive Victim–Strong Survivor? Perceived Meaning of Labels Applied to Women Who Were Raped" (2017) 12:5 PLoS ONE e0177550. https://doi.org/10.1371/journal.pone.0177550.

[210] Alison, "'In the War Front We Never Think That We Are Women'" (n. 158) 141.

[211] Ibid.

[212] Rajan (n. 136) 39: "Although male suicide bombers have been depicted as mentally unstable by scholars such as the Israeli Ariel Merari, women, in comparison, have been projected as *particularly* emotionally and mentally unstable, as excessive forms of social deviance."

[213] Michael J. Kral, "Suicide as Social Logic" (1994) 24:3 Suicide and Life-Threatening Behavior 245, 248.

to carry out their attacks. How the Sri Lankan government dealt with the attack carried out on April 25, 2006 by twenty-one-year-old Kugenthirasah is a case in point. Kugenthirasah blew herself up in the military headquarters in Colombo, killing eleven and injuring over twenty. The attack targeted the recently appointed Army Chief of Staff, Lieutenant General Sarath Fonseka, who was injured in the attack. The case garnered an excessive amount of interest, especially regarding whether she had been pregnant at the time of her death. The Criminal Investigation Department of Sri Lanka went so far as to send Kugenthirasah's blood samples abroad to determine whether she had been pregnant. Questions about Kugenthirasah's condition were finally put to rest when it was determined that she had indeed been pregnant. While this does not state anything about whether Kugenthirasah herself was aware of her pregnancy, it adds another layer of deviance and shock to her act of violence. It signals a denial of motherhood and makes her a perpetrator for targeting not only the enemy but her fetus. Especially in a context such as Sri Lanka, where abortion is considered a crime, her criminality is magnified, at least as far as domestic law is concerned.

The heightened shock of suicide by a pregnant woman also feeds into a gendered vision of how women's agency becomes limited when participating in the workforce. It is seen as acceptable for women to be excluded from work involving high levels of danger because danger to the female body constitutes a potential danger to the fetus.[214] Women who participate in military combat, therefore, potentially expose not only themselves but the life of the fetus to danger. Women's bodies cease to be just their own and within their control but instead become vessels of reproduction. Militaries have employed various measures to manage pregnancies during combat missions.[215] Revolutionary Armed Forces of Colombia (FARC), a non-State armed group in Colombia had a strong policy against pregnancy and carried out forced abortions.[216] As per IHRL, right

[214] Sally Sheldon, "Reconceiving Masculinity: Imagining Men's Reproductive Bodies in Law" (1999) 26:2 Journal of Law and Society 129, 133.

[215] April S. Fitzgerald et al., "A Primer on the Unique Challenges of Female Soldiers" Reproductive Issues in a War-Ready Culture" (2013) 178:5 Military Medicine 511, 511; Todd S. Albright et al., "Pregnancy during Operation Iraqi Freedom/Operation Enduring Freedom" (2007) 172:5 Military Medicine 511, 511; Max Fisher, "Military Pregnancy Ban: What's the Point?" The Atlantic (December 22, 2009), online: https://www.theatlantic.com/politics/archive/2009/12/military-pregnancy-ban-what-s-the-point/347173/ last accessed January 27, 2025: "Major General Anthony Cucolo, who commanded the forces in northern Iraq, officially prohibited pregnancy, a rule that would allow for punishing any military woman who got pregnant, as well as the military man responsible. This command was later rescinded." "Baby birth shock for soldier on Afghanistan deployment," *BBC News* (September 20, 2012), online: https://www.bbc.com/news/uk-19657646.

[216] CEDAW, General Recommendation 30 (n. 60); Rebecca J. Cook & Verónica Undurraga, "Article 12" Marsha A. Freeman, Christine Chinkin, & Beate Rudolf (eds.) *The UN Convention on the Elimination of All Forms of Discrimination against Women: A Commentary* (Oxford University Press 2012) 311, 320: "The CEDAW Committee has established that States parties are required to ensure that Sexual and Reproductive Health services include 'emergency contraception; maternal health services, including antenatal care ... safe abortion services; [and] post-abortion care.'"

to life begins at birth and women have the right to make decisions about their reproductive health.[217] Forced abortions would violate IHL's prohibition against violence to life and person, including mutilation, cruel treatment, torture, and outrages upon personal dignity.[218] While IHL treaties make no express reference to whether a woman has a right to abortion,[219] their provisions, which cater to protecting pregnant women, indicate that IHL does place value on preserving the life of the fetus.[220] In this larger framework of IHL, which makes the life of a woman more valuable for being pregnant, a suicide attacker who decides to terminate her life while carrying a fetus becomes a subversive actor.

Women's ability to feign pregnancy to control how others die also acts as a reversal of pregnancy being a site where the State controls women's bodies.[221] Non-State armed groups instrumentalize this tactic by training female combatants "how to walk and sit as if they were pregnant while carrying explosives around their waists".[222] Rajan unpacks how female suicide attackers generate a new site of agency for women who engage in violence, thus:

> By feigning pregnancy, women bombers not only mimic the visual register of the pregnant woman, but further reveal it to be something that can be superficially and easily presented, no different than wearing a disguise; often, women place the bomb over their abdomen to simulate pregnancy. As such, women bombers who feign pregnancy to execute attacks entirely undermine the authority of the male gaze.[223]

These women utilize the one characteristic that is inaccessible to men and, therefore, which is the marker that is used to distinguish them from the other, to engage in political violence and enter a domain reserved for men. By pretending to

[217] "Colombia's Female FARC Fighters Wage a New War, for Gender Parity" New Humanitarian (September 7, 2017), online https://www.thenewhumanitarian.org/feature/2017/09/07/colombia-s-female-farc-fighters-wage-new-war-gender-parity last accessed January 27, 2025: "If you're a guerrilla, you have to take contraception," said Victoria Sandino, a senior FARC leader who was the group's representative on a gender subcommission during peace talks in Havana, Cuba. She said it was a requirement because FARC was in an active war. If guerrillas got pregnant and wanted to keep the baby, they had to leave the group. If they wanted to stay, they had to abort, said Sandino."

[218] First Geneva Convention (n. 47) Article 3; Second Geneva Convention (n. 47) Article 3; Third Geneva Convention (n. 47) Article 3; Fourth Geneva Convention (n. 47) Article 3; Updated Commentary to the Third Geneva Convention (n. 56) para. 734.

[219] Akila Radhakrishnan, Elena Sarver, & Grant Shubin, "Protecting Safe Abortion in Humanitarian Settings: Overcoming Legal and Policy Barriers" (2017) 25:51 Reproductive Health Matters 40, 42: these authors argue that IHL provisions dealing with wounded and sick and the prohibition on cruel and inhumane treatment can be interpreted to include a requirement to provide access to safe abortions. Rome Statute (n. 69) Article 7(2)(f): according to this article, the definition of "forced pregnancy should not be interpreted as affecting national laws on pregnancy."

[220] Third Geneva Convention (n. 47) Article 14(2).

[221] Rajan (n. 136) 290–291.

[222] Bloom, *Bombshell* (n. 2) 154.

[223] Rajan (n. 136) 289.

be pregnant to increase the likelihood of carrying out a successful attack, the female suicide bomber thwarts the idea ingrained in IHL provisions that women's pregnancy makes them incapable of entering the domain of war and, therefore, must be protected from violence. They go from being the helpless pregnant mother who needs to be protected from being a victim of war to someone who uses this pregnancy trope to become a more lethal weapon.

Female suicide attackers further subvert the gendered public–private divide that IHL institutionalizes within a State-centric and hypermasculinized structure of warfare. With female combatants blowing themselves up in acts of violent resistance against the State, the separatist movement finds an opportunity to project the State as failing in its duty to exercise its gendered role as protector of the weak and vulnerable. In doing so, female suicide attackers challenge the State's masculine authority over its population. In a domain where women are made invisible by referring to them as "one of the boys" even when fighting as combatants, the female suicide attacker demands that her gender no longer remain invisible: she does not conform to the image of a soldier who bears arms openly and, therefore, does not fit into the State-centric notion of how a combatant should look or behave.[224] Bearing arms openly is a public act. Thus, militancy continues to be associated with the public domain reserved for men and governed by international law. While being incorporated within a military structure, the way female suicide attackers carry out attacks often does not conform to traditional military tactics. The way they were carried out required privacy: the weapon is concealed close to her body, in her private space, and she goes close to her target and shares in their deaths. At the same time, these attackers subvert the privacy attached to the female body by using it to carry out acts of violence in the public theater of war. Their suicidal violence co-opts the public–private divide in IHL's gendered idea of warfare to their advantage, even as they are carried out in public spaces for political purposes.

The female suicide attacker also does not attempt to hide her femininity and sexuality to become an actor of violence. Instead of suppressing their femininity, female suicide bombers use their gender and the tropes attached to it as a tool that makes them more lethal. By dressing in feminine attire, they project themselves as women in need of protection. Most often, they are dressed in conservative attire, playing into the trope that a woman's body needs to be protected to maintain her modesty. These garments serve the additional purpose of providing cover for their bomb. Without having to give up on their femininity, therefore, they use the conservative notions about female sexuality and its limits to carry out their act of violence. This act of violence gains their honor in the eyes

[224] De Mel, "Body Politics" (n. 182) 76: "It is called a terrorist attack, an act outside the mainstream 'legitimate' violence unleashed by a military force."

of the rebel movement. They exploit the inconsistency with which IHL defines the notion of honor. They instrumentalize the feminine idea of honor to gain access to the notion of honor reserved for warriors. In this manner, the female suicide attacker, through her death, simultaneously occupies the positions of an agentic warrior, a victim of self-harm borne by a patriarchal military structure, and a perpetrator who engages in violence unbecoming of a woman. She both challenges and subverts the gendered binary in IHL that frames who is deemed to be capable of exercising agency when dying in combat.

4.4. Conclusion

IHL embodies a public–private/divide that is inherently patriarchal, and the State-centric nature of IHL exacerbates this divide. When coupled with the fact that it regulates war, which is a masculinized domain, it tends to mirror patriarchal exclusionary practices as seen in military cultures. Given that in IHL, women are categorized as weak and vulnerable, it also views women through their reproductive function or as persons whose honor is contingent on sexual purity. These stereotypes that IHL attaches to women lead to women being viewed as victims of war. When women become participants of political violence, thereby deviating from the role IHL assigns to them, their agency is considered deviant or irrational. Non-State armed groups, while not devoid of patriarchy, operate outside this State-centric structure propped up by IHL. This results in a distinct relationship between these armed groups and female combatants' agency. This agency is complex and ambivalent, and it challenges the way IHL attempts to place women into neat binary categories of victims or perpetrators. The female suicide attacker subverts IHL's State-centricity by engaging in violence that challenges its public–private divide. The female suicide attacker resists the notion that women are characterized by their role as mothers and that their sexuality needs to be contained for female honor to be protected. By engaging in an inherently intentional and voluntary act, she also challenges how women who engage in political violence are perceived as irrational monsters. By claiming agency over her own death, she eschews neat boxes created by IHL for victims and perpetrators.

5

Jihadi Martyrdom Operations and IHL: Between the Secular and the Religious

5.1. Introduction

The shockwaves created by the attack of September 11, 2001, when members of Al-Qaeda intentionally crashed two planes into the Twin Towers of the World Trade Center in New York City and the American Airlines Flight that crashed into the Pentagon in Arlington, Virginia, have been etched into the collective memory of the global community and generated significant scholarly attention on suicide attacks.[1] This attack is only one of the many suicide attacks carried out by Al-Qaeda,[2] which was established in 1988 under the leadership of Osama Bin Laden to establish Islamic governments across the world.[3] Bin Laden, in his fatwas and communications, had cited religious motivations for conducting attacks against the United States and other countries that, according to him, challenge Islam.[4] Rohan Gunaratna notes that "[m]artyrdom is assigned the highest priority by Al Qaeda's volunteers" and that "[k]illing and dying for Allah are viewed as the highest form of sacrifice. . . . This explains why an unusually high percentage of Al Qaeda attacks are suicide operations."[5] Likewise, Al-Qaeda has used suicide attacks, or what have been characterized by Islamic armed groups as "martyrdom operations," in prosecuting a militant interpretation of the Islamic concept of *jihad*.

[1] Michael C. Horowitz, "The Rise and Spread of Suicide Bombing" (2015) 18 Annual Review of Political Science 69, 69.

[2] See Yoram Schweitzer & Sari Goldstein Ferber, *Al-Qaeda and the Internationalization of Suicide Terrorism, Memorandum No. 78* (Tel Aviv University, Jaffee Center for Strategic Studies 2005).

[3] For a more elaborate account, see Peter L. Bergen, *The Osama bin Laden I Know: An Oral History of al Qaeda's Leader* (1st ed., Free Press 2006).

[4] "Full text: bin Laden's 'letter to America'" The Guardian (November 24, 2002), online: http://www.theguardian.com/world/2002/nov/24/theobserver last accessed January 19, 2025; Osama Bin Laden's 1996 fatwa first published in *Al Quds Al Arabi*, a London-based newspaper, in August 1996, online: https://is.muni.cz/el/1423/jaro2010/MVZ203/OBL___AQ__Fatwa_1996.pdf last accessed January 27, 2025.

[5] Rohan Gunaratna, *Inside Al Qaeda: Global Network of Terror* (Columbia University Press 2002) 91.

Suicide Attacks and International Humanitarian Law. Vishakha V. Wijenayake, Oxford University Press.
 DOI: 10.1093/9780197812174.003.0005

At the outset, I adopt the term "martyrdom operations" to refer to suicide attacks carried out by Islamic armed groups, acknowledging that this term is ideologically loaded. This shift in terminology from suicide attacks to martyrdom operations is significant for several reasons. First, there is a distinction between the concepts of suicide and martyrdom that becomes crucial to armed groups who attempt to justify such attacks by resorting to religious texts. Suicide is considered *haram* (prohibited) in Islam as opposed to martyrdom operations carried out in the pursuit of *jihad*. The purity of intention of the person carrying out such attacks plays a crucial role in this distinction.[6] Thus, armed groups have played a role in defining martyrdom operations and distinguishing them from suicide attacks.

On the one hand, given that legal pluralism requires the recognition that wartime practices are shaped by multiple actors that go beyond nation-States, examining the narrative concepts adopted by these armed groups on their terms is important. On the other hand, it would be remiss not to underscore that many scholars have argued that these operations, whether they harm civilians or not, are contrary to Islamic principles. Reid Hutchins argues that suicide attacks are a distortion of Islamic teachings and that suicide which is *haram* in Islam has been reframed as martyrdom by terrorist organizations, which is followed by a false conflation between martyrdom and *jihad*.[7] The study of how communal interpretations of religious scripture can lead to violence does not in any way imply that religious scripture itself is permissive of it. However, in analyzing how armed groups have used martyrdom operations, this chapter does not aspire to uncover religious truths or delve into which interpretation of Islam is more accurate in relation to distinguishing between suicide and martyrdom. It merely attempts to understand the process through which armed groups have utilized religious interpretations to give meaning to specific practices they carried out during wartime. According to Clifford Geertz, "[f]or an anthropologist, the importance of religion lies in its capacity to serve, for an individual or a group, as a source of general, yet distinctive, conceptions of the world, the self, and the relations between them."[8] Similarly, this chapter focuses on how armed groups have used Islam to justify the use of martyrdom operations and how these religious justifications raise curious questions about International Humanitarian Law's (IHL) relationship with religion.

As will be elaborated later in this chapter, in interpretations of the Qur'an through *hadith*, references to the term *shahid*, meaning witness, have been used

[6] David Jan Slavicek, "Deconstructing the Shariatic Justification of Suicide Bombings" (2008) 31:6 Studies in Conflict and Terrorism 553, 555–556.

[7] Reid Hutchins, "Islam and Suicide Terrorism: Separating Fact from Fiction" (2017) 9:11 Counter Terrorist Trends and Analyses 7, 8.

[8] Clifford Geertz, *The Interpretation of Cultures: Selected Essays* (Basic Books 1973) 123.

to describe martyrs, tracing as further back as to the time of the Prophet during military action in Medina.[9] Likewise, Bernard K. Freamon notes that, although recently these attacks have been used more frequently to support the goal of a military *jihad*, their theological foundations are found in a "long and rich martyrological tradition" that predate twentieth-century militarism.[10] In modern times, the early justifications of martyrdom operations through the interpretation of Islamic principles came from Shi'a scholars. David Jan Slavicek states that "[t]he shariatic justification of suicide bombings was pioneered by Shi'ite scholars in Iraq in the 1960s and 1970s, adopted and implemented by Lebanese and Iranian militants in the 1980s, by Palestinian militants in the 1990s and subsequently globalized by Al-Qaeda."[11]

Revolutionary Iran under Ayatollah Khomeini used Shi'ite principles to frame self-sacrificial violence as both religious duty and political necessity.[12] Inspired by the martyrdom of Imam Husayn at Karbala, Khomeini encouraged acts of self-sacrifice as emblems of resistance to tyranny.[13] In 680 CE, Husayn, grandson of the Prophet Muhammad, and a small band of companions were massacred at Karbala by Yazid's Umayyad forces. Yazid, the Sunni Caliph ruling from Damascus, sought to secure his authority, but Husayn, rejecting tyranny, refused to compromise. Despite the political and military dangers, Husayn journeyed to Kufa to support the Shi'a opposition. Surrounded by Yazid's vast army at Karbala, Husayn and his group faced certain death. His speech before the final battle emphasized martyrdom as a response to oppression and injustice, declaring his mission to exemplify truth and divine purpose. Husayn and his seventy-two companions were killed, their bodies mutilated, and their heads paraded as trophies. This event shaped Shi'a theology, making Husayn's martyrdom a symbol of resistance against tyranny and a model for self-sacrifice in the path of God. Given Husayn's stand against oppression in Karbala, his martyrdom was an apt inspiration for Shi'ite ulama in light of the rise of "secularism and colonialism" attributed to Sunni leadership in Iraq, including Najaf.[14] Khomeini worked closely with the Shi'ite movement in Iraq prior to condemning the Shah's regime in Iran and propagated a reinterpretation of martyrdom that actively advocated for self-annihilation.[15] The Basij militia, comprising untrained young boys and older men, became a symbol of this ideology.[16] They participated in

[9] Bernard K. Freamon, "Martyrdom, Suicide, and the Islamic Law of War: A Short Legal History" (2003) 27:1 Fordham International Law Journal 299, 319.
[10] Ibid. 303.
[11] Slavicek (n. 6) 554.
[12] Radhika Halder, *Understanding Suicide Terrorism* (Routledge 2019) 36.
[13] Ibid.
[14] Freamon (n. 9) 337.
[15] Ibid. 340.
[16] Halder (n. 12) 37.

"human wave attacks," with death being anticipated as an honorable act. Figures like Mohammad Hosein Fahmideh, a child martyr, were glorified to inspire further self-sacrificial acts for the Iranian cause.[17]

Hizbu'llah also adopted this culture of martyrdom, conducting many suicide attacks during the early 1980s. The group's ideology was influenced by Muhammad Husayn Fadlallah who had ties to militant Shi'ite movements in Iraq and Iran, who addressed all Muslims advocating for a globalized form of *jihad*. Prominently, in 1983, a suicide truck bombing against the US embassy in Beirut was carried out by Islamic Jihad, a precursor to Hizbu'llah, an armed group formed in Lebanon, killing US military personnel among others.[18] Hizbu'llah's globalized approach to *jihad* extended to the Palestinian struggle. Palestinian armed groups, with the Palestinian Islamic Jihad (PIJ) and Islamic Resistance Movement (Hamas), started engaging in suicide attacks, including in the First and Second *Intifada*, borrowing the idea of martyrdom as interpreted by Hizbu'llah.[19]

Martyrdom operations have increased in number and been globalized in the last few decades. In the period following the 9/11 attack, affiliates of Al-Qaeda have proliferated across the globe including Al-Qaeda in Aceh, Saudi Arabia, and Yemen.[20] In Southeast Asia, an Indonesian Islamic armed group Jemaah Islamiyah trained by Al-Qaeda has since the 1990s conducted martyrdom operations in furtherance of *jihad*.[21] Al-Qaeda affiliate, Islamic Jihad in Yemen, has carried out martyrdom operations, of which one of the more well-known attacks was conducted against the US embassy in 2008. During the attack, two suicide car bombs killed sixteen persons.[22] Similarly, in Somalia, Al-Shabaab is an armed group that has maintained relations with Al-Qaeda. According to a study conducted by the Combating Terrorism Center at West Point, since their formation in 2005 through October 2017, Al-Shabaab has carried out at least

[17] Ibid. 38.

[18] Zachary Keck & Matthew Sparks, "The Shia Shift: Why Iran and Hezbollah Abandoned Martyrdom," National Interest (May 28, 2018), online: https://nationalinterest.org/feature/the-shia-shift-why-iran-hezbollah-abandoned-martyrdom-25992 last accessed January 19, 2025; Kendall Bianchi, "Letters from Home: Hezbollah Mothers and the Culture of Martyrdom," CTC Sentinel (February 15, 2018) 20; Freamon (n. 9) 355.

[19] Tamara Zieve, "This Week in History: Terror Attack on Bus 405," The Jerusalem Post, (July 1, 2012) online: https://www.jpost.com/Features/In-Thespotlight/This-Week-In-History-Terror-attack-on-Bus-405 last accessed January 19, 2025: The 1989 bus attack carried out by PIJ is considered a suicide attack even though the attacker survived; Matthew Levitt, *Hamas: Politics, Charity, and Terrorism in the Service of Jihad* (Yale University Press 2006) 11.

[20] John Rollins, "Al Qaeda and Affiliates: Historical Perspective, Global Presence, and Implications for U.S. Policy" CRS Report for Congress (Congressional Research Service 2010) 10–11.

[21] Muhaemin Latif, "A Preliminary Study of Jemaah Islamiyah in Indonesia and The Doctrine of Suicide Bombing" (2012) 1:1 Journal of Islamic Civilization in Southeast Asia 107, 114.

[22] "Yemen arrests 19 after U.S. embassy attack" *Reuters* (September 18, 2008), online: https://www.reuters.com/article/worldNews/idUSREE77062120080918 last accessed January 19, 2025.

155 suicide attacks.[23] The increase in the number of armed groups affiliated with Al-Qaeda has also meant an increasing fragmentation and factionalism among them. Perhaps the most infamous of these offshoots has been Al-Qaeda in Mesopotamia, founded by Abu Musab al Zarqawi in 2004, which became active after the US-led invasion of Iraq in 2003 (later the Jihadists' Advisory Council in Iraq).[24] Following Zarqawi's death, his successor Abu Hamza al-Muhajir joined Abu Umar al-Baghdadi's Islamic State of Iraq.[25] Splitting from Al-Qaeda, Al-Qaeda in Iraq morphed into Islamic State of Iraq and Syria (ISIS), headed by al-Baghdadi and became influential beginning in 2013.[26] In 2014, they declared that the group would be known as the Islamic State (IS). In January 2021, the group took responsibility for a suicide attack in Baghdad that killed thirty-two people and injured over one hundred, an example of one of many martyrdom operations they conducted.[27] Other armed groups have declared their allegiance to IS: Boko Haram, an armed group based in Nigeria, pledged allegiance to IS in 2015,[28] and have in turn engaged in suicide attacks, often using female suicide attackers.[29] The emergence of IS in Somalia in 201 has led to conflicts between this armed group and the Al-Qaeda affiliate Al-Shabaab.[30]

Jihadi Salafism can be seen as a common thread that ties together most of these armed groups that have engaged in suicide attacks in the last two decades. Salafism is a movement within Sunni Islam that encapsulates a wide range of actors and followers who are united by their observance of a strict interpretation of the Qur'an, which attempts to emulate Prophet Muhammad and "the first three generations of Muslims as closely and in as many spheres of life as possible."[31] Although Salafis share a common methodological approach to Islamic

[23] Jason Warner & Ellen Chapin, "Targeted Terror: The Suicide Bombers of al-Shabaab" (Combating Terrorism Center 2018) 7.

[24] Omar Mekky, *Islamic Jihadism and the Laws of War: A Conversation in International and Islamic Law Languages* (Oxford University Press 2023) 36.

[25] Ibid.

[26] Wilson Center, "Timeline: the Rise, Spread, and Fall of the Islamic State" (October 28, 2019), online: https://www.wilsoncenter.org/article/timeline-the-rise-spread-and-fall-the-islamic-state last accessed January 19, 2025.

[27] "ISIL takes responsibility for deadly Bagdad suicide bombings" Al-Jazeera (January 22, 2021) online: https://www.aljazeera.com/news/2021/1/22/islamic-state-claims-deadly-baghdad-twin-suicide-bombing last accessed January 19, 2025.

[28] Jacob Zenn, "Boko Haram's Conquest for the Caliphate: How Al Qaeda Helped Islamic State Acquire Territory" (2020) 43:2 Studies in Conflict and Terrorism 89, 89.

[29] Serwaa Allotey-Pappoe & Afua Agyeiwaa Lamptey, "Pawns, Puppets or Weapons of Choice: Examining Boko Haram's Use of Female Suicide Bombers in Nigeria" (KAIPTC Occasional Paper #42 September 2019) 5.

[30] Caleb Weiss, "Reigniting the Rivalry: The Islamic State in Somalia vs. al-Shabaab" (2019) 12:4 Combating Terrorism Center Sentinel 29, 32.

[31] Joas Wagemakers, "Jihadi-Salafism in Jordan and the Syrian Conflict: Divisions Overcome Unity" (2018) 41:3 Studies in Conflict and Terrorism 191, 191; Mohammed M. Hafez, "The Alchemy of Martyrdom: Jihadi Salafism and Debates over Suicide Bombings in the Muslim World" (2010) 38:3 Asian Journal of Social Science 364, 365.

jurisprudence, factions have emerged based on varying interpretations of contemporary.[32] Not all of the varying factions within Salafism engage in violent acts. One faction, Jihadi Salafism, is closely associated with armed groups that carry out wartime martyrdom operations.[33] They are also influenced by scholars such as Sayyid Qutb, an Egyptian Salafist and a leading member of the Muslim Brotherhood, who advocated for a radical and political interpretation of offensive *jihad*.[34] Even within armed groups that identify with Jihadi Salafism, it would be an overstatement to claim that all such groups engage in martyrdom operations. For example, in Mozambique where ISIS arguably operates, no such attacks have been recorded, at least to date.[35]

This chapter recognizes that armed groups with strong affiliations to Islam cannot be seen as being exclusively oriented toward achieving religious goals, or that even when they are, they do not operate identically. As Omar Mekky notes, Islamic law itself evolved to adapt to political and cultural contexts as they spread across diverse regions.[36] Studying suicide attacks in Mindanao, Southern Philippines, in light of the local cultural practice of ritual suicide named parang-sabil, Kenneth Yeo Yaoren argues that "the acceptance of suicide bombing is socialised within a geographic area."[37] These armed groups belong to different branches of Islam, as is the case of Hizbu'llah, which identifies with Shia Islam as compared to armed groups that are Sunni.[38] Even among the armed groups within Sunni Islam, some of them espouse territorial and nationalist aspirations that are specific to their contexts. For example, Al-Shabaab, while seeking an Islamic State, has prioritized "political and social aims in Somalia . . . through a Somali and Somalia-centric lens."[39]

[32] Quintan Wiktorowicz, "Anatomy of the Salafi Movement" (2006) 29:3 Studies in Conflict and Terrorism 207, 208.

[33] Farhana Ali & Jerrold Post, "The History and Evolution of Martyrdom in the Service of Defensive Jihad: An Analysis of Suicide Bombers in Current Conflicts" (2008) 75:2 Social Research: An International Quarterly 615, 617.

[34] Rashmi Singh, *Hamas and Suicide Terrorism: Multi-causal and Multi-level Approaches* (Taylor & Francis 2013) 98–99; Paul Rogers, *Irregular War: The New Threat from the Margins* (I. B. Tauris 2017) 28.

[35] "Mozambique Palma attack: Why IS involvement is exaggerated" BBC News, (April 16, 2021) online: https://www.bbc.com/news/world-africa-56773012 last accessed January 19, 2025.

[36] Mekky (n. 24) 12.

[37] Kenneth Yeo Yaoren, "Suicide Bombings in Mindanao" Policy Brief, International Center for Counter Terrorism (November 2021) 11: However, at the same time, he is cautious not to claim that what he terms "extremist practices" stem from local culture, noting that "[t]he local Tausug community generally do not condone suicide bombing." Also see Sajed S. Ingilan, "Tausug's Identity in Parang Sabil: A Critical Discourse Analysis" (2018) 22:1 CMU Journal of Science 37.

[38] See Kelly F. Kafeyan, "Sunni and Shiite Martyrdom: A Comparative Analysis of Historical and Contemporary Expressions" Submitted in partial fulfillment of the requirements for the degree of Master of Arts in Security Studies (Middle East, South Asia, Sub-Saharan Africa) Naval and Postgraduate School (2010).

[39] Tricia Bacon, "Inside the Minds of Somalia's Ascendant Insurgents: An Identity, Mind, Emotions, and Perceptions Analysis of al-Shabaab" Program on Extremism, George Washington University (March 2022) 39.

The Israeli–Palestine conflict, while bearing a significant religious dimension, also contains a claim to self-determination and statehood as per international law principles, negotiated in traditional sites such as the United Nations (UN). Hamas has operated within this context in pursuance of Palestinian statehood while also having distinct religious roots, its parent organization being the Muslim Brotherhood. The group has played a key role in linking the idea of sacrifice to the Islamic concepts of *jihad* and *istish'had* (martyrdom).[40] Even so, the Palestinian struggle is often characterized as a nationalist and territorial one, even by armed groups that profess motivations pertaining to Jihadi Salafism.[41] On the other hand, IS has not subscribed to international law norms such as aspiring for statehood through the UN framework and has instead advocated for a Caliphate.[42] Therefore, despite the strong religious influences within armed groups, they are influenced by other cultural, political, and economic factors that impact how they carry out their attacks and how they choose to engage with the international legal framework.

While scholars have noted that the theological interpretations used to justify martyrdom operations would not allow for female martyrs in combat operations, armed groups falling under the broad umbrella of jihadist groups have had women carrying out such attacks. The Second *Intifada* saw female martyrs affiliated to Palestinian armed groups such as the Al-Aqsa Brigades, Islamic Jihad, and Hamas engaging in martyrdom operations.[43] Similarly, the early 2000s saw suicide martyrs, also known as Black Widows, operating under the command of Chechen rebel Shamil Basayev.[44] Scholarship examining the role of female martyrs acknowledges the political nature of their acts in addition to religious influences that motivate them. Hamamra, Gould, and Mayaleh posit that "[t]he involvement of female shahids in the public sphere of politics reveals . . . the wartime reconfiguration of religion and nationalism."[45] Muhaimin Zulhair Achsin, examining the role of culture in martyrdom operations carried out by women affiliated with jihadi groups in Indonesia, argues that rather than being influenced purely by Islam, in certain regions of Indonesia, the cultural

[40] Singh (n. 34) 87.

[41] Assaf Moghadam, "Motives for Martyrdom: Al-Qaida, Salafi Jihad, and the Spread of Suicide Attacks" (2008) 33:3 International Security 46, 66: "Groups coded as mainstream Islamist groups, such as Hamas and Palestinian Islamic Jihad, differ from Salafi jihadist groups in that they participate in the political process—something that Salafi jihadist groups consider heretical, given that all power must derive from God, not from the electorate."

[42] Mekky (n. 24) 38.

[43] Bilal Hamamra, Rebecca Ruth Gould, & Asala Mayaleh, "Against the Depoliticisation of Palestinian Female Shahids" (2024) 45:13 Third World Quarterly 1929, 1930.

[44] Bill Gillespie, "The Avenging Black Widows" CBC News (March 30, 2010) online: https://www.cbc.ca/news/world/the-avenging-black-widows-1.866287 last accessed January 19, 2025.

[45] Hamamra, Gould, & Mayaleh (n. 43) 1931.

landscape constitutes an amalgamation of religious influences including Islam, Hinduism, and Christianity.[46]

Central to this chapter is the question of how, and whether, wartime practices can be framed through a religious lens (i.e., martyrdom operations) that is distinct from secular approaches to similar phenomena (i.e., suicide attacks). Given that the book approaches IHL's relationship with suicide attacks, recognizing the culturally specific nature of warfare, it is crucial to examine the notion of martyrdom that belongs to the non-Western-centric legal realms. The Islamic religion has a long-standing "martyrological tradition" central to the ideological and legal justifications used by contemporary military jihadists to rationalize self-annihilatory acts of violence.[47] While there is an assumption that martyrdom is a singular ideology, the language of martyrdom is not static or fixed.[48] It is a concept that has fragmented and gained complexity through manifold processes of meaning-making.[49] These cultural narratives are increasingly becoming globablized with armed groups often feeding into a larger narrative of supporting an offensive *jihad*, and thereby contributing to an accumulation of religious texts that support martyrdom operations. For example, the Palestinian cause has been utilized by the jihadist armed groups around the world to justify their claim that Muslims are victimized and under threat by Zionist and Western forces. Hamas has fed into this narrative by calling the Arab and Islamic masses everywhere to shoulder their duty to Palestine.[50]

While acknowledging the significant body of scholarship that analyzes not only fundamentalist Islamic militancy but also their use of martyrdom operations, this chapter notes that this phenomenon has not received sufficient attention from IHL.[51] The existing literature assessing how such suicide attacks violate IHL's prohibition on directly targeting civilians does not provide a holistic appraisal of this phenomenon.[52] As in the other chapters of this book,

[46] Muhaimin Zulhair Achsin, "Culture and Role of Women in Terrorism in Indonesia. Case Studies: Suicide Bombings in Surabaya and Sibolga" (2019) 8:5 International Journal of Engineering and Advanced Technology 873, 874.

[47] Freamon (n. 9) 303.

[48] Candida R. Moss, *Ancient Christian Martyrdom: Diverse Practices, Theologies, and Traditions* (Yale University Press 2012) 6.

[49] L. Michael White, "Review of A Noble Death: Suicide and Martyrdom among Christians and Jews in Antiquity" (1994) 113:2 Journal of Biblical Literature 358, 359.

[50] The Covenant of the Islamic Resistance Movement (1988), online: https://fas.org/irp/world/para/docs/880818a.htm last accessed January 19, 2025.

[51] Muhammad Munir, "Suicide Attacks and Islamic Law" (2008) 90:869 International Review of the Red Cross 71 discusses this issue from an Islamic *jus in bello* point of view.

[52] Donna E. Arzt, "Can Law Halt the Violence? Palestinian Suicide Bombings and Israeli 'Targeted Assassinations' under International Humanitarian Law" (2004) 11 ILSA Journal of International & Comparative Law 357; Hans-Peter Gasser, "Acts of Terror, 'Terrorism' and International Humanitarian Law" (2002) 84:847 International Review of the Red Cross 547; Roger Tansey, "A Legal Analysis of Suicide Bombing: Blowing up the Law of War?" (2004) 5 Harvard Kennedy School Review 45.

I focus on the less explored aspect of suicide attacks in terms of the death of the suicide attacker (or in this instance the martyr or *shahid*) and how the presumed secular principles of IHL interact with the religious narratives on the agency with which these attackers reached their deaths.

5.2. Warfare in the context of a secular framework

Political philosopher Charles Taylor identifies secularism as a characteristic of modern life, at least in the West or the North Atlantic world. However, secularism extends beyond this region in diverse ways.[53] Talal Asad agrees that secularism is a key aspect of modernity as a political project.[54] He also acknowledges that while secularism emerged as a reaction to religious wars in early modern Christian societies in the West, it is now a framework that extends to non-Christian societies around the world.[55] IHL also projects itself as being a secular framework of law. Its separation from the just war doctrine and its constant attempts to deny its religious roots point in this direction.[56] In IHL treaties, religion has been pushed to a place decoupled from the conduct of hostilities and into a sphere that is exclusively private or humanitarian. This reflects a secular approach to warfare, which carves out specific pockets away from the thick of the battle within which religion is accommodated, based on secular rationality as the primary frame of interacting with the world. As Lena Salaymeh argues, the secular-religious binary itself is a colonial construct, developed within Western contexts but imposed globally through colonialism, which, rather than being neutral or universal, reflects Eurocentric power structures.[57] When applied in international law, particularly IHL, this binary reinforces colonial hierarchies by marginalizing non-Western legal systems. This chapter juxtaposes the presumed secularism of IHL to examine its engagement with religiously motivated wartime practices while adopting a critical lens toward the notion of secularism.

[53] Charles Taylor, *A Secular Age* (Harvard University Press 2007) 1.

[54] Talal Asad, *Formations of the Secular: Christianity, Islam, Modernity* (Stanford University Press 2003) 13.

[55] Ibid. 2, 4: He speaks of Taylor's notion of imagined communities to argue that "[t]he modern nation as an imagined community is always mediated through constructed images."

[56] See François Bugnion, "Just War, War of Aggression and International Humanitarian Law" (2002) 84:867 International Review of the Red Cross 523; Andrew Bartles-Smith, "Religion and International Humanitarian Law" (2022) 104:920–921 International Review of the Red Cross 1725.

[57] Lena Salaymeh, "Comparing Islamic and International Laws of War: Orthodoxy, 'Heresy,' and Secularization in the Category of Civilians" (2021) 69:1 The American Journal of Comparative Law 136, 161.

5.2.1. International law's religious undercurrents

The dominant narrative of international law views it as a secular framework. Accordingly, Lauri Mälksoo states that "[t]he current predominant understanding in the field is that culture and religion are somewhat irrelevant for international law since international law became universal and a common humanity was pledged as its ontological starting point."[58] According to the conventional narrative of how international law developed, its secularization happened gradually through the contributions of various scholars.[59] This narrative strives to place religion merely as a historical influence that has little relevance to international law's current principles or structure. Likewise, David Kennedy argues that the story of the Peace of Westphalia (1648) as birthing the international legal order projects an image where nation-States, and with it order, emerge from the collapse of the Holy Roman Empire and the ruins of the Thirty Years War. Here, international law is perceived as a response to religious wars and to the inadequacies of religion.[60] From this point on, international law is primarily seen as moving forward from religion and the disharmony it created within European communities.[61] This perception that religion has been ousted from the international legal framework discourages the relationship between law and religion from being acknowledged or discussed openly.[62] Therefore, religion often only appears in the margins of international law.

This secular lens has led to (Western) legal scholars largely ignoring the relationship between religion and law, even where the division between the two cannot be maintained in practice.[63] As Carolyn Evans points out, international law's secularity is performative, concealing a more ambiguous and fraught relationship with religion.[64] First, international law's doctrines bear the structure of a belief system that does not encourage critical examinations of the "hidden patterns" of its "modes of legal reasoning."[65] One such hidden pattern that the

[58] Lauri Mälksoo, "Civilizational Diversity as Challenge to the (False) Universality of International Law" (2019) 9:1 Asian Journal of International Law 155, 161.

[59] Antje von Ungern-Sternberg, "Religion and Religious Intervention" in Bardo Fassbender & Anne Peters (eds.) *Oxford Handbook of the History of International Law* (Oxford University Press 2012) 300.

[60] David Kennedy, "Images of Religion in International Legal Theory" in Mark W. Janis & Carolyn Evans (eds.) *Religion and International Law* (Martinus Nijhoff 1999) 146.

[61] Ibid. 148; David Kennedy, "Losing Faith in the Secular: Law, Religion, and the Culture of International Governance" in Janis & Evans (n. 60) 313: "International law understands its birth as a flooding forth from the darkness of religious strife, antidote to the passions of faith, on guard against their re-emergence as ideology."

[62] Carolyn Evans, "The Double-Edged Sword: Religious Influences on International Humanitarian Law" (2005) 6:1 Melbourne Journal of International Law 1, 3.

[63] Ibid. 2.

[64] Ibid. 3.

[65] Jean d'Aspremont, *International Law as a Belief System* (Oxford University Press 2017) 14.

international legal system thrives on is the perceived "rational consensus" within the international community, though international law's truth rests neither on rationalism nor on empiricism but on "the deployment of certain transcendental validators that are unjudged and unprove[n] rationally or empirically."[66] International law's universalist logic, which mirrors religious beliefs in its propensity to view its own epistemology as applicable to all persons irrespective of their cultural or geographical position, underlies the argument that international law consists of a "common heritage with a shared language."[67] The diversity of human experience is diluted by alluding to innate humanity.[68] This illusion of consensus also shapes its relationship with plural views that may emerge from within it.[69] As argued in the introductory chapter, when the law takes the existence of a consensus for granted, it can lead to the emergence of silences in areas where diverse practices challenge that consensus.[70]

Second, international law's secularity can be understood as being performative because its normative premises cannot be separated from its historical Christian influences.[71] Francesco di Vitoria, who pioneered a universal notion of international law, was a theologian by profession and was inspired by Catholicism.[72] Antje von Ungern-Sternberg argues that "in Medieval times, the scholastic concept of natural law was based on a hierarchical set of norms closely interrelated with religion": positive law was founded on these natural law principles. Thus, even positive international law was shaped by religion.[73] Hugo Grotius is credited with presenting a "secularized restatement of natural law", which had previously been at the foundation of international law.[74] However, John D. Haskell claims that Grotius's intent was not to advocate for an agnostic political order, but to demonstrate that "Christianity was left unscathed even

[66] Ibid. 5.

[67] John D. Haskell & Pamela Slotte, "Christianity and International Law: An Introduction" in Pamela Slotte & John D. Haskell (eds.) *Law and Christianity* (Cambridge University Press 2021) 2.

[68] Ibid.

[69] Ibid. 10.

[70] Ibid. 11.

[71] Jeremy Waldron, "A Religious View of the Foundations of International Law" NYU School of Law, Public Law Research Paper No. 11-29 (April 26, 2011).

[72] See Antony Anghie, "Francisco De Vitoria and the Colonial Origins of International Law" (1996) 5:3 Social and Legal Studies 321, 322; Georg Cavallar, *Imperfect Cosmopolis: Studies in the History of International Legal Theory and Cosmopolitan Ideas* (University of Wales Press 2011) 22: He argues that Vitoria's framework of international law was theological and based on a thick Christian understanding of the good life.

[73] Ungern-Sternberg (n. 59) 300: "Human made law (*lex humana*), comprised of *ius gentium*, 'conclusions' from natural law, and *ius civile*, positive law in the form of 'determinations' from natural law."

[74] John D. Haskell, "Hugo Grotius in the Contemporary Memory of International Law: Secularism, Liberalism, and the Politics of Restatement and Denial" in José María Beneyto & David Kennedy (eds.) *New Approaches to International Law: The European and the American Experiences* (T. M. C. Asser Press 2013) 125: Haskell notes that this did not originate with Grotius, but was a common technique for earlier Catholic jurists.

through the use of human 'right reason.'"[75] By resorting to the core tenets of the faith, Grotius was attempting to avoid sectarian disputes within Christianity in Europe.[76] Similarly, Emer de Vattel argues that "the most certain and equitable means of preventing the disorders that may be occasioned by difference of religion, is a universal toleration of all religions which contain no tenets that are dangerous either to morality or to the state."[77] In making this claim, Vattel fails to acknowledge that one's understanding of morality is shaped by the dominant religion of a society, which in this case was Christianity. Likewise, not only was international law theorized initially by theologians rather than legal scholars, but it was also intended to be applied by European nations of Christian faith. The secularization of international law meant universalizing natural law principles with religious undercurrents.

These religious influences also seeped into how the notion of war was conceived in international law, connecting theological foundations of international law with sovereign power, including the power to wage war.[78] For example, the just war theory, which was developed through the writings of religious scholars such as Saints Augustine and Thomas Aquinas is inspired by medieval Christianity.[79] This medieval theory justified wars against infidels.[80] It provided legitimacy to the Crusades, which attempted to extend and enforce "Christendom's normative order, of a universalized natural law, upon neighboring societies."[81] The language of just war theory is still used by States and scholars to justify and analyze contemporary warfare. For example, Asad argues that in the post-9/11 world, there has been a renewed interest in the just war theory to legitimize violence against the non-Christian, Islamic other, whose religiously motivated violence, especially the practice of suicide attacks, is considered barbaric and labeled "terrorism."[82] Pierre-Alexandre Cardinal and Frederic Mégret posit that the otherness of Islam played a significant role in shaping the fault lines of international law according to early just war theories, with war against the Muslim "other"

[75] Ibid. 127.
[76] Ibid.
[77] Emmerich de Vattel, Joseph Chitty, & Edward Duncan Ingraham, *The Law of Nations, or, Principles of the Law of Nature Applied to the Conduct and Affairs of Nations and Sovereigns* (T. & J. W. Johnson 1867) Book I, para. 135.
[78] Costas Douzinas, "Speaking Law: On Bare Theological and Cosmopolitan Sovereignty" in Anne Orford (ed.) *International Law and Its Others* (Cambridge University Press 2006) 36.
[79] John Finnis, *Human Rights and Common Good: Collected Essays Volume III* (Oxford University Press 2011): see chapter titled "War and Peace in the Natural Law Tradition"; Jean Bethke Elshtain, "The Just War Tradition and Natural Law" (2004) 28:3 Fordham International Law Journal 742.
[80] Talal Asad, "Thinking about Terrorism and Just War" (2010) 23:1 Cambridge Review of International Affairs 3, 12.
[81] Pierre-Alexandre Cardinal & Frédéric Mégret, "The Other 'Other': Moors, International Law and the Origin of the Colonial Matrix" in Ayesha Shahid & Ignacio de la Rasilla del Moral (eds.) *International Law and Islam: Historical Explorations* (Brill Nijhoff 2018) 174.
[82] Asad, "Thinking about Terrorism and Just War" (n. 80) 818.

being considered just and validated to enable the spread of a Christian normative order and the universalization of natural law.[83] Wars among Christians, on the other hand, were prohibited.[84] On the one hand, Mekky notes that the mainstream Muslim world perceives international law as deeply rooted in colonial, Western, and Christian traditions that historically depict Islam as a chaotic and violent belief system.[85] On the other hand, Margaret Pettygrove observes that popular American culture often demonizes Islam, linking it to violence and extremism, particularly through suicide bombings, further deepening the chasm between Islamic perspectives and international legal frameworks.[86]

The spread of religion played a vital role in justifying colonial wars. It was considered the right and duty of Christians to propagate their religion and, when hindered, to resort to war against barbarians.[87] Even in the nineteenth and early twentieth centuries, Western scholars continued to identify international law with "civilized" nations, a term roughly equating to those of Christian faith.[88] The international legal order reflected a modernist, liberal, and imperialist fantasy where the colonies of the East were viewed as containing formless richness replete with confusion and with misdirected forces which, if left alone, would be destructive, while the Occident was seen as being responsible for harnessing this chaos and providing meaning and order to the colonies.[89] In this manner, modern international law, including IHL, remains outwardly "secularized," while its historical Eurocentric Christian expansionist undertones continue to be modified and applied to fit new realities.[90]

IHL, too, exists in a constant tension between its religious influences and its aspiration to be accepted as a secular framework. As per Andrew Bartles-Smith, secular narratives constructed around IHL prevent fruitful investigations on its complex relationship with religion "for fear of muddying the waters or jeopardizing the neutrality of IHL or the ICRC."[91] The case for secular and universal foundations of IHL strives to maintain itself notwithstanding the religious diversity of nations and armed groups that are called to implement IHL. The tension between IHL's Eurocentric religious underpinnings and its secular

[83] Cardinal & Mégret (n. 81).
[84] Onuma Yasuaki, *International Law in a Transcivilizational World* (Cambridge University Press 2017) 70.
[85] Mekky (n. 24) 4–6.
[86] Margaret Pettygrove, "Conceptions of War in Islamic Legal Theory and Practice" (2007) 2:3 Macalester Islam Journal 6, 34.
[87] Yasuaki (n. 84) 77.
[88] Ungern-Sternberg (n. 59) 301.
[89] Nathaniel Berman, "'The Appeals of the Orient': Colonized Desire and the War of the Riff" (2004) 2 Brown University Research Paper Series on Law, Social Thought and Global Governance 196, 198.
[90] Cardinal & Mégret (n. 81) 187.
[91] Bartles-Smith (n. 56).

image is evident in the controversy surrounding the use of the Red Cross as a protective and distinctive symbol. The use of this symbol by humanitarian actors has been the source of friction ever since the participation of IHL expanded beyond Christian nations.[92] Its adoption is tied to the role that the International Committee of the Red Cross (ICRC) played in IHL's origin story. Henry Dunant, prior to his creation of the Red Cross Movement, is also credited with having extended the Young Men's Christian Union to the world.[93] Irrespective of whether the creators of the Red Cross had religious intentions in adopting this emblem, Provost argues that what matters is that following its adoption, it was "taken to be a reference to Christianity."[94] Notwithstanding this obvious religious meaning attributed to the Red Cross by non-Christian nations, the ICRC has stuck to a narrative that promotes the nonreligious or secular nature of the emblem.[95] This demonstrates that on a symbolic level, the ICRC has attempted to distance itself from any affiliation to religion, lest it adversely affect its core principles of neutrality and impartiality. Similarly, IHL on a doctrinal level has attempted to shed principles of warfare with religious roots, such as the just war theory, by adopting a neutral approach to all parties involved in a conflict, regardless of the cause and motive of the war.[96] In this manner, IHL has adopted a humanist ethic with the potential to be universalized across cultures.

More recently, the ICRC has attempted to examine IHL principles in the context of Islam, as well as Buddhism and Hinduism. This can be seen as an effort to bring IHL within the idea of a pluralist form of secularism that is "tolerant of religion."[97] This project operates on the premise that "principles of IHL are based on humanitarian principles that are ultimately rooted in the world's religious traditions, and the role of religious leaders and institutions in promoting common humanitarian principles is therefore crucial."[98] Such endeavors are oriented to finding commonalities between religious principles and those of IHL so that the case for IHL's universality becomes strengthened. James Cockayne critiques these efforts to bridge gaps between IHL and religious traditions, noting how they tend to "exhibit subtle orientalism taking the Western system as a yardstick against which the adequacy or compatibility of the oriental Islamic

92 René Provost, "The International Committee of the Red Widget? The Diversity Debate and International Humanitarian Law" (2007) 40:2 Israel Law Review 614, 616.

93 Bernard Gagnebin & Marc Gazay, *Encounter with Henry Dunant* (Georg 1963) 18.

94 Provost, "The International Committee of the Red Widget?" (n. 92) 617.

95 Ibid. 618.

96 Theodor Meron, "The Humanization of Humanitarian Law" (2000) 94:2 The American Journal of International Law 239, 241: "The separation between jus ad bellum and jus in bello results in the uniform, neutral application of the latter, without reference to its distinctions between the rights and obligations of the parties. This separation thus contributes to the practicality of the law of war, the avoidance of preliminary disputes on the character of the war as just or aggressive."

97 Bartles-Smith (n. 56) 1732.

98 The ICRC Global Affairs Team, "Introduction" in Religion and Humanitarian Principles, online: https://blogs.icrc.org/religion-humanitarianprinciples/about/ last accessed January 19, 2025.

'other' is measured."[99] The very fact that special effort needs to be made to bridge IHL with other religious perspectives demonstrates that the Christian influences of IHL are at least subconsciously assumed.

5.2.2. Elements of IHL's secular rationality

One manifestation of how secularism operates in modern society is by framing religion as a private matter separated from the political and State structure.[100] In relation to the Western liberal societies which were the primary focus of his work, Taylor argues that public spaces have been "emptied of God"[101]: the shift to secularism meant that constitutions of States treated religious belief, sentiment, and identity as personal matters belonging to private life,[102] marking a profound disjunction between religion and public language.[103] However, this dichotomy of religion as belonging to private life separated from laws governing public life is false, given that "even if religion is often distinguished from law in Western legal and political philosophy, and largely ignored in legal writing, no such division can be neatly maintained in the real world."[104] First, even in modern Western societies, the contours of religion are often defined by the law.[105] The law actively shapes the boundaries of religion, even in societies that claim to separate the two. In these States, laws determine what qualifies as religion (e.g., in tax exemptions or religious accommodations), regulate religious practices (such as ritual slaughter or dress codes), and decide how religious freedom interacts with other rights. Thus, although often framed as a private matter, the legal system frequently intervenes in managing how religion operates in public and political spheres. Second, some societies do not clearly distinguish between the law and religious precepts. For example, Jihadi-Salafis can be seen not merely as a religious movement but also as forming "legal traditions—often around scholarly personalities—possessing digital institutions and recognized legal authorities to whom the faithful can turn."[106] Therefore, the law and religion are inextricably intertwined, making their separation impractical, if not impossible.

[99] James Cockayne, "Islam and International Humanitarian Law: From a Clash to a Conversation between Civilizations" (2002) 84:847 International Review of the Red Cross 597, 597.
[100] Taylor, *A Secular Age* (n. 53).
[101] Ibid. 2.
[102] Talal Asad, *Genealogies of Religion: Discipline and Reasons of Power in Christianity and Islam* (Johns Hopkins University Press 1993) 205.
[103] James Boyd White, *From Expectation to Experience: Essays on Law and Legal Education* (University of Michigan Press 2000) 128.
[104] Evans (n. 62) 2.
[105] White (n. 103) 130.
[106] Nathan S. French, *And God Knows the Martyrs: Martyrdom and Violence in Jihadi-Salafism* (Oxford University Press 2020) 38.

International law, too, struggles to manage these convergences between religion and law while keeping the former within its private sphere. Elizabeth H. Hurd analyzes the unquestioned acceptance of the secularist division between religion and politics as it relates to international relations.[107] She presents two constructions of secularism in international relations: the laicism model and the Judeo-Christian model. Hurd's description of the laicism model mirrors early international law's attitude toward religion, in that it perceives "[t]he mixing of religion and politics [to be] irrational and dangerous."[108] Giving into this fear of religion as being contrary to rational public relations, an early jurist of international law, Vattel, bifurcates religious worship into public and private acts: "Interior worship is necessary in its own nature; and we ought to confine ourselves to it, in all cases in which it is most convenient."[109] Through this process of excluding religion from the public sphere, the secular domain becomes associated with public authority, rational argument, and tolerance.[110] Vattel further posits that if public worship is necessary, such persons should leave the territory in question and live in a country where such worship is allowed.[111] This would present a false option today, especially as relating to international law. In a universally applicable international legal order, changing territory is insufficient to escape a framework where acts of faith are not recognized within the public sphere. This is particularly the case with IHL, wherein secular principles are universally applied despite the geographical or cultural context an armed conflict occurs.

A study of the evolution of specific IHL provisions exposes how this body of law moves religion away from the public theater of warfare. In Europe, the law of the Catholic Church prohibited its adherents from actively engaging in combat.[112] With the transformation of feudal forces into modern armies, a permanent corps of military chaplains began to emerge in Europe and Colonial America.[113] Article 2 of the Geneva Convention of 1864 offered "the benefit of

[107] Elizabeth Shakman Hurd, *The Politics of Secularism in International Relations* (Princeton University Press 2009) 1: She argues that secularism needs to be examined as a "source of political authority in its own right."

[108] Ibid. 5, 26: She argues that "laicism constantly reinscribes the boundary between public and private, secular and sacred, mundane and metaphysical. The specific contours of this separation, if made explicit, are often legitimated through reference to the dictates of logic, reason, or nature."

[109] Vattel, Chitty, & Ingraham (n. 77) para. 138.

[110] Kennedy, "Losing Faith in the Secular" (n. 61): "[R]eligion is private where the law is public. Religion is what we had before we had law. Religion is the domain of irrationality and charismatic authority, law is the realm of reason and the bureaucratic."

[111] Ibid.

[112] Stefan Lunze, "Serving God and Caesar: Religious Personnel and Their Protection in Armed Conflict" (2004) 86:853 International Review of the Red Cross 69, 70.

[113] Kristina Benson, "The Chaplaincy Exception in International Humanitarian Law: 'American-Born Cleric' Anwar Al-Awlaki and the Global War on Terror" (2014) 1:20 Buffalo Human Rights Law 1, 24.

neutrality" to chaplains.[114] Current IHL provisions maintain this separation of religion from the most public aspect of warfare: conduct of hostilities. This separation is evident in IHL rules about religious persons or objects. Religious objects are protected from attack because they are considered civilian objects or cultural property that is specially protected. Article 24 of the First Geneva Convention states that chaplains attached to the armed forces shall be respected and protected in all circumstances.[115] Chaplains are included in the armed forces and allowed to be present with combatants. The presence of religious personnel on the battlefield caters to the private and spiritual needs of combatants, often their spiritual concerns regarding death, which is a private facet of modern existence.[116] Chaplains' presence within troops acknowledges that religious norms and expectations play a role in defining the value of a soldier's life, actions, and eventual death. While chaplains are excluded from the battle to the extent that they cannot be targeted, their protection depends on their engaging in exclusive religious duties during the conduct of hostilities.[117] They are not permitted to cross the divide between attending to combatants' personal spiritual needs and entering the public domain of conduct of hostilities without losing their status as religious personnel.

The mutual exclusivity between being a chaplain and being a combatant deserves further examination. Religious personnel, by their exclusive spiritual role in IHL, are not meant to participate in hostilities directly. This is consistent with the argument that targeting a person when they do not pose a threat is not morally justifiable. However, others who do not pose a threat, such as legal advisors to armed forces, are nevertheless targetable under IHL. Therefore, chaplains' immunity seems to stem not purely from their lack of direct participation in hostilities but from the fact that IHL considers their religious duties entirely humanitarian, unlike the advisory functions of a military lawyer. If they fight, however, their role will no longer be exclusively religious. A tension is created where persons must choose whether they are combatants or religious

[114] Convention for the Amelioration of the Condition of the Wounded in Armies in the Field, August 22, 1864, Diplomatic Conference, 08.08.1864–22.08.1864, Geneva.

[115] International Committee of the Red Cross (ICRC), Geneva Convention for the Amelioration of the Condition of the Wounded and Sick in Armed Forces in the Field (First Geneva Convention), August 12, 1949, 75 U.N.T.S. 31.

[116] International Committee of the Red Cross, *Commentary on the Third Geneva Convention: Convention (III) Relative to the Treatment of Prisoners of War (Commentaries on the 1949 Geneva Conventions)* (Cambridge University Press 2020), paras. 2391–2393: "The activities of retained religious personnel may include: ministering; holding religious services; taking confessions; giving blessings; overseeing religious classes; conducting religious or spiritual study; visiting the sick; officiating at funerals in accordance with religious rites; and any other activities constituting spiritual assistance.... Religious personnel may also act as personal advisers, receive and forward the last wishes of prisoners of war and provide material assistance to them."

[117] ICRC Customary IHL Study, Rule 27 "Religious Personnel," online: https://ihl-databases.icrc.org/customary-ihl/eng/docs/v1_rul_rule27 last accessed January 19, 2025.

personnel, typifying the strict separation of religion from public acts of warfare, leaving little room for nuance. Moreover, Stefan Lunze argues that spiritual assistance is regarded as a nonpartisan service, althoughreligious personnel are often tasked with the interests of their party.[118] IHL's assumption that religion is a nonpartisan service that can assist combatants irrespective of the party to the conflict to which the combatant belongs reveals another layer of the underlying assumption that IHL is a European imagination of warfare where warring parties are religiously homogeneous.

IHL's sequestration of religion from the conduct of hostilities resonates differently when nationally implemented in diverse cultural contexts through legislation and military manuals. For example, the *Department of Defense War Manual* (2016) of the United States notes that to qualify as religious personnel, individuals must be exclusively engaged in their ministry.[119] However, a study of ICRC's database on national practice relating to religious personnel during armed conflict shows that this secular principle is often not incorporated into laws or manuals by countries that do not conform to a strict secular framework of governance. Israel's *Manual on the Rules of Warfare* (2006), which protects religious personnel as long as they do not take part in hostilities, is an exception to this trend.[120]

A stark comparison of the separation of religion from war can be seen when IHL's treatment of religion is juxtaposed with the code of conduct of the Taliban (*Laiha*). The *Laiha* does not refer to IHL but to Islamic law. There are also no provisions specifically protecting religious personnel. This may be because there is no distinction in this paradigm between those who carry out exclusively religious functions and those who engage in hostilities. According to Article 41 of the *Laiha*, anyone who is appointed as a person with responsibility within their military structure must be "inventive, pious, courageous, compassionate, and generous": "If none [of the candidates] have all these characteristics, then at least inventiveness and piety are required." In this manner, faith in Islam is integrated as a vital characteristic of a military leader. Furthermore, every military squad leader is required to spare special time for jihadi training, as well as religious education of his colleagues.[121] The *Laiha* also recommends that if there is no danger, *mujahids* should worship in the mosque collectively and if going

118 Lunze (n. 112) 79.

119 United States, *Department of Defense War Manual*, para. 4.9.1.3. note 217. Also see Australia, *The Manual of the Law of Armed Conflict*, Australian Defence Doctrine Publication 06.4, 2006, 9.88.

120 Israel, *Rules of Warfare on the Battlefield* (2nd ed., Military Advocate General's Corps Command: IDF School of Military Law 2006) 24.

121 Muhammad Munir, "The Layha for the Mujahideen: An Analysis of the Code of Conduct for the Taliban Fighters under Islamic Law" (2011) 93:881 International Review of the Red Cross 1, 38. This is stated in Article 74. The Islamic Emirate of Afghanistan. The Laiha [Code of Conduct] for Mujahids (2010), a translation of which is provided in this article. Also see Kate Clark, "The Layha: Calling the Taliban to Account," Afghanistan Analysts Network (July 4, 2011).

to the mosque is difficult, they should worship together in their places of residence.[122] Religion is intrinsically interwoven into the military affairs rather than sequestering spirituality away from the conduct of hostilities. In this manner, the *Laiha* requires that religiosity be essential to a combatant's identity.

The public and private spheres that exist in a secular international framework contain their own rationality.[123] Accordingly, in the secular world, rational agency that is not necessarily dependent on a divine explanation has gained prominence as appropriate within the public sphere.[124] This stems from the fact that the modern secular framework is founded on an "Enlightenment fear of the irrational passion and divisiveness of religion."[125] According to the conventional narrative of how international law developed, positive law replaced natural law which was premised on religious principles. It also secularized natural law, replacing its links to religion with links to reason.[126] Therefore, international law encompasses a philosophy of reason as compared to the irrational passions of religion.[127] Religion, as a result, occupies the domain of the nonrational, with connections to themes like myths, magic, and witchcraft.[128] Reason is considered a pillar that holds together an orderly society.[129] A challenge to the established order, including the established order within warfare, is likely to be deemed irrational or unreasonable. The removal of religion from the public sphere is indicative of the modern world's relationship with violence in general, but more particularly revealing of its rejection of pain and suffering that is attributable to religious motivations. Asad argues that

> [a] major motive of secularism has clearly been the desire to end cruelties . . . that religion has so often initiated and justified. . . . This firm linking of institutional religion to cruelty has its roots in Western Europe's experience of religious wars and in the complex movement called the secular Enlightenment.[130]

However, only certain kinds of suffering were sought to be eliminated, while others were considered necessary.[131]

The relationship between secular rationality and international law impacts people's attitudes toward exercising agency when their bodies undergo pain and suffering. Pain is often regarded as inimical to reason. Relatedly, suffering

[122] Ibid. 39. Translation of Article 75 of the Laiha.
[123] Taylor, *A Secular Age* (n. 53) 2.
[124] Ibid. 8.
[125] Evans (n. 62) 3.
[126] Ungern-Sternberg (n. 59) 300.
[127] Kennedy, "Images of Religion" (n. 60) 146; Evans (n. 62) 3.
[128] Asad, *Formations of the Secular* (n. 54) 22.
[129] Taylor, *A Secular Age* (n. 53) 4.
[130] Asad, *Formations of the Secular* (n. 54) 100.
[131] Ibid. 111.

is considered a human condition that secular society must eliminate.[132] John Tasioulas argues that health and human rights constitute core ideas of public reason.[133] The modern West embeds its aversion to human suffering in the notion of rights.[134] Most human rights as recognized under international law attempt to minimize suffering caused to human beings either directly or indirectly. Among these, some rights relate more patently to alleviating human suffering in the form of harm caused to the person.

Prohibition against torture is one such example and is often considered a peremptory norm,[135] indicating that aversion to human suffering is a characteristic feature of the international legal order and that any treaty or rule in international law that contradicts this principle would be void. Furthermore, the idea of universal human rights conceives people "as active cooperators in establishing and ensuring the respect which is due them."[136] Taking individuals to be active participants in this secular project of eliminating suffering translates to their being prevented from exercising their agency to waive their legally protected natural rights.[137] This idea is contained in treating human rights as inalienable. The preamble of the Universal Declaration of Human Rights (UDHR) recognizes "the inherent dignity and the equal and inalienable rights of all members of the human family is the foundation of freedom, justice and peace in the world."[138] In application to specific rights, such as the prohibition against torture as set out in Article 5 of the UDHR, it means that the right cannot be qualified in a manner that allows consenting adults to subject themselves to pain and suffering tantamount to torture.

Developments in International Human Rights Law (IHRL) have also influenced IHL, resulting in what Theodor Meron refers to as the humanization of the law of war.[139] For example, the Geneva Conventions prohibit torture both in international and non-international armed conflicts.[140] Moreover,

[132] Ibid. 67; Taylor, *A Secular Age* (n. 53) 683. According to Taylor, a feature of the modern understanding of respect is the importance of avoiding suffering. John Tasioulas, "Conceptual Overreach Threatens the Quality of Public Reason" *Aeon Essays*, online: https://aeon.co/essays/conceptual-overreach-threatens-the-quality-of-public-reason last accessed January 19, 2025.

[133] Ibid.

[134] Taylor, *A Secular Age* (n. 53) 392.

[135] See Erika de Wet, "The Prohibition of Torture as an International Norm of jus cogens and Its Implications for National and Customary Law" (2004) 15:1 European Journal of International Law 97.

[136] Charles Taylor, *Sources of the Self: The Making of the Modern Identity* (Harvard University Press 1989) 12.

[137] Ibid. 11.

[138] Universal Declaration of Human Rights, U.N. General Assembly, December 10, 1948, 217 A (III).

[139] Meron (n. 96) 245.

[140] Common Article 3 of the 1949 Geneva Conventions prohibits "violence to life and person, in particular . . . cruel treatment and torture [and] outrages upon personal dignity, in particular humiliating and degrading treatment" with respect to persons taking no active part in the hostilities, including members of armed forces who have laid down their arms and those placed *hors de combat*

some provisions in IHL demonstrate that protections in IHL are inalienable. Common Article 7/7/7/8 of the Geneva Conventions states that in no circumstances may protected persons renounce "in part or in entirety the rights secured to them" by the Geneva Conventions. As per the updated Commentary to the Geneva Conventions, this Article indicates that "the rights of protected persons are inalienable."[141] Therefore, no effect is given to any real or purported renunciation of rights by a protected person.[142] Common Articles 6/6/6/7 of the Geneva Conventions state that "[n]o special agreement shall adversely affect the situation of the wounded and sick, of members of the medical personnel or of chaplains, as defined by the present Convention, nor restrict the rights which it confers upon them." Meron argues that Common Article 6/6/6/7 clarifies that rights are granted to protected persons, so that States or armed groups cannot derogate from or limit these rights and therefore performs a similar function to *jus cogens*, resulting in the nullity of such agreements.[143] The Pictet Commentary recognizes that Common Article 6/6/6/7 has been influenced by the UDHR and takes into account the fact that persons in wartime conditions may face pressure to give up on their protections and that it would be difficult to prove such duress.[144] These articles can be interpreted to mean that "the [S]tate is not the sole holder of the rights, [and that] it cannot validly waive them for the individual; the same is true for the individual vis-a-vis the state."[145] According to these scholarly interpretations of these common articles, provisions of the Geneva Conventions are seen as nonderogable by parties to the conflict and inalienable by the individual who benefits from their protections. The ICRC writers comment on Additional Protocol I that "in the eyes of the victim all suffering is superfluous and any injury is unnecessary."[146] This statement reveals that the Commentary takes for granted that all persons would want to avoid suffering if given the choice. Yet, the drafters of IHL treaties and those writing interpretive commentaries felt the need to specify that individuals do not have the right to

by sickness, wounds, detention, or any other cause. Article 12, second paragraph of the 1949 Geneva Convention I provides that violence to wounded and sick members of the armed forces in the field shall be strictly prohibited, in particular torture. Article 12, second paragraph of the 1949 Geneva Convention II provides that violence to wounded, sick and shipwrecked members of the armed forces at sea shall be strictly prohibited, in particular torture.

141 Updated Commentary to the Third Geneva Convention (n. 116) para. 1169.
142 Ibid. para. 1176.
143 Meron (n. 96) 252.
144 Jean S. Pictet (ed.), *The Geneva Conventions of 12 August 1949, Commentary, Volume I, First Geneva Convention for the Amelioration of the Condition of the Wounded in Armies in the Field* (ICRC 1952) 76; Updated Commentary to the Third Geneva Convention (n. 116) para. 1160.
145 René Provost, *International Human Rights and Humanitarian Law* (Cambridge University Press 2002) 28.
146 Bruno Zimmermann et al., *Commentary on the Additional Protocols of 8 June 1977 to the Geneva Conventions of 12 August 1949* (Brill 1987) para. 1428.

renunciate their protections. This implies that IHL presumes that when persons give up their rights to be protected from torture or suffering, they are doing so under duress and not while exercising rational agency.

Regardless of this idea that pain and suffering are antithetical to the rational exercise of agency toward one's well-being, IHL recognizes that those who actively participate in hostilities lose the protections granted to civilians and open themselves to being targeted legally. Individuals who have assumed the role of combatants put their right to life at risk. IHL does not protect combatants from death during combat. As far as combatants exposing their lives to risk, IHL does not take this fact as a renunciation of inalienable rights. While human life is sacred, it is only so to the extent that States have deemed it to be so.[147] Therefore, during wartime, inhuman suffering, as opposed to necessary or inevitable suffering, is regarded as being gratuitous.[148] IHL's rationality mirrors a utilitarian logic which is inimical to senseless suffering inflicted on humans on account of religion.[149] Asad argues that "'[e]xcess' is a concept of measure. An essential aspect of the modern attitude to pain rests on a calculus that defines rational (calculable) actions."[150] This rational approach to suffering can be observed in the principle of proportionality. According to this rule, suffering that is excessive in relation to the anticipated military advantage is considered disproportionate.[151] This demonstrates that one way in which the cruelties of the battlefield are reconciled with modernity's aversion to pain is by treating pain as measurable.[152]

While IHL acknowledges the inevitability of certain types of suffering, its provisions deem some other kinds of suffering as "excessive" and "unnecessary." Customary IHL prohibits the use of means and methods of warfare which are of a nature to cause superfluous injury or unnecessary suffering. The prohibition of superfluous injury or unnecessary suffering has been recognized by the International Court of Justice (ICJ) as a cardinal principle constituting "the fabric of humanitarian law."[153] In doing so, the ICJ defined unnecessary suffering as "harm greater than that unavoidable to achieve legitimate military objectives."[154] According to the ICRC Commentary to Additional Protocol I, this prohibition limits the infliction of unnecessary damage or injury, or the use of violence in an irrational way.[155] Therefore, unnecessary suffering goes against the

[147] Asad, *Formations of the Secular* (n. 54) 117.
[148] Ibid. 113.
[149] Ibid. 106.
[150] Ibid. 123.
[151] Additional Protocol I, Articles 51(5)(b) and 57(2)(a)(iii).
[152] Asad, *Formations of the Secular* (n. 54) 117.
[153] *Legality of the Threat or Use of Nuclear Weapons*, Advisory Opinion, I.C.J. Reports 1996, 226, International Court of Justice (ICJ), July 8, 1996, para. 78.
[154] Ibid. para. 238.
[155] 1987 Commentary to the Additional Protocols (n. 146) para. 1411.

rationality of IHL which is formulated around measuring military necessity. This requires the weighing up of the nature of the injury or the intensity of suffering as compared against "military necessity," to decide whether there is superfluous injury or unnecessary suffering.[156] Therefore, while it is generally lawful to kill a combatant, it is unlawful to inflict suffering that is not necessary to render them *hors de combat*. The Preamble of the 1868 St. Petersburg Declaration Banning Explosive Projectiles under 400 Grammes Weight ("exploding bullets") states:

> [Considering] that the only legitimate object which states should endeavour to accomplish during war is to weaken the military forces of the enemy;
>
> That for this purpose it is sufficient to disable the greatest possible number of men;
>
> That this object would be exceeded by the employment of arms which uselessly aggravate the suffering of disabled men, or render their death inevitable;
>
> That the employment of such arms would therefore be contrary to the laws of humanity.

To locate the meaning of "superfluous injury or unnecessary suffering," it is essential to understand the meaning of the word "necessary" that is implicit in it.[157] The purpose of suffering considered legitimate or necessary within IHL is calculated in the confines of strict military advantage. The rationality of IHL, therefore, would not support a paradigm that includes practices that lead to the inevitable death of combatants in pursuit of objectives that are not measurable from the point of view of strict military advantage.

According to some critics, martyrdom operations in war violate the sanctity of life in a manner that the ordinary combatant engaging in combat of hostilities does not.[158] This distinction can be understood considering how IHL's aspiration to separate religion from the conduct of hostilities has a direct impact on how it perceives contrasting frameworks. As R. Panikkar has argued, such universalist and secular frameworks are merely "one window through which one particular culture envisages a just human order for its individuals. However, those who live in that culture do not see the window. For this they need the help of another culture which sees through another window."[159] To appraise how

[156] Ibid. para. 1428.

[157] Henri Meyrowitz, "The Principle of Superfluous Injury or Unnecessary Suffering: From the Declaration of St. Petersburg of 1868 to Additional Protocol 1 of 1977" (1994) 34:299 International Review of the Red Cross 98, 106.

[158] Meir Hatina, *Martyrdom in Modern Islam: Piety, Power, and Politics* (Cambridge University Press 2014) 204.

[159] R. Panikkar, "Is the Notion of Human Rights a Western Concept?" (1982) 30:120 *Diogenes* 75, 78–79.

martyrdom operations can relate to IHL, it is necessary to view warfare through a multitude of windows, some more religious than others, rather than looking through a purely secular frame on the narratives constructed around combatant deaths.

5.3. Martyrdom operations as religious intentionality

Modernity deems it rational that individuals would want to avoid pain and suffering. Martyrdom operations, being a voluntary form of self-harm, question this assumption. Being a religiously motivated form of self-harm, such attacks invoke the fear that modernity has concerning the perceived nonrationality of religion. Due to this affiliation with a nonlegitimate rationale for self-harm in hostilities, those who carry out martyrdom operations are more likely to be seen as perpetrators. Unlike the case where the law attributes deviant agency to perpetrators, in the case of those who carry out martyrdom operations, religious beliefs also contribute to them being seen as irrational and fanatic in the eyes of secular law. In contrast, in local narratives, combatants carrying out martyrdom operations are seen as agentic actors engaging in spiritual and heroic acts.

5.3.1. Martyrdom operations as public and religious wartime deaths

Enshrined within IHL rules is an attempt to maintain religious neutrality and to sustain the separation of religion from hostilities.[160] However, it is not always possible to separate religion from the public domain of warfare. Religiously motivated armed groups attest to this. The law's efforts to keep religion away from hostilities shape its attitude toward actors who carry out public demonstrations of religion. Hurd argues that the secularism embedded in international law leads to the construction of narratives that view political Islam as transgressing the Western secular public/private binary. The result is that "in contemporary international relations theory and practice, political Islam appears almost exclusively in a transgressive or regressive capacity."[161] Similarly, due to the marginal recognition given to religion in the narrative of international law, when there is an "other" that can be labeled "religious," their otherness is

[160] Hurd (n. 107) 5. This more covert presence of religion in IHL corresponds to the type of secularism in international relations which Hurd refers to as one that emphasizes the role of Christianity "as the foundation for secular public order and democratic political institutions."

[161] Ibid. 11. She adds: "To make this argument is not to deny that there are forms of Islam, such as Al-Qaeda and the Taliban, which are transgressive and even regressive by almost any standard of judgment."

magnified.[162] Accordingly, among different types of violence that take place in warfare, violence that does not operate within a secular model is deemed to be more excessive and extreme than the types of violence that fall within a secular rationality. IHL, in turn, supports this secular framework, and therefore, the depiction of violence as carried out by political Islam is seen as shocking. Given this element of transgression attached to religious violence, those who carry out religiously motivated attacks are more likely to be labeled "perpetrators with deviant agency." This is so as they deviate from the secular framework IHL adopts in warfare.

Martyrdom operations are paradigmatic of this friction between IHL and public religious acts during warfare. The public dimension of death is one of martyrdom's integral features. The label of martyrdom is attributed ex post facto by others.[163] For this label to be attached to death, it requires being witnessed by others. The Arabic term for martyr, *shahid*, appears in the Qur'an "primarily in the sense of "witness"—that is, Muslims should act as a living testimony for the rest of mankind."[164] Similarly, in Qur'anic interpretations an equivalency is made between martyrdom and bearing witness:

> It is often suggested that the reason the Qur'an refers to martyrs as "witnesses" is that the act of martyrdom is viewed as a clear form of testimony in support of the Islamic theological creed. It is through the testimony of the martyr that mankind is able to know the truth of the Islamic theological creed and to be able to distinguish the true believers from the non-believers.[165]

Raphael Israeli connects this notion of bearing witness to martyrdom to the ancient Hebrew idea of *Kiddush Ha-Shem*, which relates to the praising of God's name "in the public square, in speech and in deeds, on every occasion, to the point of sacrificing one's life in that endeavor."[166] Therefore, martyrdom is performed publicly.[167]

Although Islamic martyrdom is now considered a deviation from the secular sensibilities of the Western construct of law, Israeli points out that historically, the Judeo-Christian tradition also viewed martyrdom as a public act and

[162] Kennedy, "Images of Religion" (n. 60) 150–151. These others, for example, Islamic fundamentalism, appear as a powerful threat because it reminds international law of the history it has repressed: "a history that would recast relations between law and state and among our doctrines and theories as repetitions of the work of faith, distinguishing the sacred and the profane. Yet we know we are not faithful, being all reasonable men."

[163] Friedrich Avemarie & Jan Willem van Henten, *Martyrdom and Noble Death: Selected Texts from Graeco-Roman, Jewish and Christian Antiquity* (Routledge 2002) 3.

[164] Hatina (n. 158) 36.

[165] Freamon (n. 9) 319.

[166] Raphael Israeli, *Dying as a Shahid: Martyrs in Islam* (Strategic Book Publishing & Rights Agency 2019) 6.

[167] Ibid. 2.

influenced the notion of *shahid* in Islam.[168] It is not only the person who faces death who engages in the practice of bearing witness. The public nature of the death means that it is also communally witnessed. These people who witness the death sanctify and commemorate this death as heroic martyrdom.[169] It is, therefore, an act that is done in public and then given meaning by the public.

The public dimension of martyrdom makes it a performative act. Performativity relates to the repetitive nature of acts and their ability to generate new realities and meanings.[170] For Judith Butler, performative acts include those that "could and would bring about new social forms."[171] In this framework, a non-State actor who carries out performative acts is exercising agency to challenge an established framework through their act.[172] Nasser Abuharfa alludes to this performative nature of Hamas's use of martyrdom operations and how this led to the creation of a culture of martyrdom in the Palestinian context. He argues that

> [m]artyrdom is the form of contemporary Palestinian resistance that has proved meaningful and captured the imagination of Palestinian publics. To be recognized as a resistance faction, Palestinian groups are compelled to participate in the performance of martyrdom. The cultural discourse of martyrdom has achieved such power that the cultural dynamic is defining the form of engagement and resistance, forcing it on some groups and reorganizing society.[173]

Furthermore, the narratives found in *Dabiq*, a magazine issued by ISIS, memorialize the deaths of martyrs, depicting them as intentional deaths toward the revolutionary goals of ISIS's political project.[174] The deaths of martyrs are given meaning by armed groups and the larger public that views their performance and constitutes an important component of local narratives. This performative dimension of martyrdom shifts attention to the discursive power of these acts, regardless of whether they are considered faithful to Islamic scripture.

These public narratives valorizing martyrdom can incentivize others to become martyrs, thereby sustaining this performative cultural practice. Martyrs are granted an elevated place in the worldview for which they exercise their self-sacrifice. It is presented as a glorified means through which Muslims can fulfill their religious duties.[175] For example, Article 57 of the *Laiha* states that a

168 Ibid. 18.
169 Ibid.
170 Erkan Toguslu, "Caliphate, *Hijrah* and Martyrdom as Performative Narrative in ISIS *Dabiq* Magazine" (2019) 20:1 Politics, Religion & Ideology 94, 96.
171 Judith Butler, "Performative Agency" (2010) 3:2 Journal of Cultural Economy 147, 155.
172 Ibid.
173 Nasser Abufarha, *The Making of a Human Bomb: An Ethnography of Palestinian Resistance* (Duke University Press 2009) 195.
174 Toguslu (n. 170).
175 Munir, "The Layha" (n. 121) 37.

martyrdom attack should be used for important and high-value targets, given that the self-sacrificing heroes of the Islamic Ummah must not be used for low and worthless targets.[176] Accordingly, "martyrs are model figures for the groups who transmit and read the writings devoted to them" and play an important role in "the process of the formation of self-identity."[177] A martyr, facing a hostile situation, chooses death rather than complying with a demand of an authority that often does not belong to their faith.[178] Having to choose between a worldview that is religious and one that is imposed by secular authorities underlay most early Jewish and Christian martyr texts.[179] Those communities that identify with the performance of martyrdom as an act of resistance would be more likely to attribute a positive value to the public act of martyrdom. Therefore, in addition to the tactical advantages that martyrdom operations may offer, they also serve as "cultural capital" and contribute to recruitment and reinforce "collective solidarity".[180] Due to the public nature of martyrdom, it transforms the individual sacrifice of the martyr into a cultural performance that helps in the construction or preservation of the identity of a community. In doing so, martyrdom brings religion from the private sphere to the public square.

In addition to religion, modern society has relegated death to the margins. One example of how death is marginalized is Foucault's analysis in *Discipline and Punish* of how penal law in the nineteenth century shifted away from public torture as punishment to more hidden and covert domains. This indicates a transition from a "culture of spectacle" with public corporal punishment and other torture techniques to "a system where punishment and discipline are internalized and woven into the social institutions through which the character of modern man is shaped."[181] Furthermore, the use of public violence was a demonstration of State authority and the control it exercises over individual lives.[182] Avemarie Friedrich and Jan Willem van Henten posit that in modern Western societies, death has been banished from public life where dying preferably quietly and unconsciously has become the norm.[183] While public executions do take place in the twentieth-century West, by and large they are seen as

[176] Ibid. 36.
[177] Avemarie & Henten (n. 163) 7.
[178] Ibid. 3.
[179] Ibid. 44.
[180] Hatina (n. 158) 49.
[181] Bryan H. Druzin & Anthony S. Wan, "The Theatre of Punishment: Case Studies in the Political Function of Corporal and Capital Punishment" (2015) 14:3 Washington University Global Studies Law Review 357, 365.
[182] Ibid. 366: "The elaborate ceremony of corporal punishment was a drama designed to promote the idea of the State's majesty and its absolute authority in deciding the fate of the individual, displayed and acted out in the most brutal and impactful manner. Such 'performances' underscored the intense asymmetry between the power of the individual and the power of the State."
[183] Avemarie & Henten (n. 163) 1.

> shocking aberrations which have to be hidden. Even the "clean" legal executions, where the death penalty is still in force, are no longer carried out in public, but deep within prison walls. . . . We are much more sensitive to suffering, which we may of course just translate into not wanting to hear about it rather than into any concrete remedial action.[184]

When public deaths do occur, such as in the case of drone strikes, they take place in distant lands and usually against people who have been othered due to their culture, making it easy to ignore them as deaths that occur outside the public space of the modern West.[185] Martyrdom operations bring death to the public sphere and deviate from the marginalization of death to the private sphere.

Martyrdom operations challenge the framing of violence and death as needing to be hidden from the public domain. They are carried out by non-State actors in a manner that mirrors the performative dimension of public executions carried out by States to perpetuate their power over the individual. However, at the same time, they challenge the State given that these deaths are depicted as agentic acts carried out by individuals who belong to non-State armed groups. This contradicts the idea that the sovereign power of the State manages the lives and deaths of its subjects. The agency of the martyr, therefore, becomes a deviant act against the sovereign authority of the State.

Given that they are additionally religiously motivated deaths, their deviance is magnified and presented as an irrational interference with the secular management of death. The next part of this chapter delves more deeply into the notion of pain and suffering as conceived within the secular framework. It examines why, within this model, self-inflicted suffering, and more particularly, voluntary suffering in the name of religion, as seen in martyrdom operations, is considered excessive and, therefore, cannot be understood within the framework of rationality set up within IHL.

5.3.2. The rationality of voluntary suffering and martyrdom operations

Acts of martyrdom have not been exclusive to Islam. However, the way martyrdom has evolved in the context of Christianity differs from how it is perceived today by Islamic jihadist armed groups. The earliest religious texts provide examples of martyrdom, which may overlap with the modern understanding of suicide. The Jewish text, 1 Maccabees, narrates the account of Eleazar Avaran,

184 Taylor, *Sources of the Self* (n. 136) 13.
185 See Judith Butler, *Precarious Life: The Powers of Mourning and Violence* (1st ed., Verso 2004).

who attempted to kill the Seleucid king Antiochus V Eupator "during the battle of Beth-Zechariah by attacking the king's elephant (1 Macc. 6:43–46)".[186] Furthermore, the Second Book of Maccabees contains a story of martyrdom that is a suicide story (2 Macc. 14:37–46).[187] In this story (14:37), Razis, an elder from Jerusalem (14:38), was convicted of fighting for Judaism, and five hundred soldiers were sent by Nicanor to arrest him (14:40).[188] When he was about to be captured, and the mob was storming his house through the gates, he

> nobly ran up to the wall and threw himself straight down upon the mob, as a real man. (14:44).... The blood spouted from his painful wounds, but he went at a run through the mob and placed himself upon a precipitous piece of rock. (14:46) Having lost all his blood, he exposed his bowels, took them with both hands and hurled them into the mob, while he called upon the One who has the mastery over the breath of life to give them back again to him. In this way he quit his life.[189]

This example overlaps the modern idea of suicide with the ancient practice of martyrdom. Avemarie and van Henten argue that "unlike modern people the ancients did not distinguish between glorious ways of suicide and other violent deaths."[190] It is important to note that while not all examples of martyrdom would qualify as suicides in the strict sense, those that did qualify as suicide were not initially excluded from being valued as acts of martyrdom.

The historical evolution of the Christian attitude toward martyrdom and suicide demonstrates a complex understanding of active and passive voluntariness to die. The chapter acknowledges that the notion of suicide is a contested one within Christian theology. However, it is possible to evaluate the notion from a historiographical point of view. The first reference to martyrdom in the name of the Christian faith is found in Martyrdom of Polycarp (155–160 CE), about people who were executed due to their obedience to Christian faith and identity.[191] In Roman sacrifice as well as in early Christian practice, the intentionality

[186] Moss (n. 48) 40.
[187] Avemarie & Henten (n. 163).
[188] Ibid. 71.
[189] Ibid. 72; Moss (n. 48) 43: "The death of Razis has been something of a sensitive subject; he is rarely even called a martyr and is described as having either suffered a 'heroic death' or committed suicide. While the modern interpreter may distinguish between the deaths of Eleazar and the Maccabean mother and her sons on one hand and Razis on the other, it is clear that the same cannot be said for the author of 2 Maccabees, for whom the death of Razis serves the same purpose in the cycle of liberation as the deaths of the other martyrs."
[190] Avemarie & Henten (n. 163) 5: "[T]he ancient Greeks put several kinds of glorious death in one category of *biaiothanasia* ('violent death'): death on the battlefield by falling victim or forcing one's own death, execution, as well as other forms of self-sacrifice and suicide."
[191] Ibid. 2.

of the victim was an integral element of the sacrifice itself. The victim was central to the narrative and was considered an active participant of the process: "the more actively voluntary, the more effective the sacrifice. Sacrifice exalted the victim and rendered him or her divine."[192] Following Saint Augustine, for Christians, martyrdom came to be defined through the act of sacrifice of Christ. Rather than active acts of self-harm, passivity became the norm.[193] Volunteering to die was condemned.[194] One was not expected to actively volunteer for persecution.[195] To clarify the definition of suicide in early Christian thought, Darrel W. Amundsen compares two scenarios: one scenario looks at a person who is put to death for refusing to recant a belief. In relation to this, he argues that the "[w]illingness to die for a cause is not typically viewed as suicide; otherwise, all martyrs, even all soldiers who die in the line of duty, are suicides." The second scenario presents a person who "actively seeks or volunteers for martyrdom."[196] He argues that this case may well be labeled 'suicide.' Here, a distinction is made between a person who lets themselves be killed by others while defending their beliefs and those who actively harm themselves. Therefore, the determination of whether an act is considered martyrdom in the Judeo-Christian narratives depends on the active or passive nature of the act itself. Whether an act is active or passive lends itself to objective assessment without requiring an inquiry into the subjective intention of the person who dies.

The distinction between suicide and martyrdom is not exclusive to Christianity. Islam, too, differentiates between these two concepts. However, the distinction in Islam is based on different grounds from those identified in Christianity. The debate surrounding suicide and martyrdom in Islam is not settled. Islamic scholars with affiliations to different schools and sects have diverging opinions on the topic. The label of martyrdom operations plays a crucial role in this Islamic justification of acts that would otherwise have been considered suicide and, therefore, prohibited under Islam. The Arabic terms "martyrdom operation" and "martyrdom seeker" first entered discourse through the Lebanese Hizbu'llah in the 1980s. Slavicek argues that it was a concept that was "neither inherent to Islamic tradition nor culture, but rather a product of strategic cultural framing to legitimize suicide terrorism in Middle-Eastern conflicts."[197] Even when Islamists advocate for violence, they attempt to ground

[192] Margaret Cormack (ed.), *Sacrificing the Self: Perspectives on Martyrdom and Religion* (Oxford University Press 2002).

[193] Ibid. 42.

[194] See Geoffrey Ernest Maurice de Ste. Croix, "Why Were the Early Christians Persecuted?" (1963) 26 Past and Present 6.

[195] Cormack (n. 192).

[196] Darrel W. Amundsen, "Suicide and Early Christian Values" in Baruch A Brody (ed.) *Suicide and Euthanasia. Historical and Contemporary Themes* (Springer Netherlands 1989) 78: He concedes however, that distinguishing between these two scenarios present conceptual difficulties.

[197] Slavicek (n 6.) 554.

their actions in Islamic texts, allowing them to project an image of themselves "as bearers of authentic Islam and as followers of divine commandments," and circumnavigating the constraints on Muslims not to kill themselves intentionally.[198] To fall within the contours of acts allowed by Islam, narratives constructed around martyrdom operations depict them as fulfilling two requirements: "the test of intention, namely to become a martyr in the service of the faith; and the test of the result, namely causing damage to enemy forces."[199]

As a general principle, it is agreed that suicide (*intihar*) in and of itself is considered *haram* (i.e., forbidden).[200] There are three Qur'anic passages often cited by jurisconsults to establish the prohibition of suicide:

> And spend in the way of God and *do not, with your own hands, cast yourselves into ruin.* And be virtuous. Truly God loves the virtuous. (Sura 2:195)
>
> O you who believe! Consume not each other's wealth falsely, but trade by mutual consent, *and slay not yourselves.* Truly God is merciful unto you. And whosoever does that in enmity and injustice, We shall cause him to burn in a Fire; and that is easy for God. (Sura 4:29–30)
>
> Say, "Come, I will recite that which your Lord has forbidden you . . . *slay not the soul that God has made inviolable, save by right*." (6:151)

Scholars have interpreted the prohibition of suicide to not apply to a person who attacks a group of unbelievers even though he knows he will be killed.[201] These types of justifications have also been extended to justify martyrdom operations. Likewise, for martyrdom operations to be distinguished from suicide according to these shariatic justifications, they must fulfill four conditions:

> first, the "sincere devotion" (*ikhla ̄s*) of the attacker manifest in his or her "sincere intention" (*n ̄ıya kha ̄lisa*) of "seeking martyrdom" (*istishha d*); second, the necessity of a "benefit" (*maslaha/manfa'a*) to the Muslim community by "damaging" (*nika ̄ya*) the enemy; third, a state of war and *jihad* between Muslims and the enemy; finally, the inevitability of suicide bombings because other tactics seem impossible or ineffectual, that is, a condition in which "necessity permits forbidden acts" (*ad-daru ̄ra tub ̄ıh al-mahzu ̄ra ̄t*). The first two conditions are each a condition sine qua non, whereas the latter two are not absolute.[202]

198 Hafez (n. 31) 364–365.
199 Hatina (n. 158) 189.
200 Singh (n. 34)105.
201 Hatina (n. 158) 40.
202 Slavicek (n. 6) 555–556.

Given that this book has focused on issues about a suicide attack's effect on the attackers themselves, this chapter would also focus particularly on the first condition which speaks to the sincere intention of seeking martyrdom and what this means to their treatment under IHL.[203]

In Christianity, to actively engage in self-harm rather than allow someone to harm oneself are two distinct things and the former is suicide while the latter is martyrdom. Rather than determining whether the act of violence was passively accepted or actively inflicted upon oneself, Islam delves into the subjective intentionality of the person engaging in self-harm. In Islam even where one takes active measures to harm oneself voluntarily, it still constitutes martyrdom. In Islam, forms of suffering are intrinsic to "the kind of agent a devout Muslim aspires to be. The most important of these is the universal experience of dying and death."[204] Martyrdom operations focus on self-sacrifice (*istish'had*), which is considered desirable in Qur'anic teachings, commentaries, and *fatwas*.[205] While there has been opposition by Islamic scholars for providing shariatic justifications for suicide attacks, most opposition pertains to such attacks harming civilians. It does not directly engage with the intentionality of the martyrs to harm themselves.[206] Therefore, martyrdom is not distinguished from suicide based on the active or passive contribution of the martyr regarding the violence inflicted, but on an assessment of the subjective intention behind the self-inflicted violence. Islamic martyrdom deviates from the "tenacious passivism" that characterizes martyrdom in Christianity.[207] On the contrary, to label acts as martyrdom, local narratives, particularly from within jihadist armed groups, depict deaths as intentional, religiously motivated, and agentic sacrifices.

The distinction between intention and action plays a crucial role in how martyrdom is defined in Islamic thought and can be contrasted with Western secular interpretations of martyrdom as suicide. Martyrdom transforms a subjective belief in a particular worldview into a violently tangible reality. Cover writes:

> [T]he miracle of the suffering of the martyrs is their insistence on the law to which they are committed, even in the face of world-destroying pain. Their triumph—which may well be partly imaginary—is the imagined triumph of the

[203] As for the second, third, and fourth elements, these would require a discussion on IHL with regard to the damage these attacks cause to others and how an armed conflict is defined within Islam and IHL. While these are interesting topics on their own, the first one has been addressed by some scholars already, and the second issue is too broad for the scope of this chapter and is not directly relevant to the crux of this book.

[204] Asad, *Formations of the Secular* (n. 54) 90.

[205] Singh (n. 34) 106.

[206] Ibid. 106, 115.

[207] Hatina (n. 158) 36.

normative universe—of Torah, Nomos—over the material world of death and pain.[208]

Like Cover's statement, in Islam, the subjective imaginary of the martyr becomes critical to how their act is defined. Therefore, the intentionality of the person engaging in the attack plays a crucial role in distinguishing a mere suicide from what is recognized as a martyrdom operation. Nathan S. French argues, having studied *fatwas* relating to suicide and martyrdom operations, that according to some *muftis*, suicide is a matter of displaced desire and emotion toward material and temporal concerns.[209] On the other hand, martyrdom is

> an act of an intentionally performed piety constructed upon a subjectivity that seeks to realize the ideal relationship with the divine.... The intention (*niyya*) and purpose (*qaṣd*) of an operation are subjective characteristics described by the authors and muftis to differentiate between a martyr and a suicide.[210]

Likewise, actions are not judged through an objective assessment of action and consequence, but on the intention of the acting agent.[211]

This focus on the subjectivity of the attacker does not sit well with IHL, which uses more objective measures to classify acts as permitted or prohibited. The 2009 ICRC Interpretive Guidance on the Notion of Direct Participation in Hostilities examines the relevance of an individual's subjective intent in determining whether they have lost their civilian status and, therefore, are targetable. According to experts who participated in this process, there is no subjective element in direct participation. Whether an act constitutes hostilities is to be assessed, regardless of whether it was carried out intentionally or unintentionally, based on more objective factors, such as the level of harm inflicted.[212] There seems to be a unanimous agreement that "the subjective motives for carrying out an act cannot be reliably determined during the conduct of military operations and, therefore, cannot serve as a clear and operable criterion for 'split second' targeting decisions."[213] Even the notion of belligerent nexus was distinguished from subjective intent and was to be assessed based on the objective purpose of the act: "[t]hat purpose is expressed in the design of the act or operation and

[208] Robert M. Cover, "Violence and the Word" (1986) 95:8 Yale Law Journal 1601.
[209] French (n. 106) 110.
[210] Ibid. 122–123.
[211] Hafez (n. 31).
[212] Rewi Lyall, "Voluntary Human Shields, Direct Participation in Hostilities and the International Humanitarian Law Obligations of States" (2008) 9:2 Melbourne Journal of International Law 313, 323–324.
[213] International Committee of the Red Cross (ICRC), "Interpretive Guidance on the Notion of Direct Participation in Hostilities under International Humanitarian Law," May 2009, 59 note 150.

does not depend on the mindset of every participating individual."[214] When it comes to members of conventional armies, IHL does not investigate the subjective intent or their consent to fight at all. IHL, on this matter, operates on whether such a person is a member as per the local legislation of the particular country. Thereby, the subjective intention of an armed combatant is entirely shifted to the State and the rational process of lawmaking. Lawmaking, at the national level, is, in most cases, a secular activity.

The issue of voluntary human shields is a controversial case that requires assessing the intention of the participants in hostilities. Customary IHL prohibits the use of human shields. However, whether this prohibition extends to voluntary human shields is highly debatable. Article 51(7) of Additional Protocol I to the Geneva Conventions places the obligation not to direct "the movement of the civilian population or individual civilians in order to attempt to shield military objectives from attacks or to shield military operations" on the party to the conflict. It does not address the voluntariness or the intention of the persons who act as the shield. According to a judgment by the Supreme Court of Israel, civilians serving as a "human shield" if they do so of their own free will, out of support for the armed group, would be seen as persons taking a direct part in the hostilities.[215] However, according to the ICRC Interpretive Guidelines on Direct Participation in Hostilities, "[t]he fact that some civilians voluntarily and deliberately abuse their legal entitlement to protection against direct attack in order to shield military objectives does not, without more, entail the loss of their protection and their liability to direct attack independently of the shielded objective."[216] Therefore, objective factors such as the harm inflicted by the action of shielding an object is given weight in IHL rather than purely operating on the basis of the subjective intention of those involved. The mental state of civilians is only taken into account in exceptional situations such as when they are unaware of the role they are playing, such as in the case of involuntary human shields being coerced into providing cover.[217] IHL's reluctance to delve into the subjective intention of persons means that often, people are considered targetable based on an objective assessment of the impact of their actions, unless their lack of voluntariness is overwhelmingly evident. Even so, the indeterminacy of IHL on voluntary human shields itself reveals its unease with having to assess the subjective intention of those engaging in hostilities and self-assumed vulnerability. Given this attachment to objectivity, IHL struggles to directly interact with the paradigm of martyrdom operations, which emphasizes the subjective intention of the person

[214] Ibid. note 35.

[215] Israel, *Public Committee against Torture in Israel v. Government of Israel*, Case No. HCJ 769/02, December 13, 2006 para. 36.

[216] ICRC, Interpretive Guidance (n. 213) 57.

[217] Ibid. 60.

engaging in an attack. This also explains why IHL does not make a distinction between martyrdom operations and any other attack in war, thereby ignoring the peculiar nature of the death of the combatant engaging in them.

Not only is the intention of the martyr subjective, but it is also rooted within religion. As an overtly secular framework, religious motivations are not considered relevant within IHL's rationality. The secular discourse of being human also enshrines detachment from passionate belief. Therefore, commitment to religious beliefs is considered outside the ambit of rationality.[218] This understanding of rationality sits diametrically in opposition to martyrdom operations whose logic is one of renouncing individual interest as understood in secular rationality and "placing faith ahead of one's own material comfort" to seek divine providence.[219] Piety is assessed through deeds of self-sacrifice.[220] Martyrdom operation goes beyond being a mere military act and also becomes an act of worship. Moreover, the necessity of martyrdom operations are not measured solely by damage caused to military objectives by an attack but in terms of how it contributes to reviving the global Muslim community and the extent to which it is perceived as advancing Muslim interests.[221] The act of martyrdom becomes a vehicle through which individual commitment to "God who urges true believers to fight persecution and never fear death" is demonstrated.[222] Therefore, even at the individual level, such operations can be seen as acts that are used for religious, political, and military ends.[223]

While I have taken an ethnographic approach to religion, it does not imply that I subscribe to the Western-secular view that religious-motivated suicide attacks are conducted for the sole purpose of pleasing God and therefore are incompatible with tools used in secular rationality. While martyrdom operations are justified through the religious motivations of the person engaging in them, it may be argued that this does not exclude rationality from being factored into how armed groups engage in these attacks. As mentioned earlier, Article 57 of *Laiha* states that "[a] martyrdom attack should be used for important and high-value targets, [given that] the self-sacrificing heroes of the Islamic Ummah must not be used for low and worthless targets." This provision incorporates what sounds like a proportionality calculation, similar to IHL, which measures the loss of the life of the martyr as against the value of the target of attack. This indicates that even military operations simply because they are justified through religion do not become mutually exclusive with rational calculations. For example, *maslahat* is a

[218] French (n. 106) 124.
[219] Ibid. 114.
[220] Hafez (n. 31).
[221] Ali & Post (n. 33) 617.
[222] Singh (n. 34) 111.
[223] Ibid. 113.

notion rooted in Islamic religious jurisprudence and considers pragmatic and public interest considerations as integral to religion.[224] This positions rationality as a component of, rather than a binary opposite of religious norms.

Rationality can be understood as going beyond a logical and instrumental paradigm. Domenico Tosini argues that axiological rationality encompasses the assumption of "certain beliefs unconditionally, without taking into account their effects or advantages."[225] He uses the example of suicide attacks carried out based on the belief of an Islamic ideology as an exercise of axiological rationality.[226] Martyrdom operations are therefore a military practice that accommodates both the spiritual and the rational. The careful, analytical nature in which IHL manages human intention through objective rationality and separates religion as a factor relevant to the conduct of hostilities, prevents it from fully appreciating or engaging with how martyrdom operations are influenced by religion. As discussed in previous discussions in chapter 2 on the limits of embodied understandings of life and death, as well as chapter 3's examination of how cultural beliefs on the afterlife impacted narratives surrounding the deaths of Kamikaze attackers, this chapter too demonstrates how the belief in an afterlife in the Islamic tradition frames a martyr's actions. In Islam, the mortal world is brief and temporary and functions as a test for an eternal afterlife. The artificial dichotomy between the religious and the rational, as seen in IHL, which prevents such considerations impacting life-and-death decisions from being appreciated in a nuanced manner, clouds how, in the context of martyrdom operations, rational considerations are not completely excluded, thereby indicating that wartime practices can be influenced by a plural normative framework that includes both the religious and the rational.

The image of war in IHL adopts a Western secular form of rationality, and the soldier's sacrifice, too, is viewed in this light. Despite IHL's secular rationality, in cultural narratives, the soldiers' sacrifice is often intertwined with that of Christ. This narrative does not include active self-harm. Therefore, the Western narratives use the term "suicide attacks" rather than the language of martyrdom. The Western narratives deny sacral status to those engaging in martyrdom operations as classified by jihadist armed groups. In doing so, they depict the attacker as "an abject other" and their agency as "morally deviant" or criminal.[227] Kahn similarly posits that the distinction between a criminal act and an act of war,

[224] Bahman Khodadadi, "Public Interest (Maslahat) in Shi'i Theocracy: Implications for Legal and Political Decision-Making" (2025) 58:3 Iranian Studies 490.

[225] Domenico Tosini, "A Sociological Understanding of Suicide Attacks" (2009) 26:4 Theory, Culture & Society 67, 69. Also see Raymond Boudon, "Beyond Rational Choice Theory" (2003) 29 Annual Review of Sociology 1.

[226] Tosini (n. 225).

[227] Karin Marie Fierke, "Agents of Death: The Structural Logic of Suicide Terrorism and Martyrdom" (2009) 1:1 International Theory 155, 157.

and whether a combatant's death is viewed as a sacrifice, depends on diverse narratives of war constructed by multiple entities, including by States.[228] Acts of self-harm on the part of combatants that sustain the State and its liberal notion of sovereignty are labeled sacrifices while those that threaten the security of the State are termed suicide.[229] This liberal State is secular and religion is treated as a private matter. A person carrying out a public and religiously motivated act of violence acts in a manner not condoned by the secular State, and is therefore labeled a criminal.[230] Secularism denies political agency to those carrying out martyrdom operations and equates their deaths to the deviant agency of a someone perpetrating a criminal act.

5.4. Conclusion

As I have noted, contemporary Western society is made uncomfortable by voluntary, public, and violent death. This is the type of ostentatious death that martyrdom typifies.[231] Therefore, acts of martyrdom are no longer considered suitable for modern life and are seen as shocking, uncomfortable, and unusual.[232] These modern attitudes toward public and violent deaths are also reflected in how IHL treats martyrdom operations. In this chapter, I have set out the ambiguous relationship between IHL and religion. This complex relationship impacts its silence on martyrdom operations. IHL appraises attacks with a lens that is intrinsically tied to its overt adoption of secularism. It relegates religion to the private sphere and excludes it from being a factor in the conduct of hostilities. I argued that the separation of religion from public affairs in the secular age stems from a fear of the nonrational that is often affiliated with religion. Religious motivations, therefore, conflict with the rational foundations on which human well-being in IHL is framed. Martyrdom operations, which are carried out in the name of Islam, are essentially a public act that is justified through religion. The martyrs' death demands public recognition of the fact that attempting to sequester the religious into private pockets within warfare is a futile endeavor. Furthermore, martyrdom operations contradict the secular rationality that IHL promotes. Unlike the objective calculations through which IHL's rationality measures whether combatant deaths are excessive, martyrdom operations delve into the subjective intentionality of the attacker. In doing so, they valorize active and voluntary self-harm, which deviates from the Christian

[228] Paul W. Kahn, "Imagining Warfare" (2013) 24:1 European Journal of International Law 199.
[229] Ibid.
[230] Ibid. 217.
[231] Avemarie & Henten (n. 163).
[232] Ibid. 1.

notion of martyrdom that is primarily restricted to passively allowing others to harm oneself. As a religiously motivated form of self-harm, such attacks invoke the fear that modernity has with respect to the perceived nonrationality of religion. Therefore, the religiously motivated acts of agency carried out by the martyr are depicted in Western narratives as irrational or as deviant or criminal agency.

6

Beyond Binary Legal Categories

6.1. A retrospective

This book examined International Humanitarian Law's (IHL) silence on the phenomenon of suicide attackers' deaths. It did so by facilitating a conversation between IHL and insights from other disciplines, including anthropology, feminist scholarship, and sociology. Through this dialogue, the book revealed how, despite their claims to universality, the cultural biases that impose barriers to engaging with diverse and context-specific narratives surrounding suicide attackers' agency undergird IHL. One manifestation of these barriers is IHL's propensity to adopt stereotypes that classify persons as victims or perpetrators, which signal how they exercise agency in armed conflicts. Throughout the chapters of this book, I progressively demonstrated how the agency exercised by suicide attackers is constructed through cultural narratives that provide meaning to their deaths. These narratives on suicide attackers' deaths depict their agency in more nuanced ways than the binary classifications in IHL permit and, thereby, challenge and subvert its assumptions of how combatants exercise agency on the battlefield.

In this chapter, I offer an overview of the insights gleaned from this book pertaining to why IHL is silent on suicide attackers' deaths and present how these insights provide tools to unpack the impact of classifications and binary constructions on how we process complex phenomena that go beyond suicide attackers. In the following sections, first, I synthesize key findings from the three case studies in this book and elucidate how complex cultural narratives shape our understandings of the agency suicide attackers exercise in death. Second, I propose that this culturally plural approach, which challenges binary constructions, can open new avenues for IHL scholars and practitioners to examine and situate themselves in relation to other wartime phenomena. Having presented these potential applications, in the third section of this chapter, I problematize the demand placed on scholars engaging in critical work to propose policies or recommendations stemming from their findings. Rather than providing prescriptive recommendations, I discuss the importance of approaching critical scholarship as an ethical practice when challenging structural biases in normative frameworks.

Suicide Attacks and International Humanitarian Law. Vishakha V. Wijenayake, Oxford University Press.
 DOI: 10.1093/9780197812174.003.0006

6.2. Insights from case studies

A central thread of this book was the silence in IHL regarding suicide attackers' deaths. Upon closer examination, it was evident that this silence was a symptom of a broader assumption that combatant deaths are an inevitable reality of war. These underlying assumptions shape IHL's claim to universality, presenting its principles as neutral and universally applicable while, in reality, reflecting specific cultural and ideological frameworks. This presumed universality, in turn, manifests through rigid binary classifications, which structure the law in ways that obscure complexities and reinforce existing silences. Closer scrutiny of these gaps reveals challenges to both explicit and implicit legal norms, making visible what the law has overlooked or taken for granted.

While noting that the Geneva Conventions of 1949, which enshrine principles of IHL, have been universally ratified by States, this work posited that IHL cannot be understood in isolation from the historical context in which these principles were formed and the cultural norms that influence how its provisions are interpreted in different contexts. As such, the book presented arguments supported by existing critical legal scholarship, and made the case that IHL is grounded in a Eurocentric image of warfare, despite introducing its principles as universally applicable. To counterbalance this narrative of universality, this study examined how local cultural contexts impact wartime practices of armed groups.

Through the case studies in this book, it became evident that there is no one monolithic Eurocentric image of how war is to be conducted, given that even European attitudes toward wartime phenomena have changed over time, and as States deemed "Western" or "developed" themselves have diverse interests and agendas. Moreover, IHL provisions have been interpreted by States worldwide, taking into account the contexts and realities in which conflicts occur and the beliefs and ways of life of those who fight in them. Likewise, the ways that different armed groups conduct war tend to mirror the cultural constructs of the community in which they reside. Promoting a single and universal normative framework thereby makes IHL less efficient in addressing diverse wartime practices across a wide range of societies.

Legal pluralism provided a theoretical lens that meaningfully accommodated the multiplicity of normative frameworks and the complexity of narratives that commingle in wartime contexts. This pluralistic approach, which explored how IHL interacts with cultural norms that influence militaries and armed groups, was well-suited to the study of suicide attackers. First, it acknowledged that suicide attackers function within their cultural contexts, recognizing that combatants do not exclusively reflect their attitudes as members of their militaries but are also influenced by social, political, or religious norms. This book's examination of scholarship on suicide also suggested that the ways people die, especially when it is a voluntary death such as suicide, can be diverse and influenced by their experiences, further highlighting the importance of a culturally plural approach for IHL to relate to suicide attacks.

As opposed to more positivist understandings of international law, which rarely treat individuals as having norm-making capacity, critical legal pluralism also views individuals as having the agency to challenge and contribute to the creation of the normative frameworks that surround them, of which law is one among many. Critical legal pluralism, therefore, opened new avenues for this study to engage with how suicide attackers, through their performative deaths, subvert and create alternate norms around how combatant agency is perceived during hostilities.

The first chapter of this book unpacked the historical and cultural roots of IHL that shaped its understanding of combatant deaths. The second chapter of this book delved further into the notion of agency in death. Ensuing case studies of cultural narratives about suicide attackers' deaths troubled IHL's understanding of agency attached to combatant deaths. These understandings were grounded in assumptions on how individuals exercise agency, and revealed how IHL principles are propped up by compounding binary constructions, pitting victims against perpetrators, separating public from private spheres, as well as assigning secular or religious motivations to combatant deaths. In this manner, IHL frames the combatants' agency over their own deaths within a cultural comfort zone, dictating, first, the extent of this sacrifice, second, who is capable of exercising agency attributed to a warrior, and third, what can legitimately underpin the motivations of such sacrifice.

However, the book noted that this approach that IHL takes to agency is neither universal nor sufficient to account for the complex normative frameworks that shape suicide attackers' deaths in various contexts. By examining three case studies—the Kamikaze pilots of Japan, female suicide attackers in the Liberation Tigers of Tamil Eelam (LTTE), and jihadist martyrdom operations—the book illustrates how local narratives of sacrifice and agency often defy the binary frameworks of IHL. Each case study adopted a culturally informed approach toward agency while juxtaposing them with binary constructions that IHL adopts to manage combatant agency during the conduct of hostilities. In doing so, this study attempted to act as an antidote to IHL's silence on suicide attackers' deaths by providing, to the greatest extent possible, a genuine appraisal of how these combatants' deaths are given meaning in their communities.

6.2.1. The extent of IHL's recognition of combatant agency

The first case study focused on the Kamikaze pilots of World War II, whose deaths challenged IHL's boundaries around reciprocity of risk in combat. IHL is built on the premise of mutual risk: combatants are expected to expose themselves to danger in combat, but there is an underlying assumption that this risk is limited and framed within a broader context that allows for self-preservation. IHL's image of warfare is modeled after the European notion of chivalry, which presumes that combatants exercise voluntary agency when they risk their lives on the battlefield. This agency is recognized in a manner consistent with the notion of self-preservation. The possibility of surrender, for example, is a key tenet of IHL, which instills the assumption that combatants will prioritize their survival over the certainty of death. In other words, in IHL, agency on the part of the combatant is assumed if they risked their lives in a limited manner, with the possibility of surrender, rather than fought with the certainty of death.

The Kamikaze pilots' deliberate and certain deaths disrupted this framework. Rejecting reciprocal and limited risk in warfare, they presented death as an inevitable and honorable outcome of combat. This violation of the unwritten norm in IHL of reciprocal risk in combat placed Kamikaze pilots on the one hand in the role of a fanatical perpetrator of violence due to deviation from established humanitarian norms. On the other hand, they were stereotyped as victims whose capacity to exercise agency is challenged due to the hierarchical military structure whose internal policies decreed that they fight to the death. As within these conflicting narratives, they alternated between occupying two seemingly contradictory spaces: their deaths defied the presumption that the victim–perpetrator binary was mutually exclusive. This struggle to place them in either category was illustrative of the confines of how combatants are deemed to exercise agency.

Through this case study, several key findings emerged. First, despite IHL's claim to universality, the conduct of hostilities is shaped by the internal cultural ethos of militaries. While not expressly mentioned in a specific provision, a notion that is implicit in IHL provisions, including on means and methods of warfare, surrender, and taking of prisoners, when examined in relation to one another, is that combatants exercise agency when they expose themselves to mutual risk as well as when they stop fighting. However, this assumption disregards the impact of internal military rules and cultural norms that underpin the military ethos on how a combatant exposes oneself to risk and when or if at all they surrender in combat. When militaries expect their combatants to take a higher level of risk than the limited risk outlined in IHL, these combatants are likely to be seen as victims of an oppressive military structure who do not have the capacity to exercise agency over their deaths.

The case study on Kamikaze pilots showed how when persons submit themselves to authority to the extent of embracing certain death, there is a presumption in the eyes of those who value self-preservation that these fighters have ceased to exercise their rational judgment. This perception that suicide attackers are victims of an oppressive military structure would facilitate an argument for legal regulation of suicide attacks by making it illegal for local militaries to require combatants to fight until death. However, this solution supposes that when IHL prohibits such rules, combatants would choose self-preservation, ignoring the power that cultural narratives around death and sacrifice may have on individual choice.

This study offered a model of agency in Japanese narratives, where agency is not viewed as operating in competition with cultural influences. This alternative understanding acknowledges the possibility that a person's act of prioritizing their community over individual self-preservation could also constitute a socially embedded form of agency. This notion of agency also challenged the embodied conception of the self, which comes to an end with the death of its physical form, but lives on beyond physical death through communal memorialization. An embodied understanding of the self is one in which personhood is intrinsically tied to the physical body. Death, in this view, represents the ultimate loss of agency, as the body ceases to function and the self is presumed to end with it.

However, the cultural narratives surrounding Kamikaze pilots challenge this embodied notion of self by presenting the self as not ending with the death of the physical body but as persisting through communal remembrance, deification, and integration into the collective identity of the nation. If the self can endure beyond death through memorialization, then the scope of agency expands. The Kamikaze pilots' actions, rather than being viewed as a negation of agency through self-destruction, can instead be understood as an assertion of agency within a different conceptual framework where sacrificing one's body is not the end of the self but a means of securing its continued existence.

6.2.2. Those with perceived capacity to exercise agency in combat

Not only is IHL's notion of agency conditioned by the extent of risk taken by combatants, but it also limits the type of persons who are considered capable of making agentic decisions during the conduct of hostilities. The second case study, likewise, examined the female suicide attackers of the LTTE, focusing on how gendered assumptions influence IHL's understanding of agency. A masculinized image of the combatant has historically shaped IHL, framing men as warriors and women as victims of war. This essentialist perspective limits IHL's ability to recognize women as agents of violence and fails to provide a nuanced image of women's roles in warfare. The chapter recognized a tendency both in policy and in scholarship to question the agency of female combatants operating within societies labeled as conservative, on account of their actions being influenced by a patriarchal military structure. At the same time, women who engage in violent political acts are seen as deviating from the role assigned to them within the patriarchal institution of warfare and, therefore, as morally corrupt perpetrators of violence.

The narratives stemming from within the armed group present a different account of female combatants as exercising agency against an oppressive State structure. Suicide attacks carried out by female cadres were a case where these contradicting narratives of victimhood and political agency coalesced in a manner that generated cognitive dissonance when juxtaposed with IHL's depiction of how women are deemed to exercise agency in hostilities. While her gender made her an ideal candidate to be classified as a victim in IHL, the female suicide attacker weaponized this perception of vulnerability to become a perpetrator of violence, defying the victim–perpetrator binary in IHL.

The chapter studied the LTTE to understand how their ethnonationalist separatism against the State engendered a message of gender liberation for its cadres. In this analysis, I strove to maintain a balanced view regarding the claims that non-State armed groups make regarding female liberation while acknowledging that these groups, including the LTTE, reproduce many patriarchal gender biases inherent in militaries. Even while adopting this nuanced approach, it was hard to dismiss how the role that female suicide attackers played in narratives coming out of these militant structures and their adversaries, as well as the manner in which they conducted their operations, subverted many gender stereotypes in wartime hostilities.

Female combatants in non-State armed groups often face deeply constrained circumstances, with limited options shaped by the intersections of patriarchal oppression, militarized environments, and the harsh realities of war. Within these restrictive contexts, their choices may not align with traditional notions of empowerment but reflect strategic acts of agency in response to the conditions they endure. These choices, while far from ideal, represent a way to navigate oppressive systems and reclaim a degree of autonomy over their lives.

Female suicide attackers in the LTTE often described their actions as liberating, providing a sense of control over their lives and deaths. These narratives speak to an agency over the self that is not experienced by those who simply wait to die. What comes through in these narratives is that their position within a patriarchal structure did not diminish their agency; instead, it was expressed through their ability to navigate and subvert it. By adopting a relational model of agency, this study offered a more complex understanding of the roles women play in warfare as well as frames of agency that enable IHL to recognize that women can be agents while operating within patriarchal structures.

6.2.3. Permitted rationales for combatant agency in death

The third case study explored how IHL's secular framework struggles to relate to the religious and subjective intentionality of those who carry out martyrdom operations in jihadist non-State armed groups. It did so by analyzing international law as well as IHL's complicated relationship with religion. IHL's secular framework relegates religion to the private sphere, and the notion of agency in IHL is contingent on a secular rationality that assumes individuals will act to avoid pain and suffering. Martyrdom operations, which involve voluntary self-harm carried out in the name of religious belief, disrupt this framework by presenting a form of agency that is a public and spiritual embracing of violent self-harm.

Martyrdom operations carried out by non-State armed groups in the name of *jihad* show how religiously motivated self-harm conflicts with the rational foundations on which human well-being in IHL is predicated. In doing so, these combatants' deaths challenge the separation of religion from the conduct of hostilities. These deaths thereby evoke the fear of the nonrational that is often affiliated with religion. Due to this incongruency that martyrdom operations present to the secular framework of agency in IHL, those who carry out these operations are more likely to be viewed as perpetrators of violence exercising deviant agency.

This study revealed how IHL's secular assumptions about agency are not neutral but are shaped by Christian ideas of martyrdom and self-sacrifice. While IHL accommodates certain forms of self-sacrifice within its framework, it excludes others, particularly those associated with the Islamic "other." Martyrdom operations challenge IHL's cultural biases by presenting a vision of agency that is grounded in religious intentionality and collective solidarity. These acts defy IHL's secular rationality and expose the limitations of its framework in understanding the motivations of combatants from diverse cultural and religious backgrounds.

Moreover, this case study highlighted the performative nature of martyrdom operations, which transform individual acts of self-sacrifice into collective narratives of resistance. These narratives serve as a powerful form of cultural capital, reinforcing communal identities and challenging the secular State's monopoly over the management of life and death. By excluding these narratives from its framework, IHL perpetuates a narrow and exclusionary vision of agency that fails to resonate with the lived realities of combatants in diverse contexts.

6.3. The way forward: broader implications

As expounded in the previous section, this book explored underexamined cultural biases embedded within IHL. Current IHL rules and scholarship often rely on generalized assumptions about how combatants risk their lives, who is considered capable of exercising agency in warfare, and the motivations behind the sacrifices combatants make during battle. The case studies revealed that diverse cultural narratives surrounding suicide attackers' deaths depict agency in ways that challenge the biases inherent in IHL.

By understanding that combatant experiences are complex and contextualized within their cultural practices, this book aims to facilitate a shift in how we approach IHL principles, making them not only theoretically sound but also practically applicable. First, adopting a culturally plural lens within IHL offers practical tools for practitioners and humanitarian workers engaging with diverse wartime actors by encouraging them to interpret warfare through multiple frames rather than attempting to impose a rigid, predetermined vision of warfare and hostilities onto varied contexts. Second, this book enables militaries to understand the behavior of armed groups engaging in suicide attacks while acknowledging the cultural contexts that influence such actions and move toward a more nuanced engagement with these groups. At the same time, it challenges States to critically examine their own practices and the narratives surrounding how they treat their troops. Third, it underscores the importance of those involved in drafting IHL rules being aware of, if not mitigating, binary categorizations that obscure diverse experiences and meanings attributed to combatant actions. By reflecting on these dynamics, IHL can evolve into a framework whose application is meaningful in diverse operational environments.

I recognize certain limitations of this study that leave space for further research on suicide attackers within international law. The book delved into three case studies focusing on thematic analyses of IHL's structural biases, and the specific conclusions of the study are drawn from the cultural narratives pertaining to these contexts. While the findings of these case studies were insightful, examining other cultural contexts could enrich our understanding of agency in warfare and complicate the conclusions drawn in this book. I invite scholars to continue the interrogation of the cultural underpinnings of IHL's frameworks, through which we can deepen our understanding of how law interacts with the lived realities of suicide attackers.

Furthermore, in shaping the specific research questions and establishing the scope of this research, I had to set aside some questions that would merit in-depth examination, including the full potential of how International Human Rights Law (IHRL) and International Criminal Law (ICL) shape narratives on warfare. While I have referred to these branches of the law to shed light on developments that impact IHL, there is ample scope to research that examines the historical biases that underpin both ICL and IHRL in terms of how they view agency in warfare. This would complement the rich critical literature that already exists within these branches, which is shifting scholarly attention toward a more pluralist appreciation of the law.

The following sections will further establish how the insights from this book can inspire potential research beyond the study of suicide attackers. To facilitate future research, I offer two examples to portray how findings from the previous chapters can have broader resonance both within and beyond IHL. The thrust of the following examples is that the approaches used in this study to identify binary classifications can be a useful tool for unpacking complex social phenomena that are often oversimplified in legal or policy discourse. To this end, I reflect on my past experiences as an IHL practitioner to critique my thinking and writing on searching for wartime missing persons through a culturally plural lens. Going beyond IHL, I examine the concept of intersectionality, which has gained traction across disciplines in the past decades. I explore whether there is potential for cross-pollination between the ideas on overlapping binary classifications discussed here and the developing scholarship on intersectionality. Finally, having noted potential ways that legal practitioners may be able to make best use of this book, I trouble the imperative placed on critical legal scholars to offer policy recommendations or propose prescriptive solutions to complex problems. Instead, I invite both scholars and practitioners to approach critical cultural pluralism as an ethical practice for finding relevant solutions.

6.3.1. Challenging binaries: potential applications

A key insight from this book was that undergirding seemingly objective norms are binary classifications, which are socially and culturally constructed. These constructions can help us understand the world, although they fall short in contexts that demand more nuanced approaches. The fog and chaos of wartime are fertile ground for issues that defy simple binary understandings. This is particularly the case where death arrives suddenly or violently: the dead no longer being available to provide answers as to what transpired, the surrounding community is required to go through a process of translating silences and piecing together fragments of stories.

During my work as a legal advisor to the International Committee of the Red Cross, I navigated the uncertainties prevalent in the post-conflict search for missing persons. In the aftermath of a long and brutal armed conflict, Sri Lanka had established an Office on Missing Persons to trace the fate of those who had gone missing. Locating a mass grave, identifying a body, and discerning the cause of death, I soon learned, was far from being a straight-forward process. It involved weaving narrative threads from family members' testimonies, combing through their memories of the last time they saw their loved one, and tracing detention records, if the State was willing to share them. Even the land itself became a witness, with the patterns of grass and soil revealing how long a grave had been hidden. A missing person's fate, in their absence, was determined through elements that helped construct a story within a specific social milieu.

How the law, including IHL, treats missing persons illuminates its struggle to engage with liminal spaces that challenge categorical understandings of life and death. Legal rules constructed with the presumption that death is a mutually exclusive reality to being alive, and a tangible and ascertainable fact, had to make space for "ambiguous loss" experienced by families of the missing, when confronted with the uncertainty of not knowing whether their loved one is either dead or alive.[1] Moreover, my work led me to acknowledge the extent to which recognizing the rights of missing persons was often contingent upon how their families and society at large responded to this ambiguous loss, the need to find closure, and the pursuit of justice. Therefore, the social ties of a missing person, whether as a family or community member, or as symbolic figures in broader political or cultural narratives, became crucial to how the law interacted with their legal identity as a missing person.

The work around searching for missing persons, while challenging the certainty of categorizing people either as dead or alive, also brought to the fore another binary construction in legal discourse: this is the debate regarding whether the search for missing persons must be motivated by humanitarian considerations as opposed to linking them to criminal prosecutions.[2] In my previous related work titled "The Office on Missing Persons in Sri Lanka," I engaged with this debate, arguing in favor of a victim-centered approach to searching for missing persons.[3] My learnings from this book encourage me to critically examine the assumptions in my previous work, particularly regarding the classification of certain measures as humanitarian in opposition to prosecutorial action.

What struck me too is how my conversations with families of the missing were laden with emotion, and how, as I translated their words into policy

[1] Theo Hollander, "Ambiguous Loss and Complicated Grief: Understanding the Grief of Parents of the Disappeared in Northern Uganda" (2016) 8:3 Journal of Family Theory & Review 294; Vincent Bernard, "The Disappeared and Their Families: When Suffering Is Mixed with Hope'" (2017) 99:2 International Review of the Red Cross 475.

[2] Eric Stover & Rachel Shigekane, "The Missing in the Aftermath of War: When Do the Needs of Victims' Families and International War Crimes Tribunals Clash?" (2002) 84:848 International Review of the Red Cross 845.

[3] Vishakha Wijenayake, "The Office on Missing Persons in Sri Lanka: The Importance of a Primarily Humanitarian Mandate" (2017) 99:905 International Review of the Red Cross 641.

recommendations, the intimacy of that testimony was diluted in legalese. Critical legal pluralism has given me a framework to unpack the process of translation that humanitarian legal practitioners undertake in their work, bridging the gap between international legal norms and the human, cultural, and political realities on the ground. It acknowledges how the humanitarian lawyer on the field influences how legal solutions to complex issues are framed and, in doing so, engages in a jurisgenerative exercise of constructing legal meanings while operating within a wartime context.

The reflections in this book are a reminder that epistemological and normative frameworks such as the law often operate on a schema of binary logic, a mode of thought that categorizes phenomena into oppositional pairs—legal/illegal, guilty/innocent, civilized/savage, rational/irrational, male/female. While binary logic can simplify realities for the purpose of managing complexity, it also creates reductive frameworks that fail to account for contextual nuances. By juxtaposing the narratives on suicide attackers across varying contexts with IHL provisions that maintain silence of their deaths, this book uncovered the pervasive influence of binary logics in shaping how IHL interprets agency in combatant deaths.

While the victim–perpetrator binary remained central in this analysis, additional intersecting binaries—including life/death, public/private, and secular/religious—played significant roles in structuring IHL's epistemological framework. For instance, chapter 3 explored how suicide attackers defy the life/death binary by embodying culturally specific understandings of agency that view death as an extension, rather than termination, of one's active participation in a cause. Chapter 4 showed how gender binaries reinforce the public/private divide; women were predominantly categorized as victims of violence and rendered incapable of exercising agentic violence. Yet, the case of female suicide attackers in the LTTE exemplified how women navigated and subverted these binaries, weaponizing societal perceptions of their vulnerability to achieve strategic aims. Further, chapter 5 introduced the secular/religious binary, demonstrating how IHL's purported secularism is intricately tied to colonial histories. Martyrdom operations by jihadist non-State armed groups disrupt IHL's reliance on secular rationality by foregrounding intentional religious self-harm as a form of agency. Designating such acts as "irrational" or "deviant" revealed how IHL privileged seemingly secular motivations, highlighting the inadequacy of IHL's frameworks in accommodating diverse cultural and religious narratives around violence and sacrifice.

IHL's binary classifications attempt to impose an ordered framework onto the complexities of wartime contexts. However, these rigid categories marginalize those who do not fit within their boundaries. This phenomenon reflects how overlapping exclusionary frameworks manage complexity while reinforcing systemic barriers, pushing divergent perspectives to the peripheries. The manner in which these binary constructions in IHL intersect and reinforce one another parallels a central principle of intersectionality, a framework rooted in critical race theory and developed by Kimberlé Crenshaw.[4] Intersectionality has become a framework that has gained traction across disciplines and geographies in recent decades, examining how systems of oppression overlap to create distinct and compounding barriers for individuals occupying multiple marginalized identities.[5]

While intersectionality traditionally engages with social categories such as race, gender, and class, its methodological diversity also reveals the nuanced ways power and agency operate across multiple axes of exclusion. Scholars such as Leslie McCall and Paola Rebughini provide critical insights into how intersectionality engages with agency, offering valuable tools to unpack further how identities interact with normative structures.[6] McCall underlines how, as intersectionality is applied in diverse disciplines and contexts, it also faces challenges of managing the complexity of analyzing multiple categories without falling into the trap of essentializing groups.[7]

One effect of managing complexity in intersectionality is using categories as static and deterministic, thereby diluting the agencies of those operating within systemic oppressions to navigate them and find resistance. Rebughini argues that scholarship on intersectionality often underanalyzes individuals' capacity to negotiate and resist structures of oppression, especially where static or essentialized conceptions of classifications are adopted.[8] Challenging such deterministic interpretations of intersectionality can highlight the dynamic and context-dependent ways individuals assert themselves within oppressive systems.[9] Maintaining a critical eye on how agency is balanced in intersectional frameworks enables structural analyses of exclusion while opening pathways for understanding how individuals navigate, resist, and transform these systems.[10]

The analysis in this book included both systems of exclusions in international norms and oppressions that manifest in local contexts, which have compounding

[4] Kimberlé Crenshaw, "Demarginalizing the Intersection of Race and Sex: A Black Feminist Critique of Antidiscrimination Doctrine" (1989) 1989:1 University of Chicago Legal Forum 139; Kimberlé Crenshaw, "Mapping the Margins: Intersectionality, Identity, and Violence against Women of Color" (1991) 43:6 Stanford Law Review 1241.

[5] Devon W. Carbado et al., "Intersectionality: Mapping the Movements of a Theory" (2013) 10:2 Du Bois Review: Social Science Research on Race 303.

[6] Paola Rebughini, "Agency in Intersectionality. Towards a Method for Studying the Situatedness of Action" (2021) 15 Socio 189; Leslie McCall, "The Complexity of Intersectionality" (2005) 30:3 Signs: Journal of Women in Culture and Society 1771.

[7] McCall (n. 6) 1779.

[8] Rebughini (n. 6) para. 13.

[9] Ibid. para 14.

[10] Ibid.

effects on individuals. It examined how, in oppressive wartime circumstances, diverse forms of agency that subvert rigid binary classifications emerge in cultural narratives around suicide attackers. These diverse narratives on agency offer an opportunity for cross-pollination with the burgeoning research on intersectionality, enabling it to be a more culturally plural endeavor, while underscoring the importance of recognizing how marginalized communities, framed through the lens of intersectionality, resist, reshape, and reimagine oppressive structures.

6.3.2. Critical legal pluralism as an ethical practice

My approach in this book to understanding the silence on suicide attackers' deaths in IHL was to acknowledge that while legal rules influence wartime practices, the law does not have a monopoly over dictating how an individual or society engages with wartime death. The intention of this book was not to fill a silence with a new universal norm but to critically examine why no express provisions exist in IHL regarding suicide attackers' deaths and what it says about the assumptions that determine how violence manifesting in diverse ways is regulated by this body of law. Given this objective of the study, in conclusion, I am hesitant to convert its findings into prescriptive solutions.

Naz Modirzadeh's critique of Third World Approaches to International Law (TWAIL) is indicative of the pressures placed on critical scholars who focus primarily on deconstructing existing frameworks to also engage in building alternative structures.[11] She argues that TWAIL scholarship engages in diagnosing colonial roots of international law and fails to have a transformative effect on these structures by not proposing practical tools or grassroots-driven strategies:

> TWAIL has failed to produce a coherent set of new ideas about what international law should be, how it should function, what it should seek to do in the world, and how to get there. Without such a programmatic vision of what a just, moral international order would look like, those seeking to reform international law according to TWAIL's commitments are left with little guidance.[12]

While this book did not adopt a strictly TWAIL-oriented approach, this critique resonates with me as I identify gaps and reveal prevailing assumptions in

[11] Naz K. Modirzadeh, "'Let Us All Agree to Die a Little': TWAIL's Unfulfilled Promise" (2023) 65:1 Harvard International Law Journal 79.
[12] Ibid. 90.

IHL. It makes me reflect on whether I bear a corresponding responsibility to find alternatives or make constructive proposals that appeal to policymakers. In doing so, I consider that it is important to exercise this responsibility while not reproducing universalistic frameworks or binary logic.

Legal scholars are often expected to propose solutions to social issues they examine, positioning their work as a means to reform laws and institutions. While I do not want to create an artificial separation between different types of scholarship, I admit that such an expectation would align more neatly with scholarship that is more advocacy or reform-oriented.[13] Critical scholarship aims to question cultural, historical, and ideological foundations of law, challenging assumptions and exposing the structures that sustain them.[14] Paul W. Kahn emphasizes that the role of critical legal scholarship is not necessarily to fix or reform the law but to uncover its cultural and symbolic dimensions, offering insights into how law reflects societal values and beliefs.[15] To this end, Kahn argues for a separation between academics who deconstruct law and practitioners who reform it, suggesting that the former's value lies in deepening understanding rather than prescribing solutions.[16]

Demanding critical scholars to produce easily digestible recommendations risks undermining the depth and purpose of their work, as their contributions often reside in reshaping how we think about law rather than in direct policy interventions. Therefore, I posit that the absence of prescriptive norms in critical scholarship does not diminish its importance. Instead, it performs a different function of broadening the cultural discourse around law, often while bringing in knowledge from other disciplines to reframe the contours of law. Having said that, I do not deny that exemplary critical scholars may offer transformative solutions to structural issues in the law. Perhaps one day, I will be able to do the same. However, at this stage, I acknowledge that if I were compelled to envision solutions to the issues I have unpacked, I may fall into the trap of subconsciously managing the complexity of the phenomenon merely to enhance the possibility of providing a neat solution.

As Sarah Kendall points out, critical scholars are viewed by more doctrinal international law scholars as being external to the workings of the international legal framework, observing it from a distance, "sitting on the wall looking in."[17] Kendall thus writes:

[13] Paul W. Kahn, *The Cultural Study of Law: Reconstructing Legal Scholarship* (University of Chicago Press 1999) 22.

[14] Ibid. 35.

[15] Ibid.

[16] Ibid.

[17] Sara Kendall, "On Academic Production and the Politics of Inclusion" (2016) 29:3 Leiden Journal of International Law 617, 619.

> The boundaries of critical scholarship are porous and contested, and there is a risk, as Immi Tallgren observes, that self-described critical scholars perform the very things that they fault elsewhere: "constructing blind alleys of expertise and ownership" and elevating new universal truths and false idols in place of those they have unsettled.[18]

Even when they do not propose elaborate structures to replace those riddled with bias, critical scholarship offers space to take a step back and reflect on existing structures. This scholarship provides further insights from other disciplines that challenge routine methodologies and normative commitments often taken for granted by practitioners in certain legal disciplines. This transformation can happen by infusing the law with the experiences of everyday people from diverse parts of the world, and by maintaining a healthy dose of skepticism toward the coherence of law as a normative framework, including its universal truths that purport to manage complex social issues.

This requires legal scholars and practitioners to interrogate the assumptions underlying their work, particularly those shaped by dominant epistemologies. The failure to engage in this practice perpetuates a static, decontextualized view of the law, obscuring its role as a cultural and political product. For instance, IHL's categorization of actors into binaries—victim or perpetrator, combatant or civilian—relies on criteria that reflect dominant understandings of agency and morality in a given context. These frameworks fail to account for culturally plural narratives, such as those surrounding martyrdom operations, which challenge IHL's binary constructions and illuminate its limitations. I propose that an ethical form of engaging in IHL scholarship, therefore, would entail critically engaging with these narratives and considering how legal categorizations might obscure the lived experiences and intentions of actors.

In IHL's defense, it may be argued that the demand for certainty in times of chaos created by war precipitates a shyness about challenging the existing order of legal norms for fear of displacing it without having a safety net present. Writing on conflict-related issues particularly carries a dilemma that is not merely academic but is deeply tied to the power dynamics and ethical considerations of speaking about, or for, individuals and communities affected by conflict. IHL scholars consistently grapple with the implications of challenging legal principles that were constructed with the intention of, and on the field operate to, protect populations from harm.

Amidst these ethical demands, writing about war can be profoundly emotionally taxing. My research was punctuated by occasional existential crises, as only contemplations of suicide can evoke. I questioned my own memories and

[18] Ibid. 622.

childhood recollections that, with silence and the passage of time, had become hazy. My responses, as I dug into my memory bank and realized the extent to which this project was personal, at times occurred at a primal level, making it dishonest to claim that I was able to entirely decouple them from my research. The urge to rationalize and dissociate can be strong when reading about and analyzing issues such as mass violence and death.

This is facilitated by the fact that legal writing leaves little space for its scholars to navigate these emotions or consider that the capacity to empathize or hold space for others' emotional realities in a nonprescriptive manner is relevant to legal scholarship. As Kahn notes: "Cultural pluralism is not a problem to be solved, as if we could finally articulate the right set of universal values or the appropriate scope of the particular. It is, instead, a warning that normative inquiry can no longer take the form of proscription, but must turn to self-exploration."[19] Just as law was not fully equipped to accommodate my emotional self as a researcher, it was also ill-equipped to appreciate cultural, spiritual, or gendered narratives built around the deaths of suicide attackers. Accordingly, throughout the writing of this book, I have gone through a process of discovering lenses other than that of law and playing with aspects and ratios to look at wartime practices. It was also a journey of experimenting with tools and methods that would enable me to present diverse cultural narratives.

In this journey, I tried to acknowledge my positionality in how I chose to tell these stories. When juxtaposed with the stories of individuals and communities amid war, I was grateful for the luxury to step away, even temporarily, from challenging work. As a legal scholar, rather than being merely detached observer, I chose to see myself as an active participant in the discursive construction of law. Our choices—whether to focus on doctrinal analysis, historical critique, or cultural context—shape the field within which we operate. Therefore, I encourage legal scholars to engage in an ethical practice of asking ourselves: Whose voices and experiences are excluded in the way I frame research questions? Whose agencies come under threat when law attempts to regulate behavior?

6.4. Conclusion

In concluding this examination of agency and death in the context of suicide attacks, I hope that this work has prompted readers to critically reevaluate their assumptions about international law and its engagement with complex, human phenomena. If this book leaves you with lingering questions about the interplay of agency, violence, and death, this outcome is intentional. The objective

[19] Paul W. Kahn, *Putting Liberalism in Its Place* (Princeton University Press 2009) 8.

of this study was to serve as an invitation to think more deeply, to engage with the uncertainties that permeate our understanding of law, humanity, and the narratives we construct to make sense of the world.

The phenomena of suicide attacks and the questions they raise about agency and death defy simple or conclusive explanations. They make us confront the limits of our conceptual frameworks and compel us to approach them with intellectual humility. This is not to suggest that academic research is futile. Instead, it recognizes that we need to be open to ambiguity and complexity when engaging in such pursuits.

Similarly, the process of writing this book has been profoundly humbling, revealing how certainty and order can be elusive when addressing profound questions. Much of what we regard as established knowledge is, in truth, rooted in narratives—stories that are socially constructed to impose coherence on a world that frequently resists it. Legal and cultural discourses surrounding suicide attacks are no exception. They not only attempt to make sense of these actions but also reflect the values and prejudices of the societies that construct them.

Once published, this book will inevitably enter a broader discursive space, one in which it will be subject to interpretation and critique by others. In this way, the text itself exemplifies a central theme of this study: agency and meaning are never fixed but are instead negotiated within a complex web of cultural, social, and legal contexts

Bibliography

Journals

Achsin, Muhaimin Zulhair, "Culture and Role of Women in Terrorism in Indonesia. Case Studies: Suicide Bombings in Surabaya and Sibolga" (2019) 8:5 International Journal of Engineering and Advanced Technology 873.

Adinkrah, Mensah, "Anti-Suicide Laws in Nine African Countries: Criminalization, Prosecution and Penalization" (2016) 9:1 African Journal of Criminology and Justice Studies 729.

Ahearn, Laura M., "Agency" (1999) 9:1/2 Journal of Linguistic Anthropology 12.

Albright, Todd S., Alan P. Gehrich, Johnnie Wright, Jr., Christine F. Lettieri, Susan G. Dunlow, & Jerome L. Buller, "Pregnancy during Operation Iraqi Freedom/Operation Enduring Freedom" (2007) 172:5 Military Medicine 511.

Alexander, Amanda, "A Short History of International Humanitarian Law" (2015) 26:1 European Journal of International Law 109.

Ali, Farhana, & Jerrold Post, "The History and Evolution of Martyrdom in the Service of Defensive Jihad: An Analysis of Suicide Bombers in Current Conflicts" (2008) 75:2 Social Research: An International Quarterly 615.

Alison, Miranda, "Cogs in the Wheel? Women in the Liberation Tigers of Tamil Eelam" (2003) 6:4 Civil Wars 37.

Anghie, Antony, "The Evolution of International Law: Colonial and Postcolonial Realities" (2006) 27:5 Third World Quarterly 739.

Anghie, Antony, "Francisco De Vitoria and the Colonial Origins of International Law" (1996) 5:3 Social and Legal Studies 321.

Appadurai, Arjun, "Theory in Anthropology: Center and Periphery" (1986) 28:2 Comparative Studies in Society and History 356.

Appiagyei-Atua, Kwadwo, "Ethical Dimensions of Third-World Approaches to International Law (TWAIL): A Critical Review" (2015) 8:3/4 African Journal of Legal Studies 209.

Arzt, Donna E., "Can Law Halt the Violence? Palestinian Suicide Bombings and Israeli 'Targeted Assassinations' under International Humanitarian Law" (2004) 11 ILSA Journal of International & Comparative Law 357.

Asad, Talal, "Thinking about Terrorism and Just War" (2010) 23:1 Cambridge Review of International Affairs 3.

Bartles-Smith, Andrew, "Religion and International Humanitarian Law" (2022) 104:920/921 International Review of the Red Cross 1725.

Bellal, Annyssa, & Ezequiel Heffes, "'Yes I Do': Binding Armed Non-State Actors to IHL and Human Rights Norms through Their Consent" (2018) 12 Human Rights & International Legal Discourse 120.

Benmelech, Efraim, Claude Berrebi, & Esteban F. Klor, "Economic Conditions and the Quality of Suicide Terrorism" (2012) 74:1 Journal of Politics 113.

Bennoune, Karima, "Do We Need New International Law to Protect Women in Armed Conflict" (2007) 38 Case Western Reserve Journal of International Law 363.

Benson, Kristina, "The Chaplaincy Exception in International Humanitarian Law: 'American-Born Cleric' Anwar Al-Awlaki and the Global War on Terror" (2014) 1:20 Buffalo Human Rights Law 1.

Benvenisti, Eyal, & Doreen Lustig, "Monopolizing War: Codifying the Laws of War to Reassert Governmental Authority, 1856–1874" (2020) 31:1 European Journal of International Law 127.

Bernard, Vincent, "The Disappeared and Their Families: When Suffering Is Mixed with Hope" (2017) 99:2 International Review of the Red Cross 475.

Blum, Gabriella, "The Dispensable Lives of Soldiers" (2010) 2:1 Journal of Legal Analysis 115.

Boudon, Raymond, "Beyond Rational Choice Theory" (2003) 29 Annual Review of Sociology 1.

Boyle, Kaitlin M., & Kimberly B. Rogers, "Beyond the Rape 'Victim'–'Survivor' Binary: How Race, Gender, and Identity Processes Interact to Shape Distress" (2020) 35:2 Sociological Forum 323.323.

Brenneis, Donald, "Telling Troubles: Narrative, Conflict and Experience" (1988) 30:3/4 Anthropological Linguistics 279.

Brown, Gary D., "Prisoner of War Parole: Ancient Concept, Modern Utility" (1998) 16 Military Law Review 200.

Buchan, Russell, "The Rule of Surrender in International Humanitarian Law" (2018) 51:1 Israel Law Review 3.

Bugnion, François, "Just War, War of Aggression and International Humanitarian Law" (2002) 84:867 International Review of the Red Cross 523.

Burgis-Kasthala, Michelle, "Scholarship as Dialogue: TWAIL and the Politics of Methodology" (2016) 14:4 Journal of International Criminal Justice 921.

Butler, Judith, "Performative Agency" (2010) 3:2 Journal of Cultural Economy 147.

Carbado, Devon W., Kimberlé W. Crenshaw, Vicki M. Mays, & Barbara Tomlinson, "Intersectionality: Mapping the Movements of a Theory" (2013) 10:2 Du Bois Review: Social Science Research on Race 303.

Case, Andrew D., & Carla D. Hunter, "Counterspaces: A Unit of Analysis for Understanding the Role of Settings in Marginalized Individuals' Adaptive Responses to Oppression" (2012) 50 American Journal of Community Psychology 257.

Casey, Demian, "Breaking the Chain of Violence in Israel and Palestine: Suicide Bombings and Targeted Killings under International Humanitarian Law" (2005) 32:2 Syracuse Journal of International Law and Commerce 311.

Charlesworth, Hilary, "Feminist Methods in International Law" (1999) 93:2 American Journal of International Law 379.

Charlesworth, Hilary, Christine Chinkin, & Shelley Wright, "Feminist Approaches to International Law" (1991) 85:4 American Journal of International Law 613.

Chatman, Seymour, "Towards a Theory of Narrative" (1975) 6:2 New Literary History 295.

Chen, Justin A., Andrew Courtwright, & Kevin Chien-Chang Wu, "The Role of Stigma and Denormalization in Suicide-Prevention Laws in East Asia: A Sociocultural, Historical, and Ethical Perspective" (2017) 25:5 Harvard Review of Psychiatry 229.

Christman, John, "Relational Autonomy, Liberal Individualism, and the Social Constitution of Selves" (2004) 117:1/2 Philosophical Studies: An International Journal for Philosophy in the Analytic Tradition 143.

Cockayne, James, "Islam and International Humanitarian Law: From a Clash to a Conversation between Civilizations" (2002) 84:847 International Review of the Red Cross 597.

Cover, Robert M., "Foreword: Nomos and Narrative" (1983) 97:1 Harvard Law Review 4.

Cover, Robert M., "Violence and the Word" (1986) 95:8 Yale Law Journal 1601.

Crane, Susan, "Clothing and Gender Definition: Joan of Arc" (1996) 26:2 Journal of Medieval and Early Modern Studies 297.

Crenshaw, Kimberlé, "Demarginalizing the Intersection of Race and Sex: A Black Feminist Critique of Antidiscrimination Doctrine" (1989) 1989:1 University of Chicago Legal Forum 139.

Crenshaw, Kimberlé, "Mapping the Margins: Intersectionality, Identity, and Violence against Women of Color" (1991) 43:6 Stanford Law Review 1241.

Delgado, Richard, "Storytelling for Oppositionists and Others: A Plea for Narrative" (1989) 87 Michigan Law Review 2411.
De Mel, Neloufer, "Body Politics: (Re)cognising the Female Suicide Bomber in Sri Lanka" (2016) 11:1 Indian Journal of Gender Studies 75.
Denton-Borhaug, Kelly, "War-Culture and Sacrifice" (2010) 18:2 Feminist Theology 175.
Derluyn, Ilse, Wouter Vandenhole, Stephan Parmentier, & Cindy Mels, "Victims and/or Perpetrators? Towards an Interdisciplinary Dialogue on Child Soldiers" (2015) 15:28 BMC International Journal of Health and Human Rights 1.
de Sousa Santos, B., "Law: A Map of Misreading. Toward a Post-Modern Conception of Law" (1987) 14:3 Journal of Law and Society 279.
de Ste. Croix, Geoffrey Ernest Maurice, "Why Were the Early Christians Persecuted?" (1963) 26 Past and Present 6.
de Wet, Erika, "The Prohibition of Torture as an International Norm of *jus cogens* and Its Implications for National and Customary Law" (2004) 15:1 European Journal of International Law 97.
Di Marco, Francesca, "Act or Disease? The Making of Modern Suicide in Early Twentieth-century Japan" (2013) 39:2 The Journal of Japanese Studies 325.
Dörmann, Knut, & Jose Serralvo, "Common Article 1 to the Geneva Conventions and the Obligation to Prevent International Humanitarian Law Violations" (2014) 96:895/896 International Review of the Red Cross 707.
Downing, Lisa, " '(S)extremism': Imagining Violent Women in the Twenty-First Century with Navine G. Khan-Dossos and Julia Kristeva" (2020) 43:2 Paragraph 212.
Drumbl, Mark A., "Victims Who Victimise" (2016) 4:2 London Review of International Law 217.
Druzin, Bryan H., & Anthony S. Wan, "The Theatre of Punishment: Case Studies in the Political Function of Corporal and Capital Punishment" (2015) 14:3 Washington University Global Studies Law Review 357.
Durham, Helen, & Katie O'Byrne, "The Dialogue of Difference: Gender Perspectives on International Humanitarian Law" (2010) 92:877 International Review of the Red Cross 31.
Elshtain, Jean Bethke, "The Just War Tradition and Natural Law" (2004) 28:3 Fordham International Law Journal 742.
Eslava, Luis, & Sundhya Pahuja, "Between Resistance and Reform: TWAIL and the Universality of International Law" (2011) 3:1 Trade Law & Development 103.
Eslava, Luis, & Sundhya Pahuja, "Beyond the (Post)colonial: TWAIL and the Everyday Life of International Law" (2012) 45:2 Verfassung Und Recht in Übersee [Law and Politics in Africa, Asia and Latin America] 195.
Evans, Carolyn, "The Double-Edged Sword: Religious Influences on International Humanitarian Law" (2005) 6:1 Melbourne Journal of International Law 1.
Federman, Sarah, "The 'ideal perpetrator': The French National Railways and the social construction of accountability" (2018) 49:5 Security Dialogue 327.
Federman, Sarah, "Narrative Approaches to Understanding and Responding to Conflict" (2016) International Journal of Conflict Engagement and Resolution 154.
Ferry, Griffin, "Oppression through 'Protection': A Survey of Femininity in Foundational Humanitarian Law Texts" (2017) 35:1 Law & Inequality 57.
Fierke, Karin Marie, "Agents of Death: The Structural Logic of Suicide Terrorism and Martyrdom" (2009) 1:1 International Theory 155.
Fitzgerald, April S., Rita L. Duboyce, Joan B. Ritter, Deborah J. Omori, Barbara A. Cooper, & Patrick G. O'Malley, "A Primer on the Unique Challenges of Female Soldiers' Reproductive Issues in a War-Ready Culture" (2013) 178:5 Military Medicine 511.
Fleck, D., "International Humanitarian Law a Decade after September 11: Developments and Perspectives" (2011) 14 Yearbook of International Humanitarian Law 349.
Freamon, Bernard K., "Martyrdom, Suicide, and the Islamic Law of War: A Short Legal History" (2003) 27:1 Fordham International Law Journal 299.

Fuller, Lon L., "Freedom: A Suggested Analysis" (1955) 68 Harvard Law Review 1305.
Fuller, Lon L., "Human Interaction and the Law" (1969) 14:1 American Journal of Jurisprudence 1.
Gaggioli, Gloria, "Sexual Violence in Armed Conflicts: A Violation of International Humanitarian Law and Human Rights Law" (2014) 96:894 International Review of the Red Cross 503.
Gardam, Judith, "A Feminist Analysis of Certain Aspects of International Humanitarian Law" (1992) 12:1 Australian Yearbook of International Law 265.
Gardam, Judith, "Women and the Law of Armed Conflict: Why the Silence?" (1997) 46:1 International Comparative Law Quarterly 55
Gasser, Hans-Peter, "Acts of Terror, 'Terrorism' and International Humanitarian Law" (2002) 84:847 International Review of the Red Cross 547.
Gasser, Hans-Peter, "Universal Acceptance of International Humanitarian Law: Promotional Activities of the ICRC" (1994) 302 International Review of the Red Cross 450.
Gill, Paul, "A Multi-Dimensional Approach to Suicide Bombing" (2007) 1:2 International Journal of Conflict and Violence 142.
Gowrinathan, Nimmi, "The Committed Female Fighter: The Political Identities of Tamil Women in the Liberation Tigers of Tamil Eelam" (2017) 19:3 International Feminist Journal of Politics 327.
Grimland, Meytal, Alan Apter, & Ad Kerkhof, ""The phenomenon of suicide bombing: a review of psychological and nonpsychological factors" (2006) 27:3 Crisis 107.
Hafez, Mohammed M., "The Alchemy of Martyrdom: Jihadi Salafism and Debates over Suicide Bombings in the Muslim World" (2010) 38:3 Asian Journal of Social Science 364.
Hamamra, Bilal, Rebecca Ruth Gould, & Asala Mayaleh, "Against the Depoliticisation of Palestinian Female *Shahids*" (2024) 45:13 Third World Quarterly 1929.
Harris, Rachel S., "Samson's Suicide: Death and the Hebrew Literary Canon" (2012) 17:3 Israel Studies 67.
Hogg, Nicole, "Women's Participation in the Rwandan Genocide: Mothers or Monsters?" (2010) 92:877 International Review of the Red Cross 69.
Hollander, Theo, "Ambiguous Loss and Complicated Grief: Understanding the Grief of Parents of the Disappeared in Northern Uganda" (2016) 8:3 Journal of Family Theory & Review 294.
Horowitz, Michael C., "The Rise and Spread of Suicide Bombing" (2015) 18 Annual Review of Political Science 69.
Hurka, Thomas, "Proportionality in the Morality of War" (2005) 33:1 Philosophy & Public Affairs 34.
Hutchins, Reid, "Islam and Suicide Terrorism: Separating Fact from Fiction" (2017) 9:11 Counter Terrorist Trends and Analyses 7.
Ingilan, Sajed S., "Tausug's Identity in Parang Sabil: A Critical Discourse Analysis" (2018) 22:1 CMU Journal of Science 37.
Jansen, Golie G., "Gender and War: The Effects of Armed Conflict on Women's Health and Mental Health" (2006) 21:2 Affilia 134.
Jensen, Eric Talbot, "Emerging Technologies and LOAC Signaling" (2015) 91 International Law Studies Series U.S. Naval War College 621.
Jochnick, Chris, & Roger Normand, "The Legitimation of Violence: A Critical History of the Laws of War" (1994) 35:1 Harvard International Law Journal 49.
Jordan, Kim, & Myriam Denov, "Birds of Freedom? Perspectives on Female Emancipation and Sri Lanka's Liberation Tigers of Tamil Eelam" (2007) 9:1 Journal of International Women's Studies 22.
Kahn, Paul W., "Imagining Warfare" (2013) 24:1 European Journal of International Law 199.
Kahn, Paul W., "The Paradox of Riskless Warfare" (2002) 22:3 Philosophy and Public Policy Quarterly 2.
Kahn, Paul W., "War and Sacrifice in Kosovo" (1999) 19:2/3 Philosophy and Public Policy Quarterly 1.

Kasher, Asa, & Amos Yadlin, "Assassination and Preventive Killing" (2005) 25:1 SAIS Review 41.
Kendall, Sara, "On Academic Production and the Politics of Inclusion" (2016) 29:3 Leiden Journal of International Law 617.
Kendall, Sara, & Sarah Nouwen, "Representational Practices at the International Criminal Court: The Gap between Juridified and Abstract Victimhood" (2014) 76:3 Law and Contemporary Problems 235.
Khodadadi, Bahman, "Public Interest (*Maslahat*) in Shi'i Theocracy: Implications for Legal and Political Decision-Making" (2025) 58:3 Iranian Studies 490.
Kirk, Matthew D., "Islam, Veiling & Political Agency: The Visual Performativity of Palestinian Female Suicide Bombers in Broadcast News Media" (2022) 30:3 Atlantic Journal of Communication 278.
Kleinhans, Martha-Marie, & Roderick A. Macdonald, "What Is *Critical* Legal Pluralism?" (1997) 12 Canadian Journal of Law & Society 25.
Knop, Karen, "Re/statements: Feminism and State Sovereignty in International Law Symposium: Feminist Inquiries into International Law" (1993) 3:2 Transnational Law & Contemporary Problems 293.
Kral, Michael J., "Suicide as Social Logic" (1994) 24:3 Suicide and Life-Threatening Behavior 245.
Latif, Muhaemin, "A Preliminary Study of Jemaah Islamiyah in Indonesia and The Doctrine of Suicide Bombing" (2012) 1:1 Journal of Islamic Civilization in Southeast Asia 107.
Lauterpacht, Hersch, "The Limits of the Operation of the Law of War" (1953) 30 British Yearbook of International Law 206.
Linos, Natalia, "Reclaiming the Social Body through Self-Directed Violence: Seeking Anthropological Understanding of Suicide Attacks" (2010) 26:5 Anthropology Today 8.
Lunze, Stefan, "Serving God and Caesar: Religious Personnel and Their Protection in Armed Conflict" (2004) 86:853 International Review of the Red Cross 69.
Lyall, Rewi, "Voluntary Human Shields, Direct Participation in Hostilities and the International Humanitarian Law Obligations of States" (2008) 9:2 Melbourne Journal of International Law 313.
Macdonald, Roderick A., & David Sandomierski, "Against Nomopolies" (2006) 57:4 Northern Ireland Legal Quarterly 610.
Mälksoo, Lauri, "Civilizational Diversity as Challenge to the (False) Universality of International Law" (2019) 9:1 Asian Journal of International Law 155.
Mansoor, Peter R., "The Evolution of Military Ethos over the Ages" (2014) 94:2 Phi Kappa Phi Forum 10.
Margulies, Peter, "Valor's Vices: Against a State Duty to Risk Forces in Armed Conflict" (2012) 37:2 Vermont Law Review 271.
Markus, Hazel R., & Shinobu Kitayama, "Culture and the Self: Implications for Cognition, Emotion, and Motivation" (1991) 98:2 Psychological Review 224.
Markus, Hazel R., Yukiko Uchida, Heather Omoregie, Sarah S. M. Townsend, & Shinobu Kitayama, "Going for the Gold Models of Agency in Japanese and American Contexts" (2006) 17:2 Psychological Science 103.
Matusitz, Jonathan, "Symbolism in Female Terrorism: Five Overarching Themes" (2019) 23:4 Sexuality & Culture: An Interdisciplinary Quarterly 1332.
McCall, Leslie, "The Complexity of Intersectionality" (2005) 30:3 Signs: Journal of Women in Culture and Society 1771.
McFadden, Robert W., "The Ethical Aspects of Limited War" (1971) 13:1 Journal of Church and State 113.
McMahan, Jeff, "The Just Distribution of Harm between Combatants and Noncombatants" (2010) 38:4 Philosophy and Public Affairs 342.
Mégret, Frédéric, "The Humanitarian Problem with Drones" (2013) 2013:5 Utah Law Review 1283.

Mégret, Frédéric, "The Laws of War and the Structure of Masculine Power" (2018) 19:1 Melbourne Journal of International Law 200.
Meron, Theodor, "The Humanization of Humanitarian Law" (2000) 94:2 The American Journal of International Law 239.
Meyrowitz, Henri, "Les guerres de libération et les conventions de Genève" (1974) 39:6 Politique étrangère 607.
Meyrowitz, Henri, "The Principle of Superfluous Injury or Unnecessary Suffering: From the Declaration of St. Petersburg of 1868 to Additional Protocol 1 of 1977" (1994) 34:299 International Review of the Red Cross 98.
Milanovic, Marko, & Sandesh Sivakumaran, "Assessing the authority of the ICRC Customary IHL Study" (2022) 104:920/921 International Review of the Red Cross 1856.
Milgram, Stanley, "Behavioral Study of Obedience" (1963) 67:4 Journal of Abnormal and Social Psychology 371.
Modirzadeh, Naz K., "'Let Us All Agree to Die a Little': TWAIL's Unfulfilled Promise" (2023) 65:1 Harvard International Law Journal 79.
Moghadam, Assaf, "Motives for Martyrdom: Al-Qaida, Salafi Jihad, and the Spread of Suicide Attacks" (2008) 33:3 International Security 46.
Mohamed, Saira, "Of Monsters and Men: Perpetrator Trauma and Mass Atrocity" (2015) 115:5 Columbia Law Review 1157.
Munir, Muhammad, "The Layha for the Mujahideen: An Analysis of the Code of Conduct for the Taliban Fighters under Islamic Law" (2011) 93:881 International Review of the Red Cross 1.
Munir, Muhammad, "Suicide Attacks and Islamic Law" (2008) 90:869 International Review of the Red Cross 71.
Mutua, Makau, "What Is TWAIL?" (2000) 94 Proceedings of the ASIL Annual Meeting 31.
Nagel, Joane, "Masculinity and Nationalism: Gender and Sexuality in the Making of Nations" (1998) 21:2 Ethnic and Racial Studies 242.
Niezen, Ronald, "The Durkheim-Tarde Debate and the Social Study of Aboriginal Youth Suicide" (2015) 52:1 Transcultural Psychiatry 96.
Obradovic, Lana, "Comparative Analysis of Women's Military Participation in East Asia" (2015) 1 Res Militaris 1.
Oosterveld, Valerie, "Feminist Debates on Civilian Women and International Humanitarian Law" (2009) 27 Windsor Yearbook of Access to Justice 385.
Osborne, Thomas, "'Fascinated Dispossession': Suicide and the Aesthetics of Freedom" (2005) 34:2 Economy and Society 280.
Panikkar, R., "Is the Notion of Human Rights a Western Concept?" (1982) 30:120 Diogenes 75.
Parashar, Swati, "Feminist International Relations and Women Militants: Case Studies from Sri Lanka and Kashmir" (2009) 22:2 Cambridge Review of International Affairs 235.
Pettygrove, Margaret, "Conceptions of War in Islamic Legal Theory and Practice" (2007) 2:3 Macalester Islam Journal 6.
Pipes, Daniel, "The Scourge of Suicide Terrorism" (1986) 4 The National Interest 95.
Porter, Patrick, "War and the Religious Will to Sacrifice" (2005) 17:1 Peace Review: A Journal of Social Justice 17.
Posner, Eric, & Alan Sykes, "An Economic Analysis of State and Individual Responsibility under International Law" (2007) 9:1 American Law and Economics Review 72.
Provost, René, "L'attaque directe d'enfants-soldats en droit international humanitaire" (2018) 55 Annuaire canadien de droit international 33.
Provost, René, "The International Committee of the Red Widget? The Diversity Debate and International Humanitarian Law" (2007) 40:2 Israel Law Review 614.
Provost, René, & Myriam Denov, "From Violence to Life: Children Born of War and Constructions of Victimhood" (2019) 53:1 New York University Journal of International Law and Politics 1.

Provost, René, & Vishakha Wijenayake, "Collateral Kids: Weighing the Lives of Children in Targeting" (2024) 37:4 Leiden Journal of International Law 1018.
Qirko, Hector N., "Altruism in Suicide Terror Organizations" (2009) 44:2 Zygon 289.
Radhakrishnan, Akila, Elena Sarver, & Grant Shubin, "Protecting Safe Abortion in Humanitarian Settings: Overcoming Legal and Policy Barriers" (2017) 25:51 Reproductive Health Matters 40.
Rahimi, Babak, "Sacrifice, Transcendence and the Soldier" (2005) 17:1 Peace Review: A Journal of Social Justice 1.
Rajasingham-Senanayake, Darini, "Between Reality and Representation: Women's Agency in War and Post-Conflict Sri Lanka" (2004) 16:2/3 Cultural Dynamics 141.
Rebughini, Paola, "Agency in Intersectionality. Towards a Method for Studying the Situatedness of Action" (2021) 15 Socio. La nouvelle revue des sciences sociales 189.
Reeves, Shane R., & William J. Johnson, "Autonomous Weapons: Are You Sure Those Are Killer Robots—Can We Talk about It" (2014) 2014:4 Army Lawyer 25.
Riles, Annelise, "Anthropology, Human Rights, and Legal Knowledge: Culture in the Iron Cage" (2006) 108:1 American Anthropologist 52.
Robinson, Paul, "'Ready to Kill but Not to Die': NATO Strategy in Kosovo" (1999) 54:4 International Journal 671.
Salaymeh, Lena, "Comparing Islamic and International Laws of War: Orthodoxy, 'Heresy,' and Secularization in the Category of Civilians" (2021) 69:1 The American Journal of Comparative Law 136.
Sato, Makiko, "The Prohibition of Suicide for Affirmation of Human Beings by Augustine" (2015) 11 Journal of Patrology and Critical Hagiography 135.
Schmitt, Michael, "Precision attack and international humanitarian law" (2005) 87:859 International Review of the Red Cross 445.
Sheldon, Sally, "ReConceiving Masculinity: Imagining Men's Reproductive Bodies in Law" (1999) 26:2 Journal of Law and Society 129.
Şimşek, Bahar, & Joost Jongerden, "Gender Revolution in Rojava: The Voices beyond Tabloid Geopolitics" (2018) 26:4 Geopolitics 1023.
Slavicek, David Jan, "Deconstructing the Shariatic Justification of Suicide Bombings" (2008) 31:6 Studies in Conflict and Terrorism 553.
Smith, Leonard V., "War and 'Politics': The French Army Mutinies of 1917" (1995) 2:2 War in History 180.
Somers, Margaret R., "The narrative constitution of identity: A relational and network approach" (1994) 23:5 Theory and Society 605.
Stevenson, Lisa, "The Psychic Life of Biopolitics: Survival, Cooperation, and Inuit Community" (2012) 39:3 American Ethnologist 592.
Stover, Eric, & Rachel Shigekane, "The Missing in the Aftermath of War: When Do the Needs of Victims' Families and International War Crimes Tribunals Clash?" (2002) 84:848 International Review of the Red Cross 845.
Strawser, Bradley Jay, "Moral Predators: The Duty to Employ Uninhabited Aerial Vehicles" (2010) 9:4 Journal of Military Ethics 342.
Swann, William B. Jr., & Jolanda Jetten, "Restoring Agency to the Human Actor" (2017) 12:3 Perspectives on Psychological Science 382.
Taft, William H. IV, "The Law of Armed Conflict after 9/11: Some Salient Features" (2003) 28:2 Yale Journal of International Law 319.
Tansey, Roger, "A Legal Analysis of Suicide Bombing: Blowing up the Law of War?" (2004) 5 Harvard Kennedy School Review 45.
Taylor, Chloë, "Birth of the Suicidal Subject: Nelly Arcan, Michel Foucault, and Voluntary Death" (2015) 56:2 Culture, Theory and Critique 187.
Tierney, Thomas F., "The Governmentality of Suicide: Peuchet, Marx, Durkheim, and Foucault" (2010) 10:4 Journal of Classical Sociology 357.

Toguslu, Erkan, "Caliphate, *Hijrah* and Martyrdom as Performative Narrative in ISIS *Dabiq* Magazine" (2019) 20:1 Politics, Religion & Ideology 94.

Tosini, Domenico, "A Sociological Understanding of Suicide Attacks" (2009) 26:4 Theory, Culture & Society 67.

Trawick, Margaret, "Reasons for Violence: A Preliminary Ethnographic Account of the LTTE" (1997) 20:1 South Asia Journal of South Asian Studies 153.

van Dijk, Boyd, "Internationalizing Colonial War: on the Unintended Consequences of the Interventions of the International Committee of the Red Cross in South-East Asia, 1945–1949" (2020) 250:1 Past and Present 243.

van Wijk, Joris, "Who Is the 'Little Old Lady' of International Crimes? Nils Christie's Concept of the Ideal Victim Reinterpreted" (2013) 19:2 International Review of Victimology 159.

Montanari Vergallo, Gianluca, & Matteo Gulino, "End-of-Life Care and Assisted Suicide: An Update on the Italian Situation from the Perspective of the European Court of Human Rights" (2022) 21 Ethics, Medicine and Public Health.

Wagemakers, Joas, "Jihadi-Salafism in Jordan and the Syrian Conflict: Divisions Overcome Unity" (2018) 41:3 Studies in Conflict and Terrorism 191.

Walker, Jeffrey K., "Old Laws and New Wars" (2000) 94 Proceedings of the ASIL Annual Meeting 312.

Watts, Sean, "Regulation-Tolerant Weapons, Regulation-Resistant Weapons and the Law of War" (2015) 91 International Law Studies Series U.S. Naval War College 540.

Webber, Jeremy, "Legal Pluralism and Human Agency" (2006) 44:1 Osgoode Hall Law Journal 167.

Weiss, Caleb, "Reigniting the Rivalry: The Islamic State in Somalia vs. al-Shabaab" (2019) 12:4 Combating Terrorism Center Sentinel 29.

White, James Boyd, "Economics and Law: Two Worlds in Tension" (1987) 54 Tennessee Law Review 161.

White, L. Michael, "Review of A Noble Death: Suicide and Martyrdom among Christians and Jews in Antiquity" (1994) 113:2 Journal of Biblical Literature 358.

Wijenayake, Vishakha, "The Office on Missing Persons in Sri Lanka: The Importance of a Primarily Humanitarian Mandate" (2017) 99:905 International Review of the Red Cross 641.

Wiktorowicz, Quintan, "Anatomy of the Salafi Movement" (2006) 29:3 Studies in Conflict and Terrorism 207.

Williams, Joan, "Market Work and Family Work in the 21st Century" (1999) 44 Villanova Law Review 305.

Zenn, Jacob, "Boko Haram's Conquest for the Caliphate: How Al Qaeda Helped Islamic State Acquire Territory" (2020) 43:2 Studies in Conflict and Terrorism 89.

Ziv, Bohrer, "The Superior Orders Defense: A Principal-Agent Analysis" (2014) 41:1 Georgia Journal of International Comparative Law 1.

Book Chapters

Alexander, Amanda, "Narrative Contingency and International Humanitarian Law" in Ingo Venzke & Kevin Jon Heller (eds.) *Contingency in International Law* (Oxford University Press 2021).

Alison, Miranda, "'In the War Front We Never Think That We Are Women': Women, Gender, and the Liberation Tamil Tigers of Eelam" in Laura Sjoberg & Caron E. Gentry (eds.) *Women, Gender, and Terrorism* (University of Georgia Press 2011).

Amundsen, Darrel W., "Suicide and Early Christian Values" in Baruch A. Brody (ed.) *Suicide and Euthanasia. Historical and Contemporary Themes* (Springer Netherlands 1989).

Bass, Daniel, "Making Sense of the Census in Sri Lanka: Up-Country Tamils and Sri Lankan Tamil Nationalism" in R. Cherana (ed.) *Pathways of Dissent: Tamil Nationalism in Sri Lanka* (Sage 2009).

Berman, Nathaniel, "'The Appeals of the Orient': Colonized Desire and the War of the Riff" in Karen Knop (ed.) *Gender and Human Rights* (Oxford University Press 2004).
Bille-Brahe, Unni, "Sociology and Suicidal Behaviour" in Keith Hawton & Kees van Heeringen (eds.) *The International Handbook of Suicide and Attempted Suicide* (Wiley 2000).
Blum, Gabriella, "The Individualization of War: From War to Policing in the Regulation of Armed Conflicts" in Austin Sarat, Lawrence Douglas, & Martha Merrill Umphrey (eds.) *Law and War* (Stanford University Press 2013).
Bosma, Alice, Eva Mulder, & Antony Pemberton, "The Ideal Victim through Other(s') Eyes" in Marian Duggan (ed.) *Developments in Critical Victimology* (Bristol University Press 2018).
Cardinal, Pierre-Alexandre, & Frédéric Mégret, "The Other 'Other': Moors, International Law and the Origin of the Colonial Matrix" in Ayesha Shahid & Ignacio de la Rasilla del Moral (eds.) *International Law and Islam: Historical Explorations* (Brill Nijhoff 2018).
Charlesworth, Hilary, "Worlds Apart: Public/Private Distinctions in International Law" in Margaret Thornton (ed.) *Public and Private: Feminist Legal Debates* (Oxford University Press 1995).
Childs, John, "Surrender and the Laws of War in Western Europe, c. 1660–1783" in Holger Afflerbach & Hew Strachan (eds.) *How Fighting Ends: A History of Surrender* (Oxford University Press 2012).
Christie, Nils, "The Ideal Victim" in Ezzat A. Fattah (ed.) *From Crime Policy to Victim Policy* (Macmillan 1986).
Cook, Rebecca J. & Verónica Undurraga, "Article 12" in Marsha A. Freeman, Christine Chinkin & Beate Rudolf (eds.) *The UN Convention on the Elimination of All Forms of Discrimination against Women: A Commentary* (Oxford University Press 2012)
Douzinas, Costas, "Speaking Law: On Bare Theological and Cosmopolitan Sovereignty" in Anne Orford (ed.) *International Law and Its Others* (Cambridge University Press 2006).
Evangelidi, Anna, "Restraint in Bello: Some Thoughts on Reciprocity and Humanity" in Mats Deland, Mark Klamberg, & Pål Wrange (eds.) *International Humanitarian Law and Justice: Historical and Sociological Perspectives* (Routledge 2018).
Foucault, Michel, "The Order of Discourse" in Robert Young (ed.) *Untying the Text* (Routledge & Kegan Paul 1981).
Gambetta, Diego, "Can We Make Sense of suicide Missions?" in Diego Gambetta (ed.) *Making Sense of Suicide Missions* (Oxford University Press 2006).
Gillingham, John, "Surrender in Medieval Europe—An Indirect Approach" in Holger Afflerbach & Hew Strachan (eds.) *How Fighting Ends: A History of Surrender* (Oxford University Press 2012).
Grear, Anna, "'Sexing the Matrix': Embodiment, Disembodiment and Law: Towards the Regendering of Legal Rationality?" in Jackie Jones, Anna Grear, Rachel A. Fenton, & Kim Stevenson (eds.) *Gender, Sexualities and Law* (Routledge 2011).
Haskell, John D., "Hugo Grotius in the Contemporary Memory of International Law: Secularism, Liberalism, and the Politics of Restatement and Denial" in José María Beneyto & David Kennedy (eds.) *New Approaches to International Law: The European and the American Experiences* (T. M. C. Asser Press 2013).
Haskell, John D., & Pamela Slotte, "Christianity and International Law: An Introduction" in Pamela Slotte & John D. Haskell (eds.) *Law and Christianity* (Cambridge University Press 2021).
Hassig, Ross, "How Fighting Ended in the Aztec Empire and Its Surrender to the Europeans" in Holger Afflerbach & Hew Strachan (eds.) *How Fighting Ends: A History of Surrender* (Oxford University Press 2012).
Hill, Peter, "Kamikaze" in Diego Gambetta (ed.) *Making Sense of Suicide Missions* (Oxford University Press 2005).
Hunter, Rosemary, "Contesting the Dominant Paradigm: Feminist Critiques of Liberal Legalism" in Vanessa E. Munro & Margaret Davies (eds.) *The Ashgate Research Companion to Feminist Legal Theory* (Taylor & Francis 2013).

Jaworski, Katrina, "Suicide, Agency, and Limits of Power" in Ludek Broz & Daniel Münster (eds.) *Suicide and Agency: Anthropological Perspectives on Self-Destruction, Personhood, and Power* (Routledge 2016).

Jug, Steven G., "Mourning Deaths and Constructing Afterlives in the Red Army at War" in Candi K. Cann (ed.) *The Routledge Handbook of Death and the Afterlife* (Routledge 2018).

Keely, Lawrence H., "Surrender and Prisoners in Prehistoric and Tribal Societies" in Holger Afflerbach & Hew Strachan (eds.) *How Fighting Ends: A History of Surrender* (Oxford University Press 2012).

Kennedy, David, "Images of Religion in International Legal Theory" in Mark W. Janis & Carolyn Evans (eds.) *Religion and International Law* (Martinus Nijhoff 1999).

Kennedy, David, "Losing Faith in the Secular: Law, Religion, and the Culture of International Governance" in Mark W. Janis & Carolyn Evans (eds.) *Religion and International Law* (Martinus Nijhoff 1999).

Kita, Yoshito, "The Japanese Military's Attitude Towards International Law and the Treatment of Prisoners of War" in Ian Gow, Yoichi Hirama, & John Chapman (eds.) *The History of Anglo-Japanese Relations, 1600–2000* (Palgrave Macmillan UK 2003).

Kortüm, Hans-Henning, "Surrender in Medieval Times" in Holger Afflerbach & Hew Strachan (eds.) *How Fighting Ends: A History of Surrender* (Oxford University Press 2012).

Liivoja, Rain, "Chivalry without a Horse: Military Honour and the Modern Law of Armed Conflict" in Rain Liivoja & Andres Saumets (eds.) *The Law of Armed Conflict: Historical and Contemporary Perspectives* (Tartu University Press 2012).

Lonnqvist, Jouko K., "Psychiatric Aspects of Suicidal Behaviour: Depression" in Keith Hawton & Kees van Heeringen (eds.) *The International Handbook of Suicide and Attempted Suicide* (Wiley 2000).

Lye, Kit Ying, & Terence Heng, "Introduction" in Kit Ying Lye & Terence Heng (eds.) *Death and the Afterlife: Multidisciplinary Perspectives from a Global City* (Routledge 2024).

MacKinnon, Catharine A., "Feminism, Marxism, Method, and the State: Toward Feminist Jurisprudence" in Katharine T. Bartlett & Rosanne Kennedy (eds.) *Feminist Legal Theory: Readings in Law and Gender* (Westview Press 1991).

Mackenzie, Catriona, & Natalie Stoljar, "Introduction: Autonomy Refigured" in Catriona Mackenzie and Natalie Stoljar (eds.) *Relational Autonomy: Feminist Perspectives on Autonomy, Agency, and the Social Self* (Oxford University Press 2000).

Markus, Hazel R., & Shinobu Kitayama, *Cross-Cultural Differences in Perspectives on the Self* (University of Nebraska Press 2003).

Mégret, Frédéric, "From 'Savages' to 'Unlawful Combatants': A Postcolonial Look at International Humanitarian Law's 'Other'" in Ann Orford (ed.) *International Law and Its Others* (Cambridge University Press 2006).

Munir, M., "Suicide Attacks: Martyrdom Operations or Acts of Perfidy?" in Marie-Luisa Frick & Andreas T. Müller (eds.) *Islam and International Law* (Brill Nijhoff 2013).

Münster, Daniel, & Ludek Broz "The Anthropology of Suicide: Ethnography and the Tension of Agency" in Daniel Münster and Ludek Broz (eds.) *Suicide and Agency: Anthropological Perspectives on Self-Destruction, Personhood, and Power* (Routledge 2016).

Niezen, Ronald, & Sarah Federman, "Introduction: Narrative in the Aftermath of Mass Atrocity" in Ronald Niezen & Sarah Federman (eds.) *Narratives of Mass Atrocity: Victims and Perpetrators in the Aftermath* (Cambridge University Press 2022).

Oshana, Marina, "Is Social-Relational Autonomy a Plausible Ideal?" in Marina Oshana (ed.) *Personal Autonomy and Social Oppression* (Routledge 2014).

Pictet, Jean, "Humanitarian Ideas Shared by Different Schools of Thought and Cultural Traditions" in Henry Dunant Institute, *International Dimensions of Humanitarian Law* (Martinus Nijhoff 1988).

Prestwich, Patricia E., "Suicide and French Soldiers of the First World War: Differing Perspectives 1914-1939" in John C. Weaver & David Wright (eds.) *Histories of Suicide: International Perspectives on Self-Destruction in the Modern World* (University of Toronto Press 2009).

Provost, René, "Asymmetrical Reciprocity and Compliance with the Laws of War" in Benjamin Perrin (ed.) *Modern Warfare: Armed Groups, Private Militaries, Humanitarian Organizations, and the Law* (UBC Press 2012).

Provost, René, "Enfants-soldats, civils ou combattants? Expériences et réflexions canadiennes" in Oonagh Fitzgerald, Valerie Hughes, & Mark Jewett (eds.) *Réflexion sur le passé, le présent et l'avenir du Canada en droit international* (CIGI Press 2018).

Provost, René, "Interpretation in International Law as a Transcultural Project" in Andrea Bianchi, Daniel Peat, & Matthew Windsor (eds.) *Interpretation in International Law* (Oxford University Press 2015).

Provost, René, & Colleen Sheppard, "Introduction: Human Rights through Legal Pluralism" in René Provost & Colleen Sheppard (eds.) *Dialogues on Human Rights and Legal Pluralism* (Springer Netherlands 2013).

Satkunanathan, Ambika, "Whose Nation? Power, Agency, Gender and Tamil Nationalism" in Asanga Welikala (ed.) *Sri Lankan Republic at 40: Reflections on Constitutional History, Theory and Practice* (Centre for Policy Alternatives 2012).

Sharpe, Dean, & Natalia Linos, "Dying to Live in Palestine: Steadfastness, Pollution and Embodied Space" in John C. Weaver & David Wright (eds.) *Histories of Suicide: International Perspectives on Self-Destruction in the Modern World* (University of Toronto Press 2009).

Sheftall, Mordecai G., "Kamikaze Warfare in Imperial Japan's Existential Crisis, 1944–5" in Holger Afflerbach & Hew Strachan (eds.) *How Fighting Ends: A History of Surrender* (Oxford University Press 2012).

Sjoberg, Laura, "Introduction" in Laura Sjoberg (ed.) *Gender and International Security: Feminist Perspectives* (Routledge 2009).

Smith, Patricia, "Four Themes in Feminist Legal Theory: Difference, Dominance, Domesticity, and Denial" in Martin P. Golding & William A. Edmundsom (eds.) *The Blackwell Guide to the Philosophy of Law and Legal Theory* (John Wiley & Sons 2008).

Strachan, Hew, "Introduction: Surrender in Modern Warfare since the French Revolution" in Holger Afflerbach & Hew Strachan (eds.) *How Fighting Ends: A History of Surrender* (Oxford University Press 2012).

Sykes, Stephen, "Sacrifice and the Ideology of War" in Robert A. Hinde (ed.) *The Institution of War* (Palgrave Macmillan 1992).

Traskman-Bendz, Lil, & J. John Mann, "Biological Aspects of Suicidal Behaviour" in Keith Hawton & Kees van Heeringen (eds.) *The International Handbook of Suicide and Attempted Suicide* (Wiley 2000).

von Ungern-Sternberg, Antje, "Religion and Religious Intervention" in Bardo Fassbender & Anne Peters (eds.) *Oxford Handbook of the History of International Law* (Oxford University Press 2012).

Walter, Tony, "Facing Death without Tradition" in Glennys Howarth & Peter C. Jupp (eds.) *Contemporary Issues in the Sociology of Death, Dying and Disposal* (St. Martin's Press 1996).

Books

Abufarha, Nasser, *The Making of a Human Bomb: An Ethnography of Palestinian Resistance* (Duke University Press 2009).

Alison, Miranda H., *Women and Political Violence: Female Combatants in Ethno-National Conflict* (Routledge 2009).

Arendt, Hannah, *Eichmann in Jerusalem: A Report on the Banality of Evil* (1st ed., Penguin Classics 2006).

Asad, Talal, *Formations of the Secular: Christianity, Islam, Modernity* (Stanford University Press 2003).

Asad, Talal, *Genealogies of Religion: Discipline and Reasons of Power in Christianity and Islam* (Johns Hopkins University Press 1993).

Austin, John, *The Province of Jurisprudence Determined*. Edited by Wildrid E. Rumble (Cambridge University Press 2009).
Avemarie, Friedrich, & Jan Willem van Henten, *Martyrdom and Noble Death: Selected Texts from Graeco-Roman, Jewish and Christian Antiquity* (Routledge 2002).
Balasingham, Adele Ann, *Women Fighters of Liberation Tigers* (Thasan Printers 1993).
Barak, Eitan, *Deadly Metal Rain: The Legality of Flechette Weapons in International Law: A Reappraisal Following Israel's Use of Flechettes in the Gaza Strip (2001-2009)* (Brill 2011).
Barnett, Hilaire, *Sourcebook on Feminist Jurisprudence* (Taylor and Francis 2012).
Bergen, Peter L., *The Osama bin Laden I Know: An Oral History of al Qaeda's Leader* (1st ed., Free Press 2006).
Best, Geoffrey Francis Andrew, *War and Law since 1945* (paperback ed., Oxford University Press 1997).
Bloom, Mia, *Bombshell: Women and Terrorism* (University of Pennsylvania Press 2011).
Bloom, Mia, *Dying to Kill: The Allure of Suicide Terror* (Columbia University Press 2007).
Borges, Jorge Luis, *A Universal History of Infamy*. Translated by Norman Thomas di Giovanni (Penguin Books 1975).
Bouris, Erica, *Complex Political Victims* (Kumarian Press 2007).
Bruner, Jerome, *Acts of Meaning* (Harvard University Press 1990).
Butler, Judith, *Gender Trouble: Tenth Anniversary Edition* (Routledge 2002).
Butler, Judith, *Precarious Life: The Powers of Mourning and Violence* (1st ed., Verso 2004).
Butler, Judith, *Undoing Gender* (Routledge 2004).
Carpenter, Charli, *Forgetting Children Born of War: Setting the Human Rights Agenda in Bosnia and Beyond* (Columbia University Press 2010).
Cavallar, Georg, *Imperfect Cosmopolis: Studies in the History of International Legal Theory and Cosmopolitan Ideas* (University of Wales Press 2011).
Chinkin, Christine, & Mary Kaldor, *International Law and New Wars* (Cambridge University Press 2017).
Clements, Jonathan, *A Brief History of the Samurai: A New History of the Warrior Elite* (Robinson 2010).
Coates, Anthony J., *The Ethics of War* (1st ed., Manchester University Press 1997).
Constable, Marianne, *Just Silences: The Limits and Possibilities of Modern Law* (Princeton University Press 2005).
Cormack, Margaret (ed.) *Sacrificing the Self: Perspectives on Martyrdom and Religion* (Oxford University Press 2002).
Cover, Robert M., *Narrative, Violence, and the Law: The Essays of Robert Cover*. Edited by Martha Minow, Michael Ryan, & Austin Sarat (University of Michigan Press 1995).
d'Aspremont, Jean, *International Law as a Belief System* (Oxford University Press 2017).
de Charny, Geoffroi, Richard W. Kaeuper, & Elspeth Kennedy, *A Knight's Own Book of Chivalry* (University of Pennsylvania Press 2013).
De Mel, Neloufer, *Militarizing Sri Lanka: Popular Culture, Memory and Narrative in the Armed Conflict* (SAGE 2007).
de Vattel, Emmerich, *Le droit des gens ou Principes de la loi naturelle, appliqués à la conduite et aux affaires des nations et des souverains* (1758).
de Vattel, Emmerich, Joseph Chitty, & Edward Duncan Ingraham, *The Law of Nations, or, Principles of the Law of Nature Applied to the Conduct and Affairs of Nations and Sovereigns* (T. & J.W. Johnson 1867).
de Vitoria, Francisco, *Relectiones Theologicae*. Translated by Joseph B. Bogen (Bobbs-Merrill 1964).
Douglas, Mary, *Purity and Danger: An Analysis of Concepts of Pollution and Taboo* (Routledge & Kegan Paul 1966).
Douglas, Mary, *Risk and Blame: Essays in Cultural Theory* (1st ed., Routledge 1992).
Dunant, Henry *A Memory of Solferino*. Translated by the American Red Cross (American Red Cross 1959).

Durkheim, Émile, *On Suicide*. Translated by Robin Buss (Penguin Books 2006).
Enloe, Cynthia, *Bananas, Beaches and Bases: Making Feminist Sense of International Politics* (2nd ed., University of California Press 2014).
Enloe, Cynthia H., *Maneuvers: The International Politics of Militarizing Women's Lives* (University of California Press 2000).
Finnis, John, *Human Rights and Common Good: Collected Essays Volume III* (Oxford University Press 2011).
Finnis, John, *Natural Law and Natural Rights* (Oxford University Press 1980).
French, Nathan S., *And God Knows the Martyrs: Martyrdom and Violence in Jihadi-Salafism* (Oxford University Press 2020).
Gagnebin, Bernard, & Marc Gazay, *Encounter with Henry Dunant* (Georg 1963).
Gardam, Judith Gail, & Michelle J. Jarvis, *Women, Armed Conflict, and International Law* (Kluwer Law International 2001).
Geertz, Clifford, *The Interpretation of Cultures* (Basic Books 1973).
Gentry, Caron E., & Laura Sjoberg, *Beyond Mothers, Monsters, Whores: Thinking about Women's Violence in Global Politics* (Bloomsbury 2015).
Glenn, Patrick, *The Cosmopolitan State* (Oxford University Press 2013).
Glenn, Patrick, *Legal Traditions of the World: Sustainable Diversity in Law* (5th ed., Oxford University Press 2014).
Goldstein, Joshua S., *War and Gender: How Gender Shapes the War System and Vice Versa* (Cambridge University Press 2001).
Graves, Robert, *Good-Bye to All That: An Autobiography* (2nd rev. ed., Vintage 1958).
Green, Leslie C., *The Contemporary Law of Armed Conflict* (Manchester University Press 2018).
Greenspan, Morris, *The Modern Law of Land Warfare* (University of California Press 1959).
Grotius, Hugo, *De Jure Belli ac Pacis*. Translated by Francis W. Kelsey (The Carnegie Institution 1925).
Gunaratna, Rohan, *Inside Al Qaeda: Global Network of Terror* (Columbia University Press 2002).
Halder, Radhika, *Understanding Suicide Terrorism* (Routledge 2019).
Hallam, Elizabeth Jenny Hockey, & Glennys Howarth, *Beyond the Body: Death and Social Identity* (Routledge 1999).
Hamilton, V. Lee, & Herbert Kelman, *Crimes of Obedience: Toward a Social Psychology of Authority and Responsibility* (rev. ed., Yale University Press 1990).
Harmon, Christopher C., *Terrorism Today* (Routledge 2000).
Hart, H. L. A., *The Concept of Law* (Oxford University Press 1994).
Hassan, Riaz, *Suicide Bombings* (Routledge 2011).
Hatina, Meir, *Martyrdom in Modern Islam: Piety, Power, and Politics* (Cambridge University Press 2014).
Hecht, Jennifer Michael, *Stay: A History of Suicide and the Philosophies Against It* (Yale University Press 2013).
Henshall, Kenneth G., *Historical Dictionary of Japan to 1945* (Scarecrow Press 2014).
Hobbes, Thomas, & Henry Morley, *Leviathan: Or, the Matter, Form, and Power of a Commonwealth Ecclesiastical and Civil* (4th ed., G. Routledge and Sons 1894).
Howarth, Glennys, *Death and Dying: A Sociological Introduction* (Wiley 2007).
Hoyt, Edwin P., *Warlord: Tojo against the World* (Cooper Square Press 2001).
Hughes, Michael J., *Forging Napoleon's Grande Armée: Motivation, Military Culture, and Masculinity in the French Army, 1800-1808* (NYU Press 2012).
Hume, David, *On Suicide* (Penguin 2005).
Huntington, Samuel P., *The Soldier and the State: The Theory and Politics of Civil-Military Relations* (Harvard University Press 1957).
Hurd, Elizabeth Shakman, *The Politics of Secularism in International Relations* (Princeton University Press 2009).

Ignatieff, Michael, *The Warrior's Honor: Ethnic War and the Modern Conscience* (Metropolitan Books 1997).
Israeli, Raphael, *Dying as a Shahid: Martyrs in Islam* (Strategic Book Publishing & Rights Agency 2019).
Jacomet, Robert, *Les lois de la guerre continentale* (2nd ed., L. Fournier 1913).
Jamison, Kay Redfield, *Night Falls Fast: Understanding Suicide* (Vintage 1999).
Kahn, Paul W., *Putting Liberalism in Its Place* (Princeton University Press 2008).
Kahn, Paul W., *Sacred Violence: Torture, Terror, and Sovereignty* (University of Michigan Press 2008).
Kahn, Paul W., *The Cultural Study of Law: Reconstructing Legal Scholarship* (University of Chicago Press 1999).
Kastner, Philipp, *Legal Normativity in the Resolution of Internal Armed Conflict* (Cambridge University Press 2015).
Kelsen, Hans, *Pure Theory of Law* (University of California Press 1967).
Kinsella, Helen, *The Image before the Weapon: A Critical History of the Distinction between Combatant and Civilian* (Cornell University Press 2016).
Koskenniemi, Martti, *The Gentle Civilizer of Nations* (Cambridge University Press 2001).
Levitt, Matthew, *Hamas: Politics, Charity, and Terrorism in the Service of Jihad* (Yale University Press 2006).
Malathy, N., & Radha d'Souza, *A Fleeting Moment in My Country: The Last Years of the LTTE De-Facto State* (Clarity Press 2012).
Marsh, Ian, *Suicide: Foucault, History and Truth* (Cambridge University Press 2010).
McMahan, Jeff, *Killing in War* (Clarendon Press 2009).
Mekky, Omar, *Islamic Jihadism and the Laws of War: A Conversation in International and Islamic Law Languages* (Oxford University Press 2023).
Melzer, Nils, *International Humanitarian Law: A Comprehensive Introduction* (International Committee of the Red Cross 2019).
Minois, Georges, & Lydia G. Cochrane, *History of Suicide: Voluntary Death in Western Culture* (Johns Hopkins University Press 1999).
Morrissey, Susan K., *Suicide and the Body Politic in Imperial Russia* (Cambridge University Press 2007).
Moss, Candida R., *Ancient Christian Martyrdom: Diverse Practices, Theologies, and Traditions* (Yale University Press 2012).
Nader, Laura, *The Life of the Law* (University of California Press 2005).
Nedelsky, Jennifer, *Law's Relations: A Relational Theory of Self, Autonomy, and Law* (Oxford University Press 2012).
Nietzsche, Friedrich, *Thus Spake Zarathustra*. Translated by Thomas Common (Dover Publications 1999).
Nitobe, Inazo, *Bushido, the Soul of Japan* (12th ed., Teibi Publishing 1907).
O'Donovan, Katherine, *Sexual Divisions in Law* (Weidenfeld & Nicolson 1985).
Ohnuki-Tierney, Emiko, *Kamikaze, Cherry Blossoms and Nationalisms: The Militarization of Aesthetics in Japanese History* (University of Chicago Press 2002).
Ohnuki-Tierney, Emiko, *Kamikaze Diaries: Reflections of Japanese Student Soldiers* (University of Chicago Press 2006).
Omara-Otunnu, Amii, *Politics and the Military in Uganda, 1890–1985* (Palgrave Macmillan 1987).
O'Rourke, Catherine, *Women's Rights in Armed Conflict under International Law* (Cambridge University Press 2020).
Ortbals, Candice D., & Lori M. Poloni-Staudinger, *Gender and Political Violence: Women Changing the Politics of Terrorism* (Springer 2018).
Oshana, Marina, *Personal Autonomy in Society* (Routledge 2006).
Osiel, Mark J., *Obeying Orders: Atrocity, Military Discipline and the Law of War* (Routledge 2001).
Pape, Robert, *Dying to Win: The Strategic Logic of Suicide Terrorism* (Random House 2006).

Pictet, Jean, *Development and Principles of International Humanitarian Law* (Brill Nijhoff 1985).
Provost, René, *International Human Rights and Humanitarian Law* (Cambridge University Press 2002).
Provost, René, *Rebel Courts: The Administration of Justice by Armed Insurgents* (Oxford University Press 2021).
Rajan, Julie, *Women Suicide Bombers: Narratives of Violence* (Routledge 2011).
Raz, Joseph, *The Authority of Law: Essays on Law and Morality* (Oxford University Press 1979).
Rogers, Paul, *Irregular War: The New Threat from the Margins* (I. B. Tauris 2017).
Rosen, Lawrence, *Law as Culture: An Invitation* (Princeton University Press 2008).
Rundle, Kristen, *Forms Liberate: Reclaiming the Jurisprudence of Lon L Fuller* (Bloomsbury 2012).
Said, Edward, *Orientalism* (Vintage Books 1979).
Schmitt, Michael N. (ed.) *Tallinn Manual on the International Law Applicable to Cyber Warfare* (Cambridge University Press 2013).
Singh, Rashmi, *Hamas and Suicide Terrorism: Multi-causal and Multi-level Approaches* (Taylor & Francis 2013).
Sivakumaran, Sandesh, *The Law of Non-International Armed Conflict* (Oxford University Press 2012).
Skaine, Rosemarie, *Suicide Warfare* (ABC-CLIO 2013).
Smith, Leonard V., *Between Mutiny and Obedience: The Case of the French Fifth Infantry Division during World War I* (Princeton University Press 1994).
Smith, Russell, & Bronislaw Malinowski, *Crime and Custom in Savage Society* (1st ed., Routledge 2013).
Solis, Gary D., *Law of Armed Conflict: International Humanitarian Law in War* (3rd ed., Cambridge University Press 2022).
Stevenson, Lisa, *Life beside Itself: Imagining Care in the Canadian Arctic* (University of California Press 2014).
Tamanaha, Brian Z., *Legal Pluralism Explained: History, Theory, Consequences* (Oxford University Press 2021).
Taylor, Charles, *A Secular Age* (Harvard University Press 2007).
Taylor, Charles, *Sources of the Self: The Making of the Modern Identity* (Harvard University Press 1989).
Thiranagama, Sharika, & Gananath Obeyesekere, *In My Mother's House: Civil War in Sri Lanka* (University of Pennsylvania Press 2013).
Tsunetomo, Yamamoto, *Hagakure: The Book of the Samurai*. Translated by William Scott Wilson (Kodansha International 2002).
von Clausewitz, Carl, *On War* (Princeton University Press 1984).
Walzer, Michael, *Arguing about War* (Yale University Press 2004).
Walzer, Michael, *Just and Unjust Wars: A Moral Argument with Historical Illustrations* (3rd ed., Basic Books 2006).
White, James Boyd, *From Expectation to Experience: Essays on Law and Legal Education* (University of Michigan Press 2000).
White, James Boyd, *The Legal Imagination* (abridged ver., University of Chicago Press 1985).
Wood, Reed M., *Female Fighters: Why Rebel Groups Recruit Women for War* (Columbia University Press 2019).
Yasuaki, Onuma, *International Law in a Transcivilizational World* (Cambridge University Press 2017).
Zedalis, Debra D., *Female Suicide Bombers* (University Press of the Pacific 2004).

Commentaries

International Committee of the Red Cross, *Commentary on the First Geneva Convention: Convention (I) for the Amelioration of the Condition of the Wounded and Sick in Armed Forces in the Field (Commentaries on the 1949 Geneva Conventions)* (Cambridge University Press 2016).

International Committee of the Red Cross, *Commentary on the Third Geneva Convention: Convention (III) Relative to the Treatment of Prisoners of War (Commentaries on the 1949 Geneva Conventions)* (Cambridge University Press 2020).

Pictet, Jean S. (ed.) *The Geneva Conventions of 12 August 1949, Commentary, Volume I, First Geneva Convention for the Amelioration of the Condition of the Wounded in Armies in the Field* (International Committee of the Red Cross 1952).

Pictet, Jean S. (ed.) *The Geneva Conventions of 12 August 1949, Commentary, Volume II, Second Geneva Convention for the Amelioration of the Condition of Wounded, Sick and Shipwrecked Members of Armed Forces at Sea* (International Committee of the Red Cross 1960).

Pictet, Jean S. (ed.) *The Geneva Conventions of 12 August 1949, Commentary, Volume III, Third Geneva Convention relative to the Treatment of Prisoners of War* (International Committee of the Red Cross 1960).

Zimmermann, Bruno, Claude Pilloud, Claude F. Wenger, Hans-Peter Gasser, Jean de Preux, Philipe Eberlin, Sylvie S. Junod, & Yves Sandoz, *Commentary on the Additional Protocols of 8 June 1977 to the Geneva Conventions of 12 August 1949* (Brill 1987).

Media Articles

Anderson, Kenneth, "The Case for Drones," Commentary (June 2013).

"Birth Shock for Soldier on Afghanistan Deployment," *BBC News* (September 20, 2012).

Bell, David A., "In Defense of Drones: A Historical Argument," *New Republic* (January 2012).

Boustany, Nora, "20 Killed, 100 Injured in Explosion at Iraqi Embassy in Lebanese Capital," *The Washington Post* (December 16, 1981).

Fisher, Max, "Military Pregnancy Ban: What's the Point?" *The Atlantic* (December 22, 2009) online: https://www.theatlantic.com/politics/archive/2009/12/military-pregnancy-ban-what-s-the-point/347173/.

"Full Text: bin Laden's 'Letter to America,'" *The Guardian* (November 24, 2002) online: http://www.theguardian.com/world/2002/nov/24/theobserver.

Gillespie, Bill, "The Avenging Black Widows," *CBC News* (March 30, 2010) online: https://www.cbc.ca/news/world/the-avenging-black-widows-1.866287 139.

"ISIL Takes responsibility for deadly Baghdad suicide bombings," *Al-Jazeera* (January 22, 2021) online: https://www.aljazeera.com/news/2021/1/22/islamic-state-claims-deadly-baghdad-twin-suicide-bombing.

"Kamikaze Typhoons Spared Japan from Kublai Khan," *EARTH Mag* (March 2, 2015).

Katzenberg, Lauren, "40 Stories from Women about Life in the Military" *New York Times* (March 8, 2019).

Keck, Zachary & Matthew Sparks, "The Shia Shift: Why Iran and Hezbollah Abandoned Martyrdom," *National Interest* (May 28, 2018) online: https://nationalinterest.org/feature/the-shia-shift-why-iran-hezbollah-abandoned-martyrdom-25992.

Lekshmi, Priya S., "Velu Nachiyar & Kuyili: The Women Who Took Down the British 85 Yrs before 1857!" *The Better India* (August 28, 2018).

"Mozambique Palma Attack: Why IS Involvement Is Exaggerated," *BBC News* (April 16, 2021) online: https://www.bbc.com/news/world-africa-56773012.

"SC Looks at Clash in Legal Clauses on Suicide," *The Hindu* (September 12, 2020).

Sinha, Badra, "Is Attempt to Suicide Punishable? Two Laws Have Opposing Views, SC Seeks Govt's Response," *The Print* (September 11, 2020).

"Slobodan Praljak Suicide: War Criminal 'Took Cyanide' in Hague Court," *BBC News* (December 1, 2017).

"Tamil Nadu to Build Memorial for Freedom Fighter Kuyili," *The Times of India* (May 6, 2013).

"Yemen arrests 19 after U.S. embassy attack," *Reuters* (September 18, 2008) online: https://www.reuters.com/article/worldNews/idUSREE7706212008091.

Walzer, Michael, & Avishai Margalit, "Israel: Civilians & Combatants," *The New Yorker* (May 14, 2009).

Zieve, Tamara, "This Week in History: Terror Attack on Bus 405," *The Jerusalem Post* (July 1, 2012) online: https://www.jpost.com/Features/In-Thespotlight/This-Week-In-History-Terror-attack-on-Bus-405.

Online Sources

"Colombia's Female FARC Fighters Wage a New War, for Gender Parity," New Humanitarian (September 7, 2017) online: https://www.thenewhumanitarian.org/feature/2017/09/07/colombia-s-female-farc-fighters-wage-new-war-gender-parity.

Covenant of the Islamic Resistance Movement (1988) online: https://fas.org/irp/world/para/docs/880818a.htm.

Customary IHL Study, "Customary IHL Rule No. 154: Obedience to Superior Orders" ICRC–IHL Database, online: https://ihl-databases.icrc.org/customary-ihl/eng/docindex/v1_rul_rule154 33.

Customary IHL Study, "Customary IHL Rule No. 3: Definition of Combatants" ICRC–IHL Database, online: https://ihl-databases.icrc.org/customary-ihl/eng/docs/v1_rul_rule3#Fn_91C058A1_00015.

Customary IHL Study, "Customary IHL Rule No. 47: Attacks against Persons Hors de Combat" ICRC–IHL Database, online: https://ihl-databases.icrc.org/customary-ihl/eng/docs/v1_rul_rule47.

Customary IHL Study, "Customary IHL Rule No. 65: Perfidy" ICRC–IHL Database, online: https://ihl-databases.icrc.org/customary-ihl/eng/docs/v1_rul_rule.

Customary IHL Study, "Customary IHL Rule No. 72: Poison and Poisoned Weapons" ICRC–IHL Database, online: https://ihl-databases.icrc.org/customary-ihl/eng/docs/v1_rul_rule.

Gittleman, Idit Shafran, "Female Service in the IDF: The Challenge of an 'Integrated' Army," Lawfare (February 28, 2018) online: https://www.lawfareblog.com/female-service-idf-challenge-integrated-army.

ICRC Customary IHL Study, "Rule 27: Religious Personnel," online: https://ihl-databases.icrc.org/customary-ihl/eng/docs/v1_rul_rule27.

ICRC Global Affairs Team, "Introduction," Religion and Humanitarian Principles, online: https://blogs.icrc.org/religion-humanitarianprinciples/about/.

Mailänder, Elissa, "The Violence of Female Guards in Nazi Concentration Camps (1939-1945): Reflections on the Dynamics and Logics of Power | Sciences Po Mass Violence and Resistance–Research Network" (December 3, 2015) online: violence-female-guards-nazi-concentration-camps-1939-1945-reflections-dynamics-and-logics-p.html.

National Defence, "Statistics of Women in the Canadian Armed Forces," online: https://www.canada.ca/en/department-national-defence/services/women-in-the-forces/statistics.html.

Papendick, Michael, & Gerd Bohner, "Passive Victim–Strong Survivor? Perceived Meaning of Labels Applied to Women Who Were Raped" (2017) 12:5 PLoS ONE e0177550, online: https://doi.org/10.1371/journal.pone.0177550.

Tasioulas, John, "Conceptual Overreach Threatens the Quality of Public Reason" *Aeon Essays*, online: https://aeon.co/essays/conceptual-overreach-threatens-the-quality-of-public-reason.

Wilson Center, "Timeline: The Rise, Spread, and Fall of the Islamic State" (October 28, 2019) online: https://www.wilsoncenter.org/article/timeline-the-rise-spread-and-fall-the-islamic-state.

Unpublished Work

Gardam, Judith, "More of the Same–Feminist Interactions with IHL" Paper presented at Center for International Governance Justice Workshop: Recent Developments in Feminist Thinking in International Law and International Rights, Australian National University (December 3, 2014).

Herath, Tamara, "Women Identity in Contemporary Conflicts: The Case of the LTTE" (Ann Arbor: UMI Dissertation Publishing 2011).

Kafeyan, Kelly F., “Sunni and Shiite Martyrdom: A comparative Analysis of Historical and Contemporary Expressions” Submitted in partial fulfillment of the requirements for the degree of Master of Arts in Security Studies (Middle East, South Asia, Sub-Saharan Africa), Naval and Post-Graduate School (2010).

Other Sources

Allotey-Pappoe, Serwaa, & Afua Agyeiwaa Lamptey, “Pawns, Puppets or Weapons of Choice: Examining Boko Haram’s Use of Female Suicide Bombers in Nigeria,” KAIPTC Occasional Paper #42 (September 2019).

Australia, *The Manual of the Law of Armed Conflict* (Australian Defence Doctrine Publication June 4, 2006).

Bacon, Tricia, “Inside the Minds of Somalia’s Ascendant Insurgents: An Identity, Mind, Emotions, and Perceptions Analysis of al-Shabaab,” Program on Extremism, George Washington University (March 2022).

Berman, Nathaniel, “‘The Appeals of the Orient’: Colonized Desire and the War of the Riff” (2004) 2 Brown University Research Paper Series on Law, Social Thought and Global Governance.

Bianchi, Kendall, “Letters from Home: Hezbollah Mothers and the Culture of Martyrdom,” CTC Sentinel (February 15, 2018).

Census of Population and Housing, Department of Census and Statistics of Sri Lanka (2012).

Clark, Kate, “The Layha: Calling the Taliban to Account,” Afghanistan Analysts Network (July 4, 2011).

Crowe, Anna, “‘All the Regard Due to Their Sex’: Women in the Geneva Conventions of 1949,” Research Working Paper Series (December 2016).

Esquirol, Jean-Étienne Dominique, “Suicide” *Dictionaire des Sciences Médicales* (Panckoucke 1821).

Gisel, Laurent, “International Expert Meeting Report: The Principle of Proportionality,” International Expert Meeting 22–23 June 2016 Quebec, International Committee of the Red Cross (2018).

International Committee of the Red Cross, “Henry Dunant (1828-1910)” (April 6, 1998).

International Committee of the Red Cross, “Interpretive Guidance on the Notion of Direct Participation in Hostilities under International Humanitarian Law” (May 2009).

Israel, *Rules of Warfare on the Battlefield* (Military Advocate General’s Corps Command, IDF School of Military Law 2nd ed., 2006).

Law Commission of India, “Humanization and Decriminalization of Attempt to Suicide,” Report No. 210 (October 7, 2008).

Office of the Deputy Assistant Attorney General, “Re: Military Interrogation of Alien Unlawful Combatants Held Outside the United States,” U.S. Department of Justice (March 14, 2003).

Rollins, John, “Al Qaeda and Affiliates: Historical Perspective, Global Presence, and Implications for U.S. Policy,” CRS Report for Congress (Congressional Research Service 2010).

Schweitzer, Yoram, & Sari Goldstein Ferber, *Al-Qaeda and the Internationalization of Suicide Terrorism, Memorandum No. 78* (Tel Aviv University, Jaffee Center for Strategic Studies 2005).

Switzerland, Federal Council, “Report on IHL and Armed Conflict” (September 17, 2010).

United States, Instructions for the Government of Armies in the United States in the Field, prepared by Francis Lieber, promulgated as general order No. 100 by President Abraham Lincoln, Washington, DC (April 24, 1863).

United States, *TM E 30-480 Handbook on Japanese Military Forces, 1944* (U.S. Government Printing Office 1944).

United States, War Department: Office of the Chief of Staff, *Rules of Land Warfare* (U.S. Government Printing Office 1914).

United States, *Department of Defense War Manual* (General Counsel of the Department of Defense, May 2016).

Waldron, Jeremy, "A Religious View of the Foundations of International Law" NYU School of Law, Public Law Research Paper No. 11 (April 26, 2011).

Warner, Jason, & Ellen Chapin, "Targeted Terror: The Suicide Bombers of al-Shabaab" (Combating Terrorism Center 2018).

Yaoren, Kenneth Yeo, "Suicide Bombings in Mindanao," Policy Brief, International Center for Counter Terrorism (November 2021).

Index

For the benefit of digital users, indexed terms that span two pages (e.g., 52–53) may, on occasion, appear on only one of those pages.